D0045841

MORTAL GAMES

Also by Fred Waitzkin

Searching for Bobby Fischer

MORTAL GAMES

THE TURBULENT GENIUS OF
GARRY KASPAROV

FRED WAITZKIN

G. P. PUTNAM'S SONS
New York

G. P. Putnam's Sons
Publishers Since 1838
200 Madison Avenue
New York, NY 10016

Library of Congress Cataloging-in-Publication Data

Waitzkin, Fred.
Mortal games: the turbulent genius of Garry Kasparov/by Fred Waitzkin.
p. cm.
ISBN 0-399-13827-7
1. Kasparov, G. K. (Garry Kimovich) 2. Chess players—Russia
(Republic)—Biography. I Title.
GV1439.K38W35   1993   93-10814   CIP
794.1'59—dc20

Printed in the United States of America

1 2 3 4 5 6 7 8 9 10

This book is printed on acid-free paper.
∞

I would like to acknowledge the contribution of Bonnie Waitzkin, whose creative input, smart editorial judgments and loving encouragement made this book possible.

My thanks also to Bruce Pandolfini, a gifted man, who spent many hours helping me translate the drama and daunting intricacy of Garry Kasparov's chess into accessible language.

For Stella, Bonnie, Katya and Josh

1

BEGINNINGS

In late September, 1990, world chess champion Garry Kasparov and I were walking along the broad South Beach of Martha's Vineyard Island off the coast of Massachusetts. It was a sunny morning that was both warm and chilly, depending on the blustery ocean breeze, and the air was so clear that Noman's Island, nine miles to the south, seemed to be sitting just off the beach. Kasparov, on the short side of medium height, shirtless and muscular, walked along the water's edge at a pace that was nearly a run. He had been smiling for the past few minutes, enjoying an idea.

"I'm going to crush him this time," he said.

In ten days the world champion would begin a three-month intellectual and emotional battle against a man he considered morally and politically evil, "a symbol of the communist system." He pronounced the name slowly, rolling the "r," "K-A-R-R-R-P-O-V," so that it dripped with disgust, as if the challenger, one of the great players in chess history, were something vile and foul-smelling. "He is a creature of darkness," Kasparov said, with Miltonic distaste.

The fifth title match between these two chess giants would begin in New York in ten days and would conclude in Lyon, France, at

Christmastime. Kasparov's strategy going in was rather simple: "I want to kill him immediately." To this end, Kasparov was planning to begin the match with "a blitzkrieg," a first-round knockout. In the early games he intended to use several lethal new opening ideas that he had developed on Martha's Vineyard; chess players call them "novelties." After overwhelming Karpov, a former world champion and defensive genius, in two or three of the early games, the champion predicted that the challenger would be unable to recover psychologically. "K-A-R-P-O-V." He repeated the name with disdain, but this time flashed a mischievous smile.

As I struggled to keep up with him on the soft sand, Kasparov savored his victory as if it were a *fait accompli* and Karpov were already squashed like a roach, once and for all out of his life. Sea gulls wheeled overhead, yapping and diving for sand eels. Kasparov waved at them like a heedless child and then inhaled the sea air deeply and theatrically as if it were great French food. This past month on Martha's Vineyard, the hard work and island living had brought a feeling of renewal and confidence. For the last few weeks, he had been saying to close friends that he would win by a lopsided margin. But, privately, his friends were uneasy about the match.

Political changes in the Soviet Union had distracted Kasparov from chess and he had not trained nearly as much as he had planned. Objectively, there was no reason to expect that the match would be easy. Kasparov had been unable to overwhelm Anatoly Karpov in their previous four championship bouts, each of them exhausting and very competitive, which in aggregate encompassed 120 games, about 600 hours of play—if you can call it play to plot the demise of another man's spiritual and psychological well-being. In 120 games, Kasparov had managed to win only a single game more than Karpov. Incredible. There had never been such a competition in all of professional sports: so many encounters, so many hours, so much on the line, so much hatred seeping from a game into life and then back into a game.

On Martha's Vineyard, it seemed to Kasparov that he had spent half of his twenty-seven years and sacrificed much of his life's joy trying to rid himself of this sallow, physically frail man who stuck to him like a shadow. Half a lifetime sitting across from Karpov, whom

he loathed, toes practically touching, conceiving his finest ideas—
which chess players would surely revere 100 years from today—
while smelling Karpov's smells, listening to his digestion or to the
incanting sound of Karpov's counting while he calculated variations,
glimpsing the quivering of Karpov's stretched, nerve-wracked face
when he was losing, or his preening, apple-cheeked self-admiration
when he was winning. Half a lifetime watching closely for Karpov's
mood swings as crucial clues to the game and to Kasparov's own
well-being, for if Kasparov won he would feel like a god afterwards,
and if he lost, his dejection, the blackness and rage closing upon him,
would resist all forms of consolation from his friends, his wife, his
mother. Such depths of despair and humiliation! After losing a game,
Kasparov seemed to shrink in size. Then, as he wrestled with self-
doubt, he would be vulnerable in the next game. Karpov would know
this, of course, and would be ready to pounce.

In ten days, the fifth world championship match between them
would begin, and Kasparov would strain to sense the meaning of
Karpov's body English, the blankness of his face, his twitches and
devious relaxations. For five hours in the evening, these two men
would feel each other's hidden meanings as keenly as any two lovers
while all the while hating one another, but not so loudly that it might
interfere with the flow of ideas.

Eight months before coming to this island, Kasparov, whose father
was Jewish and mother was Armenian, had been forced to flee from
his training camp in Baku, the city where he had been born and
raised, when Azerbaijani hooligans had begun systematically slaughtering Armenians. He had experienced this nightmare not merely as
the loss of home and training camp but as the loss of his heritage,
part of himself. The event had shaken him, at least for a time dislodg-
ing the fundamental order in his life. When he had returned to
Moscow, feeling, as he put it, "like a refugee," chess hardly seemed
important anymore. This game which had made him wealthy and
powerful, which had been at the center of his life for twenty years
and at which he had become arguably greater than any other man in
history, had suddenly felt trivial to him.

In Moscow, with the match growing closer, there had been a
choice to make each day: to study openings in preparation for

Karpov, or to attend a political rally or an organizational meeting for a new political party, or to debate the policies of Gorbachev with visiting Western journalists. Chess was never his choice. According to his closest friends, prior to the loss of his home, his interest in the politics of his country, his anticommunist bias, had been somewhat cerebral and theoretical. But in January of 1990 the new Russian revolution had taken possession of his imagination. Soviet history was suddenly evolving at the speed of light after decades of bleak, punishing stasis. It was thrilling to Kasparov, who sensed that the end of communism was close. He told this to skeptical Western journalists and warned that support of Gorbachev's reactionary politics could force a bloody civil war. He felt most purposeful when writing political columns for Soviet and Western newspapers or giving rousing speeches in front of large crowds. When he thought about it, it seemed odd that he wasn't nervous before his speeches, though he wasn't exactly sure what he would say until he began. This life came easily to him, as though he had spent his years in the political trenches instead of leaning over a chessboard quietly calculating variations. In the fight against communism he felt connected with his passionately anticommunist father, who had died when he was seven, and found himself thinking back twenty years to nightly political discussions at the dinner table with his grandfather, who had been a staunch Party member for nearly fifty years.

But the winter and spring of 1990, a year before the fall of communism, was an injudicious time for the world champion to be plunging into frontline Moscow politics. Each political meeting, each interview, pushed him a little farther from chess. "Chess is not important now," he had said to friends and to his nervous manager, Andrew Page, who wanted him to begin his training for Karpov. It was a confusing and emotional time. Turning his back on chess was both liberating and frightening. Kasparov felt depressed, homeless, and yet he was wholly committed.

To distance himself, finally, from what he considered the charade of *perestroika*, from the daily heart-rending sight of Armenian refugees wandering Moscow streets, from the constant snare of his telephone and from the intoxication over what he sensed were the dying days of communism, Kasparov had chosen Martha's Vineyard for the final month of preparation for the world championship match.

"This time it will be easy," Kasparov said to friends who visited him on the island. Andrew Page, Kasparov's closest friend in the West, grimaced and bit his tongue when Garry boasted that he would destroy Karpov. Page worried that Garry was putting additional pressure on himself and that if he couldn't live up to his inflated claims, he might fall apart altogether. Page had his fingers crossed that Garry could eke out a win against the former world champion, who had been training for months without distraction.

On the beach, Kasparov tried to put Karpov out of his mind: thinking about his enduring enemy was a blight on this postcard-perfect morning. The ocean air was clear, the sky wonderfully blue, and just offshore fishing boats slowly dragged their nets. As we walked at his furious pace, we began talking about his grand plans for the chess world after he won the match. "The public must come to see that chess is a violent sport," he said. "The stakes are very high in an important chess game. When you beat your opponent you destroy his ego; for a time you make him lose confidence in himself as a person. If the general public understood that chess players were plotting to crush one another, don't you think they'd be interested? In this match you'll feel it. The two greatest intellects in the chess world trying to destroy one another. People in the theater will be shivering."

Piqued by the gorgeous day, and the closeness of the match, ideas gushed out of him. We must do away with dry, technical games between grandmasters, he argued, gesturing with his hands as if before an audience. Grandmasters must play on the edge, risk defeat in order to create masterpieces. We were both sweating from our long walk and from the conversation, which held a sense of urgency and importance, but which also seemed a little absurd to me. Yes, yes, I nodded, as if I were an ambitious young grandmaster. No more dry grandmaster games. This must be changed. "Look," Garry insisted, "This is the way I play. I always search for the best move, but this way there is a chance to lose. A chance for greatness and a chance for disaster."

A chance for greatness and a chance for disaster. This is the kind of chess I love as well. It reminds me of the great basketball in the NCAA tournament, when players dive and bleed for each point. It is the kind of uncompromising chess that I wanted my thirteen-year-old son Joshua to play, though I could not begin to play it myself. Likewise, I have always believed that great writing involves taking risks. I was about to say this, but Kasparov's mind had suddenly moved somewhere else—maybe he was thinking about Gorbachev, maybe about a novelty in the King's Indian defense.

When I talk to Kasparov about chess, there are moments when I cannot get past the hilarity of my situation. I think, isn't our dialogue at least as farfetched as if I were chatting about encyclicals with the pope or about military strategy with Norman Schwarzkopf? Yet, since we met in the fall of 1989, there have been many afternoons when Kasparov and I have sat at the chess board and he has shown me all the variations that he might have played in games cherished around the world: attacks, intricate parries, chessic paradoxes, wondrous possibilities that chess lovers will never see. I have felt fretful, even guilty, while he showed me his magnificent ideas. I have wanted to write them down for the world, but his delicate fingers moved much too quickly and the pieces squirted around the board like animated characters. They rushed ahead, demonstrating an attack that failed, then a slightly different attack. "Better," he said quietly, and nodded his head. Better, but why was it better? I could not begin to figure it out. Maybe if I had a month. Once while I was trying to understand one position, he set up another and asked absently if I recalled this from a game in 1968. I grunted. I felt like an idiot. Clearly, everyone should remember this position from '68. "Fred, this is really incredible," and the pieces squirted around. Somehow I could feel that it was incredible.

While trying to follow Kasparov's moves, I have caught myself marveling at the wild and unexpected turn my life had taken. I am not a tournament player myself, and relative to a chess professional, I know little about the game, but in the last half-dozen years, chess has come to dominate my life. I love to watch chess more than almost anything and to talk about exciting games and the quirky habits and hang-ups of players during evening walks around Washington

Square Park with my patzer friends, but mostly I love to talk chess with my son, who is a chess master, and with the world chess champion, Garry Kasparov, who knows that I understand very little about grandmaster-level tactics and modern opening theory but doesn't seem bothered by it. To the contrary, attempting to transform deep and often highly technical ideas into ordinary language seems to engage his imagination. Sometimes Garry calls my apartment from Europe to tell me about a tournament or some game he has just played against Ivanchuk or Anand. He is a good storyteller, and I feel as if I am in his skin, sweating, plunging ahead into a promising but dangerous position. My chess life is very rich.

In the summer of 1972, like many Americans, I fell under the spell of the Bobby Fischer–Boris Spassky match for the chess world championship. Several times a week, my friends and I sat glued to my television, as national master Shelby Lyman duplicated the moves that Fischer and Spassky were making in Reykjavik, Iceland. I hardly knew how to move the chess pieces, but Shelby Lyman had a gift for simplifying the game's complex strategies and tactics. With boyish charm, he convinced millions of chess-apathetic Americans that, by trying a little, not only could they appreciate Bobby and Boris's games, but—who knows?—within weeks they might be playing such masterpieces themselves.

After a few of Shelby's shows, everyone I knew wanted to play like Bobby Fischer, who spoke of the game as intellectual warfare and said shyly that he loved to crush his opponent's ego. Almost overnight, chess clubs began cropping up across America, Little League kids were pleading for chess sets, young men were deciding to forgo college for careers as chess masters. Bobby was a role model, a chess player loved for his smile, his secret power, for moves that were thrilling and sexy. There were chess groupies who craved Bobby but settled for sallow preoccupied masters who spent their days poring over dense books in clubs and coffee shops. It was the time of Muhammed Ali, Joe Namath, the Beatles and Bobby Fischer. Imagine, a chess genius holding the land in thrall like a rock star. Bobby was on the cover of *Time, Life* and *Newsweek.* Commercial sponsors

were lined up to give him millions. He had singlehandedly taken on
the Soviet chess establishment, which during the Cold War seemed
like taking on the Soviet Union itself. The Central Sports Committee
had virtually all of the top chess minds in the Soviet Union working
on plans to help Spassky defeat Fischer, who worked by himself at
night in his room in Iceland and matter-of-factly told the world that
he would win. . . . Bobby, the chess monk who once refused a hotel
room with a scenic view because it might distract him from his work.
Bobby thrilled us with ideas we could never understand, with a chess
victory that felt like a political and moral triumph.

Bobby. Poor Bobby. In a few years he would be standing on street
corners in Pasadena, disguised by a beard, wearing a shabby overcoat
and the same shoes he had worn in the brilliant 1971 candidates
match against Tigran Petrosian, handing out anti-Semitic literature.
After deciding not to defend his title against the young Anatoly
Karpov, Fischer went underground for two decades, living in grimy
rooming houses in Pasadena and Los Angeles. The grandmaster Pal
Benko, who visited him in one of his hideouts, said that he believed
Bobby was afraid that if he had defended against Karpov in 1975, the
Russians would have had him murdered. Fischer showed Benko, who
had spent more than a year in a Nazi labor camp in Hungary, his
treasured color photograph of Adolf Hitler. To his close friends, who
were directed never to discuss him with the press, he expounded
upon the illusion of the Holocaust. It was the Jews who had driven
him out of chess, he claimed to one friend, who kept hoping Fischer
would rid himself of this obsession and return to chess. Bobby
dressed in disguises and cursed the Jews in buses and cheap Chinese
restaurants, and sought out the newest anti-Semitic classics as he had
once accumulated volumes on the chess openings.

But who could imagine this ugliness from Bobby at a time when
grandmaster chess seemed as American as rock and roll? Who could
imagine that Fischer, half Jewish himself, would drop out of chess to
live for two decades in poverty, isolation and delusion after his
stirring victory against Spassky? And who could ever imagine that
twenty years after the great match, in September, 1992, Fischer, by
now much more legend than man, would emerge from our dreams
once again to push wood against Spassky, this time earning millions?

That he would show us a time-weakened version of his clean and deceptively simple game, while seizing the opportunity of a handy international press corps to lambast the Jews, Israel and Garry, whom he labeled a fraud and a cheater? But this is jumping ahead of the story.

In 1972, Bobby Fischer and Boris Spassky had played in a league above all other players in the world, but the deepest meaning of that, translated as it was by Fischer's John Wayne shyness and macho one-liners, and by Lyman's charm, excitement and determination to make chess popular, had been lost for most Americans, including me and my friends who were off buying chessboards and fancy wooden pieces in order to enter the international chess wars. It seems now as if Shelby had intuited that the Fischer phenomenon would be chess's big chance in America, a country too slick and fast for the royal game. While Bobby had taken a half-hour contemplating his position, Shelby and his guests had spoken reassuringly, hyping how accessible this game was: maybe he would move the knight, maybe the bishop—it hardly seemed to matter—there were many good moves. Inspired by their patter, I quickly decided how I would play and couldn't figure out why the two grandmasters were taking so long.

Years later, I would learn that at the highest level chess demands a staggering amount of homework, and that during games a vast library of knowledge is referred to and sometimes inventively rejected. World champions have learned numerous positions, axioms and exceptions. By memory they can play over thousands of games, and can set up positions that they happened to have glanced at years before. Many grandmasters study six or seven hours a day. I know one who studies twelve hours a day, who takes his meals in front of a computer screen while he ponders games played the day before in Europe. There are many thousands of books and journals containing opening analysis, known as "theory," and this information is constantly added to by grandmasters working around the world to improve upon or to refute old ideas. A chess world champion must know both the old and the newest theory, or he stands the risk of being beaten before the game begins.

In addition to a considerable advantage in knowledge, a world champion's mind works differently from mine, which virtually aches from the effort of trying to peer one or two moves ahead while the pieces keep swimming off their squares (Waitzkin, years ago, that ought to have been the clue). The strongest grandmasters are truly intellectual wizards. In certain positions with few pieces on the board, they can look ten or even fifteen moves ahead, accurately calculating and evaluating the entire intricate tree of possible variations. According to chess master Bruce Pandolfini, Lyman's regular guest on the PBS Fischer-Spassky broadcast and today a leading chess author, the deepest calculations of the world's best players are the equivalent of doing a Sunday *New York Times* crossword puzzle in one's head.

But to listen to Kasparov, the question of how many moves one can see ahead—a question which the world champion is asked again and again—is misleading and simplistic. The great player does not think only linearly. The highest art in chess takes place in the creating and evaluating of unbalanced positions—when, let us say, one player has less material than the other but his smaller army is attacking more effectively than the larger, when less is actually more. To conceive of such dynamic imbalances, according to Kasparov, a player must think of the game in three dimensions, and during the course of play continually invent and reject chessic constructions of enormous complexity and beauty. To do this, he must be something of an artist, trusting intuition and aesthetic judgment at least as much as raw calculating ability. "This is too beautiful to be true," a grandmaster fretted to me recently, about an inspired middlegame tactic. He couldn't calculate whether the move was sound or only a pretty illusion. "Intuition and profound ideas win chess games at the highest level, not counting," says Kasparov.

After the 1972 Fischer-Spassky match was over, I studied a little, and even tried my hand in a couple of chess clubs. But without the soothing voice of Shelby I didn't seem to be the same player. I couldn't rearrange the pieces in my head as Bobby could. Without Shelby's gentle nudging, I didn't know where to place them to initiate my attacks. After losing ignominiously one afternoon to a pimply adolescent who read the newspaper while I strained and sweated, I retired as an active player. I put my elegant wooden pieces on a top shelf and didn't touch them for ten years, until the afternoon my six-year-old son Josh begged me to take them down. That was the beginning of a great adventure in my life.

As fate would have it, my three-foot son could see where his father was blind. Within days, it was clear that Josh could calculate more quickly and more accurately than I could. He had a sense for where to place his knights and bishops so that they worked together to make threats. Try as hard as I might, my pieces were simply here and there, weak isolated soldiers fighting to survive, while Josh's were helping one another and ultimately closing in on my king—it felt like my throat. Clever combinations played themselves out beneath Josh's dimpled hand while I strained to defend. Within weeks, my six-year-old was beating me and my friends, the same crew that a decade earlier had been ready to follow Bobby to the top.

Soon my little boy began to take chess lessons with Bruce Pandolfini and to play experienced adults in Washington Square Park and in chess clubs in New York. It was clear to chess masters who observed him that Josh was a special little player. By the age of seven, he was winning most of his games in scholastic tournaments. By nine, he was the strongest for his age in the United States, the winner of the national scholastic primary championship for third grade and under.

During the early years of my son's chess life, my emotional investment was very large, almost as if I were playing the games and not he. When Josh played poorly, I felt hopeless and absurd for having allowed, no, for having urged him to devote so much of his young life to a board game. But when he was inspired, sacrificing his pieces and mating elegantly, it felt as if Josh and I were shadowing Fischer and Kasparov and all the other great ones—Alekhine, Botvinnik, Capablanca, Karpov, Keres, Korchnoi, Petrosian—names that Josh struggled to pronounce, but which coursed through my head like old friends. While other fathers fantasized big-time careers for their boys in baseball and basketball, I dreamed of my son becoming a grandmaster.

Being the father of a chess prodigy was thrilling but also disturbing. By the time he was seven, I had started writing about the chess world in magazines and later in a book, *Searching for Bobby Fischer*, which chronicled my chess adventures with Josh and was made into a movie by Paramount. I had discovered that in the eighties in America, chess professionals were a tiny underclass, a group of brilliant men who could not support themselves at their life's work, and who, by and large, were not respected for their gifts of mind. The Fischer phenomenon had been short-lived. When Bobby retired to begin his dark political work, chess seemed to dry up in the United States. The chess clubs quickly shrank in size or disappeared altogether. Without Bobby, chess was no longer on television or in our national magazines, and many tournaments were played in out-of-the-way places offering the most meager prize funds, only a few hundred dollars. Whereas in Europe and the communist countries, top players made a good living and were sought out for autographs and venerated by fans as celebrities, in the United States players simply couldn't make it, and some of our best were forced to give up the game in their prime in order to try to earn a living at something else. Those who continued to try to survive as professionals were bitter about their lot in life. When they couldn't earn enough in tournaments, some took menial part-time jobs and others spent their days in parks like Washington Square near our home in New York City, hustling games against passersby for a dollar or two in order to eat.

I suspect that such romanticism and excessive devotion to my son's chess would never have evolved without Fischer. I could never quite get over him. I kept thinking that Bobby would show up some day soon, cured of his problem, to stride onto a stage and contemptuously push ahead his king pawn against this Kasparov fellow (who would ever have guessed that war-torn Yugoslavia, hideously dotted with concentration camps, would be Bobby's venue of choice for his second coming against Boris Spassky?). The idea of Bobby's crushing Garry Kasparov gave me goosebumps. At the time, Kasparov was only a Russian name to me, and great as he surely was, I was convinced that he held center stage only because Bobby Fischer was temporarily indisposed.

Then Garry Kasparov came into my chess life. On Monday, February 22, 1988, the world champion visited the South Bronx to play a simultaneous exhibition against fifty-nine school kids, to promote the introduction of chess into the public school system by the newly-created Manhattan Chess School. The gym of P.S. 132 was near-bursting with little players and their parents readying cameras for Kasparov, who was late. There was considerable media interest in the world champion's first appearance in the United States. Scores of serious-looking journalists from New York papers and national magazines vied with TV crews from the three networks and several cable channels for interviews with nervous kids. Shelby Lyman, bathed in lights, grayer and a little more portly than during those Bobby Fischer afternoons, was angling with one of the organizers for an interview with the world champion. At least for this afternoon, chess was big-time again.

Kasparov came into the gymnasium surrounded by an austere group of men—his business manager and several friends from the Russian-American community—but at the time I didn't know who they were. Their faces were joyless, all business, as was his, and I fancied that they were his bodyguards, maybe even KGB. Kasparov was solidly built, like a soccer player, handsome, unsmiling. He talked seriously for a few moments with the organizer about rules. He wore a stylish sweater and a green scarf hung around his neck, suggesting that the match against fifty-nine little ones would be over before it began and then he would be flying off to the chill and gloom of Russia to continue his inexorable struggle against Karpov and the Russian chess establishment.

During the introductory speeches, Kasparov looked distracted, bored. When the crowd applauded, his smile was forced. The man must be all chess, I thought, a hard core of chess variations and unbeatable ideas. No emotions, no love, no humor. In truth, I was not a calm and detached observer. For me, the events of that afternoon were distorted by years of thinking about all the great players and by my rooting for my son. Kasparov was the man who was maybe better than Bobby Fischer, and my kid, wearing a yellow and blue polo shirt, telling NBC News that he wasn't nervous, would soon be playing against him. It would probably be the only time in his life Josh would play the world champion. My heart was pounding in my ears.

The exhibition began and Kasparov seemed to explode from his detachment. He progressed from one chessboard to the next in a kind of choppy run, pushing his pieces ahead in a flash. The children had been instructed to move at precisely the moment that the world champion appeared in front of them, but he was there and gone so quickly that some kids, shaking with anticipation and worry, toppled their pieces trying to accomplish a move. Kasparov would re-create the position from memory and move instantly. He was all pace and action, banging a pawn ahead while looking at the next board, racing around the room grabbing material, his scarf swinging from his neck. He was tailed around and around by a jangling slew of TV sound booms, cameras and cables. Some of the kids became stage-struck when he stood impatiently before them, the forbidding attacker they had seen on the cover of chess magazines. They couldn't move, although they had decided what the move should be. Kasparov understood his effect and rapped hard with his knuckle on the table three times and said sharply, "Move, move." When he hesitated at a board where the position had become complicated, everyone in the gymnasium felt this power stopped in place like a roped horse.

I shall never forget the moment when he first paused in front of my son. Garry bent over the board until his head was only a few inches from Joshua's, and then after about a half a minute he stood up straight and made a funny expression with the corners of his mouth turned down, what do we have here? Then he rocked from side to side, calculating, considering. The noisy gym became very quiet. What is Kasparov doing? He smiled a little and looked at Josh, who peeked up at him. Then he scratched his head and rocked some more, and wiped the back of his hand across his mouth. Kasparov recognized that Josh had successfully fended off his attack and that their positions, after many moves, were equal. After that, each time he came around the room to Josh, he considered the board deeply, rocking, scratching his head, appraising Josh with an affectionate glance that said, a clever defense, this little kid is a player. After a few more moves, Josh offered the world champion a draw, and Kasparov accepted with a terrific smile. And after Kasparov had raced off from Josh, winning games with one hand while he scribbled autographs with the other, Josh pumped his fist in the air as if he had just scored the winning shot for his basketball team. The world champion won fifty-seven games and drew two that afternoon.

*   *   *

In October of 1989, I attended a party for Kasparov in the Upper East
Side apartment of Olga Capablanca, the widow of the former world
champion, Jose Raul Capablanca. This unusual place was crammed
with chess players and well-to-do patrons of the game who hoped
for a handshake and a word with the champion. Kasparov, who
earlier in the evening had easily beaten the fifteen-year-old prodigy
Gata Kamsky in an exhibition, spoke earnestly to Mrs. Capablanca.
She was nearly ninety and wore red lipstick and a faded flowing
gown from wonderful parties long ago. Doubtless, they exchanged
words about Capablanca, who like Garry had been an unusually
gifted prodigy, known for his uncanny intuitive play and lightning-
fast vision of the board. There were other similarities between the
two great world champions. Capablanca had been a moody man and,
according to his wife, had a talent not only for seeing deeply into a
chess position, but for correctly predicting events in the future.
Kasparov prided himself on the ability to predict political develop-
ments.

They talked for quite a while. Mrs. Capablanca held Kasparov's
hand, and they seemed to be measuring one another, the champion
perhaps looking for intimations of his future, the lady for a fresh scent
of the past. I knew that she would tell Kasparov about the afternoon
almost sixty years before when she had berated another world
champion, Alexander Alekhine, Kasparov's favorite player, for refusing to give her frustrated husband a rematch after taking the championship from Capablanca ten years before. I wondered if the world
champion would find her story quaint or disturbing.

Olga Capablanca peered into Kasparov's eyes as they spoke. What
a bewitching beauty she had been. Sitting on an end table beside
them was a photograph of her in the twenties, when she had looked
like a young Marlene Dietrich. I wondered if Garry also reminded her
of her first husband, a physical powerhouse, a horseman and adven-
turer, a descendant, she liked to say, of Genghis Khan. Like Garry,
this dashing young man had championed the cause of Armenians. In
the 1920s he had been a pioneer aviator in the Caucasus, and had
eventually taken over the fledgling air force of Armenia at a time
when the Turks had been slaughtering Armenians by the thousands.

Olga Capablanca's dark apartment, cluttered with relics from her storybook past, was a place chess luminaries visited to look at photographs of Capablanca and to try to know him through his wife and her stories. She sometimes said, coquettishly, that buried in her papers she kept a Capablanca masterpiece that had never been published, a private game played in the thirties between her husband and a top grandmaster of that time. Her husband had dedicated it to her, and Olga would not show it to anyone, a Rembrandt hidden in her closet.

But Olga had her own story to tell, and the Cuban world champion was but one chapter, though she pointed out softly, "I was with him until his last breath." I wondered if, knowing Kasparov's interest in military history, she had also told him about another of her husbands, Admiral Jocko Clark, commander of the Pacific Fleet during the Second World War. I got the impression that she loved Jocko a little more than the others. On the walls and end tables, along with photographs of the Armenian aviator—freedom fighter and Capablanca smiling calmly beside his chessboard, were many photographs and oil paintings of Jocko Clark aboard his warships: the admiral heroically turning on the lights, and thus risking submarine attack, in order to save his planes from running out of fuel over the Pacific; the admiral shaking hands with Admiral Nimitz at the signing of the peace treaty with Japan. Kasparov, with his passion for history, could not help but have felt the evocative and odd mixing of memorable events from the past. However, he and the other guests could not have suspected that at Mrs. Capablanca's there was a contemporary subtext that was both a little sinister and sad.

Just off the living room where Olga held Kasparov in thrall was a door with a brutal-looking police lock. Behind this door lived a hundred-year-old man, Hamilton Fish, and his much younger wife. Fish had been a longtime United States congressman, best known for his political battles with Franklin Delano Roosevelt. According to Mrs. Capablanca, he had inherited a share of this apartment from her deceased sister, to whom he had been married. Mrs. Capablanca said that over the years she and Fish had become mortal enemies, and claimed that, among other vicious things, the congressman had discarded her treasured photographs and papers, and waited for her to die so that he could take sole claim to the apartment. She was tormented by Fish. She whispered—lest he hear—that the congress-man's young wife had worked in a butcher shop before entering into this unlikely relationship. Mrs. Capablanca's home, this temple of fighting men, was also a battleground on which two feisty old people were making a last stand.

Kasparov had been in New York for several days prior to the exhibition and party. I had hoped to interview him, but each time I had called Andrew Page at the Regency Hotel, he had put me off. I approached the Englishman at the party and asked for an hour in the world champion's schedule. Page's eyelids drooped with weari-ness from journalists asking him for Kasparov interviews. "They all think that they are so bright, that their point of view is bold and sparkling, but they all ask the same boring questions," he told me some time later, in his British drawl. He explained that it would be impossible to talk to Garry during this trip. Kasparov was much too tired, and tomorrow they would be flying off to Europe. His demeanor reflected the weariness of living the high life, too many five-course meals at Lutèce and the Four Seasons, too many Con-corde flights sipping champagne. Oxford-educated, Andrew Page is suave, handsome and eloquent in the style of Peter Jennings. At that moment he also came across as slick, smart and unreflective. Over time, though, I learned that he is very thoughtful, and not infrequently stopped in his tracks by self-doubt, but that he enjoys portraying himself as a rake and power broker. Page is apt to dis-miss a proposition as impossible and then upon reflection, embrace it as utterly wonderful. Whereas Kasparov is set in his points of view like granite, Page is buffeted by his own keen sense of irony—indeed, he sometimes appears amused by his own whimsi-cality and crumbling convictions, and perhaps that is what makes their close relationship viable.

Just when I was thinking that here was someone who controlled a piece of greatness and wasn't going to dole it out unless he could turn a profit, Page's musical voice stopped me in my tracks. "Why don't you have a word or two with him now, while he is standing around?" At that moment, Kasparov had finished his conversation with Olga Capablanca and was approaching us, looking haggard at the end of his long day, signaling Page that he was ready to leave.

It was difficult for me to introduce myself. Where to begin after so many years of thinking about chess world champions, and wondering particularly what Garry Kasparov might have to say about Bobby Fischer and whether he regretted having devoted his childhood to the game—questions that were at the center of my life. But mainly, I felt afraid of him. During the past half-dozen years, I had derived so much happiness thinking about the chess greatness of my son, planning for the day when he would become world champion. For me, much of the fun of Joshua's chess life had to do with my preposterous daydreams, and maybe that wouldn't work so well after knowing the real thing.

"Do you recall that two years ago you gave a simultaneous exhibition in the South Bronx?" A clumsy beginning. Of course he remembered, he remembered everything. Kasparov tensed with impatience or perhaps with the anticipation of another person he didn't know asking for something: an autograph, an interview, a chunk of his time for a worthy cause. "My son was the eleven-year-old who drew against you."

"Your son is Josh?" he said, suddenly interested. "You should have come right over." I was dumbstruck. How could he have recalled my son's name from a twenty-second conversation and a handshake two years before?

We left the party together and spoke for perhaps fifteen minutes. What struck me most during our first meeting was the powerful draw of his concentration. For the most part, I asked him questions about Kamsky, the fifteen-year-old defector from the Soviet Union whom he had beaten in two games a few hours before. Kamsky's life was entirely dominated by his father's dream for him to become world chess champion. This remarkably gifted teenager was not allowed to go to school, so that he could study chess twelve hours a day, and his progress had been so stunning that many predicted he would someday be a challenger for the title.

I asked, "Does a father have a right to ask his young son to study all the time, to give his childhood to chess?"

"It is a kind of risk," he said. "Later you regret the lost childhood. I have regrets. But when I was very young I knew that chess would be my profession. I felt that there was no choice and my mother said okay. I needed chess like a drug."

Kasparov's face was flushed with emotion. "You must ask your kid," he said, wiping aside the pretense that my primary interest was journalistic, a story I was writing about this other boy. "It's up to Josh. If he feels very strongly about it, he will do it. For some, chess is stronger than the sense of childhood."

The following spring I traveled with the champion to research an article for *The New York Times Magazine,* and Garry and I became friends. During the ensuing months there were many dinners, walks, car, plane and train rides together, scores of late-night conversations, some of them emotional and for me thrilling. As we toweled off in front of the red cliffs which border the South Beach of Martha's Vineyard, just ten days before the beginning of Karpov-Kasparov V, I remembered that twenty years before I had entertained the fantasy of being friends with Bobby Fischer.

"On the white side, I feel I'm in very good shape," Kasparov reflected. We had just come out of the frigid water after half an hour of riding the waves, switching off on his boogie board. The surf was up this morning, and Kasparov had attacked the breakers with a persistent seriousness.

"I only wish I could have spent another month training. I would have done more preparation with the black pieces."

"Too bad you didn't begin training in Moscow last January after Baku." At the mention of his home in Azerbaijan, Garry looked as though I had struck him. His face grew dark and I could imagine his train of thought: Why are you talking to me about chess training? I have lost my home. Friends are dead or lost somewhere—I don't know where they are. Why did you bring up Azerbaijan? Are you trying to ruin me? Kasparov pulled at his nose with his thumb and forefinger, as he does sometimes when he plays a chess position which is menacing and unclear. His prior good mood and optimism about the match were hard to recall. He looked out at the ocean, but I knew that he wasn't seeing it. I said something or other, and he didn't reply. We walked for about half an hour, back to the huge rented house set on a bluff above the water, without saying a word.

The world champion's moods are very loud and entirely dominating. I have frequently seen his happiness cheer a crowded room. When he is alive with energy and ideas, I feel inspired to argue, listen or laugh with him. But his despair can make a friend feel entirely helpless and chaotic. When Kasparov is angry and brooding, the air around him seems thinner. Sometimes he turns his face away and won't look at me, as if I had sinned, hideously sinned. At such moments, I would prefer to be anywhere else.

2

CHESS TRAINING AND
GENOCIDE

Because Kasparov is a strikingly candid person, when he exercises reserve about an issue the effect is teasing. For the first year that I knew Garry, he wouldn't speak to me about his last days in Baku, and I knew only fragments about this harrowing time. Whenever I raised questions about the loss of his home, he became angry or silent or directed the conversation elsewhere. Then one afternoon in New York, months after Karpov-Kasparov V, he grimaced at my question, which over time had grown into something of a dare, a long oh-what-the-hell expression, and then he told the story with remarkable detail and craft. It was apparent that the events in Azerbaijan in late December, 1989, and early January, 1990, had darkly colored Kasparov's championship year. I have placed this recollection at the beginning of this narrative, long before he told it to me, so that the reader can feel something of Kasparov's state of mind as he trained and then played against Karpov.

* * *

"At the end of December 1989, two months after we met at the party in New York, I was in Moscow preparing to leave for Baku to begin my training for Karpov. However, my mother and I received disturbing phone calls from home. My aunts and cousins in Baku said that I shouldn't come: ethnic tension between Azerbaijanis and Armenians was building, it could be dangerous.

"I decided to go to Baku anyhow. I said to myself, 'These problems will never affect me. I am a hero there.' Bad. Very bad. Sometimes being world champion makes a man lose perspective, as if he is above normal concerns. When I think now of this attitude, it makes me embarrassed.

"I left Moscow happy to be going home, looking forward to seeing my friends. I had spent much of the past year abroad giving speeches and exhibitions. I was mentally tired. I wanted to return to the Baku of my childhood. Maybe I didn't want to hear the bad news.

"During the past year, relatives of mine had been fired from their jobs, as had most Armenians. They were worried about violence and had decided to leave Baku. I had made arrangements for several to move to Moscow, for my cousin Eugene to transfer universities. But these problems seemed remote: their problems, not mine. I wasn't in Baku at the end of 1988, when Azerbaijani fanatics were chanting 'Death to the Armenians' in the streets. I wasn't there in 1989 when they destroyed an Armenian church. Of course I had heard accounts of the atrocities in 1988 against Armenians in Sumgait, forty kilometers to the north. But if you are far away, a pogrom is only a word. You must be there to feel it. I simply could not imagine my neighbors trying to harm me. Despite the fact that I am half Armenian by birth, the Azeris accept me as a friend—they take pride in my accomplishments. When I play matches they pray for me. I am part of that city and it is my heritage.

"But to tell the truth, the problems of the region weren't very much in my mind. In the days before leaving Moscow, I had been embroiled in bitter disagreements within the GMA [the Grandmasters Association, the organization he had founded to improve the way of life of professional chess players around the world]. Also, throughout December, I had been attending meetings with intellectuals and political leaders in Moscow who opposed the direction of the Gorbachev government. My friends were cautioning me that I was thinking about everything but chess, and that Karpov would be studying without distraction. It was time to turn my attention to the match.

"There is a special sanitarium north of Baku that I have used for my training since 1980. I rent a block of rooms. Though a half year might pass between visits, my furniture, books and clothing are always exactly where I left them. I know every cat and dog in the place. There are doctors and therapists on hand for any problem. When I think of it now, this camp seems like a paradise. While I study, I can hear the steady sound of small waves and smell the fresh Caspian Sea, which is close to the buildings. The air is fragrant with olive, mandarin orange and pine trees. I concentrate very well there. When I need to relax in the afternoon, I take long walks along the beach.

"I planned for Baku to be the first of several training sessions for the match. Actually, it would be a pre-training session. Along with my team, I intended to devise a general strategy. We would look at some of the games Karpov had played during the past two years to see how his style had evolved since I last played him, and to get a sense for his vulnerabilities. In general terms, we would talk about which opening systems I should concentrate on for this fifth meeting. My regular crew was assembling at the camp. As always, my mother would be in charge. She has great wisdom and experience. She would establish schedules, maintain discipline and oversee the entire training session. Alexander Shakarov, who lives in Baku, would bring our computers. He has been working with me for fifteen years. Whenever I need to look at a game or an opening variation played years ago, he quickly finds it in our large data base. My friend Kadzhar Petrosean, also from Baku, would oversee many details, do some cooking and also provide a tennis sparring partner for my afternoon workout. The grandmaster Zurab Azmaiparashvili was driving from Georgia, and I was certain he had ideas to discuss with me about Karpov's recent games. But we never got a chance to talk about them.

"When I arrived, Baku was a city of fear. All the Armenians wanted to leave, but it was hard to understand why. Nothing much was happening.

"My first day at the camp, the official ministry assigned two policeman to protect me, a major and a sergeant. I had never had protection before. These two carried handguns. They said that it would be wise for me to learn to shoot. Normally when I am in training, I run on the beach, swim or play tennis to increase my stamina for long games, but in the early days of this unusual training session I spent my time shooting bottles of sand on the beach. I became quite good at it. There were bad days ahead when I was thankful to have had this training."

To appreciate Kasparov's account of the events in Baku during the early days in January, 1990, the reader must understand a little about the history of ethnic violence in the region. In A.D. 301, Armenia became the first nation to accept Christianity. Under Tigran the Great, Armenia became a great power, conquering territories as far south as Palestine. Beginning in the eleventh century, however, Turkic peoples, who were fierce fighters, infiltrated the area, creating the Turkish Ottoman empire. Turks and Armenians lived side by side, but the Armenian ethnic composition of Nagorno-Karabakh, an area larger than Rhode Island in the center of what is now Azerbaijan, remained intact, because the fortresslike mountains were impenetrable to the invaders. In the eighteenth century, Russian armies operating against the Ottomans entered Transcaucasia, a bridge of land connecting Asia and Europe which Russia coveted for military purposes, ending Ottoman domination of the region. Armenia remained under Turkish control, but in the latter part of nineteenth century, fighting broke out between Turks and Armenians, who were impatient with Turkish rule, culminating in the massacre of a million and a half Armenians in 1915. Little notice was taken of it internationally. Kasparov points out with irony that when Hitler was warned in the thirties that genocide of the Jews would cause problems for Germany, Hitler remarked, "Who cares about the Armenian genocide now?"

In 1918, when the Turkish empire was being partitioned after World War I, an independent Armenia was created. In 1920, however, the Red Army invaded, and Transcaucasia came under communist domination. In 1923, Stalin drew the borders of the

Transcaucasian states, giving the Nagorno-Karabakh region, which was eighty-five percent Armenian, to Armenia, but then reversed his decision later in the year, leaving Karabakh to Azerbaijan. Many believe that he created this and other border disputes with the hidden agenda of keeping the nationalities at each other's throats. Over the ensuing years, the Soviet government apparently found it useful to incite pogroms to quell nationalistic impulses. When they were not manipulated by the Moscow government, Armenian and Turkic peoples got along quite well. "I can attest to this firsthand," Kasparov says. "To this day I still count Azeris among my closest friends."

During the Russian era, many Armenians migrated from Karabakh to Baku and Sumgait because of the oil industry and the opportunities of the modern city. The Armenians did not assimilate with the Muslim populations, but rather became a prosperous, highly educated class, holding large business interests and skilled jobs. Russia regarded Transcaucasia as a "colony." Many Russians settled there, and it was natural for Armenians to become allies of the Russians, who were also Christian. In Baku, the better-paid jobs were, by and large, held by Russians and Armenians. The Turkic peoples of Baku directed their resentment of Russification towards the Armenians.

"After the First World War, nationalist movements were stifled in the Soviet Union by ironclad communist rule," Kasparov explained. "That changed with *glasnost* and *perestroika*. The Karabakh Armenians were the first to exercise their new freedom. At the end of 1987, Armenians living in the Nagorno-Karabakh called for reunification with Armenia. At first, Moscow seemed sympathetic and then, following outcries from Azerbaijani leaders, the central government reversed itself and jailed Armenian leaders known as the Karabakh Committee. These men were seeking democratic rule as well as the reunification of Armenia. I believe that they were sent to jail by Gorbachev because they were demanding the end of communism in their country. Many in the Russian intelligentsia, including myself, signed a letter to support the dissidents. I might add, one year later, when I visited Baku in March of 1989, I was quietly threatened for supporting them. A group of local communists came and said that unless I repudiated my support, it might not be safe for my grandmother and cousins, who lived year-round in Baku. 'Don't you care about your family anymore?' they asked. 'Something can happen to them.'

"The tragedy of genocide struck Sumgait, a short distance north of Baku, in February, 1988. Before the slaughter of Armenians by Azerbaijani hooligans began, there were well-organized rallies, headed not by Azerbaijani leaders but by men who spoke perfect Russian and claimed that Armenians were killing Azerbaijanis in Yerevan, the capital of Armenia. According to eyewitness accounts, drugs, alcohol and iron bars were handed out to the crowds from trucks. Despite what you might have read about in the West, there was nothing helter-skelter about this violence. It was a well-organized campaign. For three days, Armenians were beaten, raped and murdered throughout the city, their apartments looted and burned. The mobs knew exactly which apartments to come to. All evidence indicates that the pogrom was incited, not by Azerbaijanis, but by the KGB with the knowledge of Gorbachev. While the slaughter went on, Soviet troops stood by and did nothing. Then after the entire Armenian population had been driven from the city, the troops stepped in and slaughtered Azerbaijanis and afterwards declared martial law. Why did the Soviet central government participate in this bloody charade? To stifle a nationalist pro-democratic movement. To maintain control."

"In the beginning of January, 1990, while we were in the training camp trying to study chess we would hear reports about the mood in Baku, forty kilometers to the southwest. The central government was paralyzed; there were no services, friends called on the phone to tell us. Buses had stopped running. Newspapers, television and radio stations were seized by nationalists, so that it was impossible to get true information. Planes were still flying from Baku, but they were filled. There were no tickets to buy. Taking a train was dangerous. You had to pass through Azerbaijani territory, and if you were Armenian, maybe you would be dragged off; no one knew.

"Armenians were in a panic. They thought that something terrible was closing in around them. For months there had been a black market business which packed the possessions of Armenians in large

containers and shipped them to Moscow. All of a sudden, this
business was finished. Armenians feared that this was orchestrated,
part of a sinister plot. Two years before, there had been two hundred
and forty thousand Armenians living in the city, but after the Sumgait massacres many had left, and now the Armenian population was
down to forty thousand. Only the weakest remained, old people,
poor people who couldn't afford to move, pensioners, and members
of mixed families, like my mother's younger sister, who was married
to an Azeri. These people were anguished. Should they abandon
their possessions and try to flee the city? It is very difficult to leave
home with only the clothes on your back. People didn't know what
to do. They were losing their minds.

"January thirteenth was a beautiful day. There was a rainbow
hanging over the sea. I will never forget it. This was the day the
pogrom started. Rumors reached the camp that Armenian apartments
in the city had been taken by mobs of killers. Was it true? It was
difficult to accept these reports. Genocide? It must be a mistake. This
was the twentieth century. We heard the news report from Moscow
which described some minor dispute between Armenians and Azerbaijanis. We spoke to our friends in the police and KGB, and they
assured us that everything would be fine. There was no danger.
Friends of mine in Moscow wanted me to return, but I decided to
stay a while.

"Gorbachev was in Vilnius, Lithuania, talking about the new federation, how Soviets had wonderful times ahead, there would be new
freedoms. What a charade. Gorbachev knew what was happening. I
will believe to the end of my life that he was responsible.

"We received phone calls from the city, describing unimaginable
horrors. Azerbaijanis were systematically burning the apartments of
Armenians. Bands of men would come to a large apartment house
and break down the doors of Armenian apartments. They knew
exactly which apartments to come to. Neighbors watched while flats
were robbed and then burned. Armenian girls were raped and burned
to death. It was Sumgait all over again. Women offering their bodies
to save their families. Armenian men, women and children were
bludgeoned in the courtyard, while their neighbors watched in horror. An Azeri friend came to the camp and told me of one Armenian

woman who was raped and then dropped from the window of her eighth-floor apartment. This happened very close to the big square in Baku. Soviet troops were guarding the square, watching. They observed this murder and did nothing.

"Many Azerbaijanis tried to save their neighbors by hiding them from the murderers. Some did nothing. If you watch the police and the army stand by idly while murder is being committed, what would you do?

"Shakarov, my old friend, was in despair. His mother, brother, and elderly uncle and aunt lived in the center of the city. They were the only Armenians in a complex of two hundred apartments. They would be the target. He tried to reach them on the phone and the line was dead. He was certain that they were murdered. All day he lay on the bed crying.

"We heard from the city that the pogromists had taken the apartment of my aunt. Fortunately, she and her husband had left the apartment. They were living with my grandmother in an apartment rented by a relative who had married an Azeri man. His name was on the door, and this gave them a little safety. But the pogrom was all around them and they were terrified. My grandmother was seventy-eight and had lived her entire life in Baku. She had buried her husband here. She didn't want to leave. She said, 'Even if they take me, I don't want to go.'

"By now, of course, I knew I must leave, and I was trying to figure out how to save my family and friends. I chartered a plane from Moscow. The phone was ringing day and night. People I knew from the city were asking, 'Save us. Please save us.' Azeri friends were smuggling Armenians to the camp. Soon we had forty people living with us. Sleeping, crying everywhere. Everyone scared to death. It was very dangerous for the director of the sanitarium. Probably he would not have allowed us to do this, except that he had the same problem. His son had married an Armenian girl and he was thinking how to bring them from the city. Finally, I managed to get my grandmother to come to the camp. I lied to her. I said that later on we would return to town.

"We found out that Shakarov's family had managed to survive by a stroke of luck. When their door was beaten down by the killers, they happened to see a fax machine, which Shakarov mainly used for getting information for me from different chess tournaments. But for some reason the crowd decided that they had broken into the apartment of American spies. About that time, two of my friends from the KGB arrived, and one of them was very clever. He said, 'Yes, yes, they are American spies. We are arresting them.' My friends rescued Shakarov's family from the killers. They took them to a small refugee camp and later to our training camp. But they had lost all their possessions—money, passports, everything in their lives. Soon after, these KGB guys and many others like them left the city. The situation was completely out of control. Baku was in the hands of the pogromists.

"The night of January fifteenth was the most difficult time. I was playing cards with Kadzhar, my driver Kolia Garaev, and another chess professional who worked with me. Our two police guards sat beside us watching the game. About half past midnight, we got a phone call that killers were coming in buses to our district from the city. The pogromists had heard that the police were protecting some Armenians. I imagined them coming to us along the road I had traveled hundreds of times, the sea on one side, oil wells on the other. We kept playing cards. Everyone seemed to be pretending that this was not happening. But of course no one could sleep.

"Some time during the night, I asked the major, 'If they break in here, will you shoot?' He didn't answer, and so I dealt the cards to Kadzhar, we played a while longer. Then, I asked him again, 'If they come, will you shoot?'

" 'You know, I have a family. I have three daughters,' he said quietly. He didn't look up at me.

"After a while, I said, 'Will you give me your gun?' He thought for a while, and then he answered, 'If they come, you have to hit me on the side of the head. Make it look like you took it from me.' It was like a scene in a gangster movie. He was a good guy and it was nice that he said he would give me the gun. Who knows if he really would have done it?

"The crowd never reached the sanitarium. The explanation is quite interesting. The area north of the city is controlled by a kind of mafia who do a huge volume of illegal business in flowers and sturgeon eggs. This 'fish mafia,' as I call them, is powerful and well-armed. They have their own code of honor. They did not want the murder of Armenians taking place in their area. When they heard that the killers were on their way, they sent out patrols. The mob was intercepted, and when they saw guns they turned back. Of course the army could have done the same as the fish mafia, but it didn't serve their purpose.

"The next day, I drove to the city. I wanted to see my flat and maybe take a few things. I drove in one car with Kadzhar and an Azeri friend, and a special Azeri police car drove in front of us, supposedly providing protection. But as soon as we began driving, they sped ahead of us, way out of sight. They didn't want to be connected to us. If we had been attacked, they wouldn't have known.

"Kadzhar wanted to go to his apartment to get some clothes, but when we reached his neighborhood we saw that most of the Armenian apartments had been taken. We decided not to stop. My apartment was one of the few that hadn't been broken into. It has a very strong steel door, and there were marks, they had tried to pry it open. I told my friends that I wanted to collect a few of my most memorable things. They said, there's no need, you'll come back here when things settle down, but I knew I would never come back. So I took a few pictures of my mother and father, some of my chess notebooks from when I was a kid, a couple of my favorite works of literature, a chess set, a few prizes. We were there for an hour. It was a very nervous hour.

"The next day, January seventeenth, the plane arrived. The plan was for a bus to take my mother, family and friends from the sanitarium. But I was worried that something might happen along the road, so I went ahead to check. Near the airport there were troops and tanks, and after we passed I could see that the tanks had rolled onto the road and stopped. Nothing could pass by them.

"The airport was all chaos and panic. Everyone who had an Armenian member of their family, a mother, a father, was trying to send them away, but all the planes were filled. Nobody knew what to do. Hundreds of Armenians were waiting for a ticket to go anywhere. They were sitting in a hangar, waiting. At the same time, Azerbaijani nationalist groups were trying to send their fighters to other districts to battle against Armenians. Everything was out of control. Our chartered plane was on the ground, a small plane with sixty-eight seats, hidden among larger ones. But the crew wouldn't fly us out. They were afraid. We got another crew. I convinced them to take us with money. Lots of money.

"I talked to a KGB man at the airport and told him that the bus with my family and friends was coming. I asked if he could help get them past the blockade on the road. He said, 'Sorry, it's your problem.' What to do? If the bus had been stopped, probably they would have been attacked by the mob. Who knows what would have happened? My mother and grandmother. All of my friends. It's better not to guess.

"Then the driver of our car remembered that there is a very old and broken road which leads to the airport. It is almost never used. You must open a gate to pass. I called the sanitarium and told them to bring the bus this way.

"The weather was very bad. It was cold and windy. It was about seven o'clock when they arrived. We were still waiting for some other people. Soon nine members of my family came from town in a small bus. Somehow they got through. It was pitiful. Two of them were very old. These confused and frightened old people were trying to take care of their granddaughter, a little girl born with Down's syndrome. The driver of their bus was an Azerbaijani. A very brave man. If the bus had been stopped he might have died with his passengers.

"There had been many phone calls to the camp, and my mother was trying to figure out where people she knew might be hiding. Every time we called someone's flat, there was no answer or the line was dead. We had some free seats on the plane. Who to take? A terrible decision. Later some Armenian nationalists criticized me for taking my driver instead of someone else. It's bullshit. My driver is Armenian. He lost his flat. There are so many terrible stories. My driver often talked to me about his best friend, who was a dentist. Kolia had been staying in this friend's home before I arrived to begin my training. The man had a large house and was quite wealthy—maybe he did some shady business, but he was a good guy. He was a perfect target for the pogromists. They came to his house and he called to them from his window, 'Come on in. I will shoot.' He had automatic weapons. When they saw this, they left him alone. The next morning the police came to this man's house and arrested him for illegal use of weapons. Can you imagine? Police, KGB, pogromists—they were in it together. I called the chief of police and asked the man to bring my driver's friend to the camp. The chief said, 'Yes, yes,' but didn't do it. A few days later they let him go and he came to the airport to try to get out. He was getting on a plane when two policeman dragged him away. The next day his body was discovered.

"We had eight free seats on the plane. Which people to chose? I asked my driver to go to the hangar and select eight of the weakest. My friends and relatives, more than sixty people, rushed to climb up a wobbly little ladder that was there for the crew. No one could bear to wait for the normal boarding ladder. Three hours after we took off for Moscow, the Baku airport was closed.

"When we arrived in Moscow it was very cold. We brought people to hotels, to the Armenian embassy. Some stayed with me. These people were uprooted, lost souls. They had lost their past. Shakarov's aunt—she was one of the ones that my KGB friends had saved from the pogromists—became sick and died ten days later. She died of trauma. In Moscow they wouldn't allow us to bury her because she had no documents. Everything had been stolen by the pogromists. Finally, I was able to get permission.

"I approached the editors of one of the biggest newspapers and said that I wanted to give a press conference to report what I had seen. They organized a press conference and many journalists came. Almost nothing was published. One very incomplete article. That was it. This was the time of *glasnost*, the end of state censorship. One TV journalist promised to do a show with me about the tragedy in Baku. Weeks passed. He came back to me and said, 'I'm sorry, Garry, it's impossible.'

"I managed to get a meeting with Gorbachev and a few of his advisors. I described what I had seen, but Gorbachev wasn't listening. It was like shouting in a desert. Afterwards I realized that their plan was to punish the nationalists and to show the Lithuanians and others who wanted to break from the central government, 'Look what happened in Baku—this will happen to you if you persist in your demands.' This was an example for the Baltic states, but in Moscow people responded, 'Okay, Azerbaijan. Something happened. But exactly what happened? Some Armenians died. Then they brought troops. It's very complicated.'

"I gave speeches that began, 'Today Baku, tomorrow Vilnius, the day after tomorrow Moscow.' Unfortunately not too many listened. I could tell people were thinking, 'The kid is only twenty-seven. And he's a chess player. What does he know?'

"I discussed the events in Baku with journalists from the West, well-informed men. We watched videotapes together showing the disaster in Baku. One or two of them said to me, 'So what? It will not be shown in the West.' Why not? 'Because it is no big deal. People in southern California are not concerned about Azerbaijan.' No big deal.

"Maybe no big deal, but it changed my life. Two hundred and forty thousand Armenians lived in Baku in 1988. By the end of the pogrom, almost all were gone. I saw it with my eyes—the face of communism is the face of death. After there were no more Armenians left in Baku to protect, government troops came into the city and slaughtered Azeres. They came into the city to preserve the communist government. That was the plan from the beginning. Incite ethnic unrest and then use it as a pretext to destroy anticommunist independence movements.

"Because of Baku, I decided to start a political life. Maybe it's one drop, but it's something I can do. My priorities changed. I saw that there are things more important and less important. When I was in Baku and people were dying, chess seemed trivial. Before this, for as long as I could remember, chess had been the center of my life.

"When I became world champion I was asked many times, 'Garry, do you want to leave Baku? It is so little. It is out of the way, provincial. You should live in Moscow. To grow as a person you need to spend time in Western Europe and America.' I said, 'No, no. It is my home. Leaving Baku would be an insult to my friends.' I had this problem. Life solved this problem. Now my wife, my mother and I live in Moscow. I don't like it there very much. I am a refugee, a wealthy refugee, to be sure. I can afford to stay at the St. James Club when I visit Paris and at the Regency Hotel when I come to New York. But I lost my home. . . .

"That was the beginning of 1990."

3

A TROUBLEMAKER AND
A TROUBLED SOUL

April, 1990. "If you don't want to listen, it's your problem," said
Kasparov. He was in the front passenger seat of a black Mercedes
which was speeding north from Paris to Lille near the Belgium
border, where he was to play a chess exhibition. I had made the error
of asking a few questions which to him seemed tainted by America's
infatuation with Mikhail Gorbachev, and now Kasparov held me in
his glare as if I were the primary architect of American foreign policy.
"America closes its eyes and says the Baltic states are an internal
problem, your business. Send troops. Kill people. We won't bother
you. Fine." Kasparov's face was steel-hard and his short sentences
were pungent with threat. "But if you continue to give this blind
support to Gorbachev you'll increase the chances of civil war, and
don't be upset if we won't shake your hand in the future, because this
hand will be in the blood."

I was far from alone among Americans in thinking that Gorbachev
was a modern hero. I suggested that it was difficult to dismiss his
accomplishments. He had established an unprecedented environment

of liberalism in his country, which had set off a chain reaction of communist downfalls throughout eastern Europe. I also mentioned that he was admired in the United States for liberalizing emigration restrictions for Jews and for bringing free press to the Soviet Union.

"Listen, we cannot find a common language [exasperated pause] . . . You Americans have a history of loving our dictators. For a while Khrushchev was a hero in your country, and Stalin as well. You want to believe that they are doing a good job. It is true that Gorbachev is doing a good job for the West. He takes the troops from Afghanistan. He takes the troops from Eastern Europe. Fine. What does he do with them? He sends them to the Baltics. Is he doing this for peace? Did he slaughter women and children in Azerbaijan for peace?

"Gorbachev has succeeded in convincing the West that his is the fight of a decent man for a better future. This is a lie. He is the last leader of the communist state, trying to save everything he can. When you in the West make the opponent king, it is betrayal."

For a moment he was silent, and I tried to take things in. I had arrived in Paris a couple of hours before, sleepy but eager to interview the world champion about chess and about Anatoly Karpov, whom he would meet in five months for the title. When I had brought up the match at the start of the drive, he had said with a hint of reproach that people in the Soviet Union weren't interested in chess today, they were concerned with survival—end of chess talk. At the time the world champion was a virtual stranger to me. We had spoken for perhaps fifteen minutes at Olga Capablanca's party in New York half a year before. I knew, of course, of his interest in politics, but I was unprepared for his passion and anger.

"Bush can support him—the entire West can support him—but the leader without the support in his own country is dead [disgusted pause].

"The so-called freedom of the press is very useful to Gorbachev. It is a charade. I could tell you about the freedom of the press in my country."

I asked what he meant and he shook his head, no. We had no common language. This was not shaping up to be the trip I had looked forward to. Paris was still visible in the rear view mirror, and Kasparov was angry with me about American public opinion and had made it clear that he didn't want to discuss chess. What were we going to talk about for the next two weeks while traveling through France?

With a gesture of his hand, he waved off my naive inquiry about his training camp in Baku. At the time I knew almost nothing about his aborted training session in Azerbaijan four months earlier. Despite an addiction to newspapers and TV news shows, like most people in the United States, I would have been hard-pressed to find the Nagorno-Karabakh region of Azerbaijan on a map, and I knew little about the long history of ethnic conflict between Armenians and Azeris. Kasparov found this irritating. During this trip to France, with the exception of one emotional exchange when I raised questions about the loss of his home, he shook his head, no, forbidden subject.

"The Soviet correspondent from Moscow was on the radio this morning, criticizing me heavily for speaking out against Gorbachev in the West," he said, "It made me very happy. They are taking me seriously." A few weeks later in Moscow, Kasparov would become deputy chairman of a new opposition political movement called Democratic Russia. He described it as a loose coalition of individuals, including prominent intellectuals and politicians, who wished to change the existing social system to a democratic society with a free market system. Within the spectrum of membership there were those such as himself who advocated immediate and radical change, and others who favored a more moderate course. Kasparov's huge popularity in the USSR and his connections in the West gave the new party instant credibility, and from its inception it was described in Western publications as the most organized and prominent anticommunist party.

I asked Kasparov about the danger of his daily attacks on Gorbachev. "If you were to lose the match against Karpov, would you be vulnerable for reprisals?"

"If you play a big game, there is always a big risk." There was no fun, no adolescent posturing in these words. The dangers for a Soviet citizen criticizing the system were, of course, well-documented. Even during the past decade of relative liberalism, there had been examples of outspoken Soviet sportsmen having lost their privileges, their state subsidies and more, for attacking the communist system or for leveling criticisms at the central Sports Committee, which controlled the lives of Soviet athletes. One famous example was that of the chess grandmaster Boris Gulko, who in the late seventies had twice been Soviet champion and was among the several best players in the world. In 1978, when the grandmaster had become a dissident and made public his desire to leave the Soviet Union, Gulko had lost his state subsidy and had not been allowed to practice his profession.

Kasparov was convinced that if he had lost to Karpov in 1985 in the first match or in the rematch, the repercussions to him would have been grave, perhaps similar to Gulko's. "They would have tried to destroy me." Nevertheless, since becoming champion, Kasparov had relentlessly and systematically used his title to gain time on Western talk shows and newscasts, and to obtain meetings with newspaper editors and government officials, to criticize the Soviet Sports Committee, the communist system, and eventually the Secretary General himself, becoming in effect Vladimir Posner's opposition in the Western media.

As he traveled the globe, giving speeches and press conferences, writing articles for *The Wall Street Journal, The European* and other publications, he accepted the fact that repercussions, including assassination, were possible. In Moscow, where Kasparov was as recognizable on the streets as Michael Jordan or Bill Bradley in the United States, he lived his life surrounded by six bodyguards.

"Listen to me, Fred, in my country the fight against communism is nearly over," he said, turning my way from the front seat of the Mercedes. "Communism is dead."

Perhaps he noticed my surprise. At the time no one in the United States was predicting the immediate collapse of Soviet Communism, nor the dismantling of the country. Opposition to Soviet power was still at the philosophical center of American foreign policy. My generation had eaten breakfast while reading about the intricacies of the Cold War and nuclear arms race. After decades of articles and editorials decrying the evils of communism, we had come to feel that communism was immutable and perhaps even necessary, like the devil. To me, Kasparov's predictions seemed gratuitous, even frivolous.

"Next year, in 1991, the Soviet Union will not exist. Definitely. Mark my words. Next year, there will be no more evil empire. We will have private property in my country. Many of the republics will have their independence." Kasparov laughed at the outrageousness of his prophecy.

"In October, 1989, I was at a party with Henry Kissinger and Jonathan Bush, the president's brother, and the president of IBM was there also. They asked for my prognosis about Europe. I said there would be no communist regime in Europe by the end of the year. They laughed at me. But I could feel the mood of the people." Kasparov inhaled deeply through his nose a couple of times to demonstrate the new political smell in the air.

Kasparov was much more relaxed now, tapping his finger to the beat of music pulsing from fine speakers and quietly enjoying the speed of the Mercedes, which weaved past cars and trucks as if they were standing still. I noticed that the speedometer was edging past 190 and I nervously tried to remember my kilometers. Wasn't that more than 100 miles per hour?

There was no pressing appointment that evening in Lille. What was the rush? Why were we racing ahead? Over time, I would discover that Kasparov needed to speak, eat, walk, drive fast, that speed drove his ideas and brought a sense of well-being, that moving slowly made him edgy.

His young life was a Cinderella story with dark and ironic turns, many of them self-created. Imagine a young man from a poor family in the provincial republic of Azerbaijan suddenly becoming as famous and powerful as a king. At twenty-seven years old, he was the greatest living practitioner of his art, perhaps the greatest of all time. He was wealthy. But he felt dissatisfaction more than success. He craved other things, different forms of expression, vaster audiences, bigger and more dangerous opponents. In a few months, he would play a deadly match against Karpov, with millions of dollars on the line, not to mention the prestige, but he could barely bring himself to think about chess. While his fans around the world wondered which opening variations he would play, Kasparov was obsessed with Gorbachev, at times so much so that he could not smile, could not taste his food. Months later, the focus and passion was likely to shift again. He seemed to know that about himself.

"This life I lead, it's like drugs," he reflected in the car. "I know that the way I live is bad. I'm taking from the future. But I need it. My mind and nervous system need the tension. I don't think that I could live the normal life. A house in the country. I need the big stage. I need to be at the front of the event.

"I am like the raider, the soldier who uses the parachute and attacks from the rear. It is a very risky profession, but it is thrilling because there is a chance for a big result." He added, "But a raider cannot make a mistake, because the first mistake is normally the last one."

"Does a raider feel fear? Does he fear death?"

"Yeah, but what can I do?"

On that somber note, the world champion dozed off in the front seat, and I was the only one fearing death. My fear was nothing so extravagant as political assassination by the KGB. I envisioned the blowout and the tumbling Mercedes. A lengthy obituary in *The New York Times* about the tragic early loss of the greatest chess player of all time, with a brief mention of a journalist who was accompanying him to an exhibition in Lille. No more going to chess tournaments with my kid, the two of us dreaming about the day he would win the world chess championship. I thought it was a little strange that this man, who didn't miss the subtlest nuance of a complex chess position, hadn't noticed that I was terrified.

"That's the advertisement for my tournament," said Dan-Antoine Blanc-Shapira, the thirty-year-old organizer of Kasparov's next event, from the driver's seat. The following weekend in Paris, he was producing the most lavish and technically sophisticated chess tournament of all time, featuring Kasparov. He turned up the volume on the radio. "The theme song," he shouted above the pounding bass and electronic piano, an undulating refrain that seemed more a call for lust than an advertisement for an elite grandmaster chess tournament.

Dan-Antoine was a handsome man who possessed the accommodating genius of Felix Krull. During each of the world champion's trips to France, Dan-Antoine shepherded him around, attending to his tiniest needs with conviviality and élan. He arranged Kasparov's travel schedule, selected restaurants, handled the press, drove the Mercedes. If Kasparov wanted speed, Dan-Antoine gave him speed.

Dan-Antoine kept glancing my way as he translated the words of the radio announcement. "The strongest action tournament ever held . . . the biggest prize fund . . . infra-red earphones." In this event, the Immopar Trophée, he would endeavor to convey the turbulent emotions of grandmaster chess through the use of larger-than-life video images—a media montage of the sometimes-agonized, some-times-elated players, and state-of-the-art graphics demonstrating chess positions—as well as with sensuous rock music and intense nontechnical commentary coming over earphones to fans seated in the elegant Théâtre des Champs Elysées. When Kasparov was feeling interested in chess, he loved Dan-Antoine's ideas for popularizing the game. As the Frenchman enthusiastically described the Immopar Trophée, I hunkered down behind the driver's seat and tried to appear casual as I suggested that he keep his eyes on the road. The speedometer was sitting on 210.

Kasparov slept like a baby, looking invulnerable in a sloppy-fitting leather jacket. We slowed down when we reached the outskirts of Lille. Kasparov woke up and scratched his head. Now he was a much softer man, younger. His face was slack, his eyes liquid and sad. He looked outside at the blackness and didn't speak until we arrived at the hotel.

Sometime later, I asked what he had been thinking about. "In a way, the trip to Lille was a journey back to the past for me," he reflected. "Nineteen seventy-six was my first trip abroad, and I came to a small village near Lille. I remember small details—a soccer game, a dinner. I don't remember the games, for some reason. Usually when I recall my early trips, I think of the games.

"I had been growing up without a father and spent much time with my grandfather, my mother's father. I loved him very much. We had a very small flat, but there was a big map in our dining room. We would look at this map and talk about distant places. I remember conversations about African revolutions, Latin America, Vietnam, Angola. Inevitably the discussion came around to communism. He was an old communist, almost fifty years in the Communist Party. Sometimes we quarreled, but they were great discussions. I felt that some things he said were wrong. I felt it, but I didn't understand, I was too young.

"And then I received this good news. I would be sent to France to play in the 1976 world junior championship at Wattigny. I was thirteen. I was so pleased to be going. For people in my country, it was unusual to travel even to Bulgaria or Rumania. But France . . . I had read many books, and understood that France was important for European culture. But we arrived at this village and it was so ordinary, a village anywhere. I had imagined something like Disneyland, but life is life."

Kasparov was born in Baku in the Soviet Republic of Azerbaijan on April 13, 1963. From his earliest years, it was apparent to members of his family that Garry was an unusual child. "When he was a little boy, still unable to speak, everyone noticed that he had thoughts in his eyes," recalled his eighty-year-old grandmother, Suzanne Kasparova, a slight woman with white hair and a mind brimming with memories. She recalled that baby Garry made subtle distinctions and manifested decisiveness that was almost shocking. "The house was always crammed with people; Garry would enter the room and decide whom he wanted to be with. If there was no one, he just left," she said, with an amused expression that I took to mean, "and he is the same way today," for the world champion chooses his conversations with care and will sometimes avoid chitchat, even at the cost of being rude.

When he was only a few months old, family members read to him; and when he started to talk, he had already accumulated a great deal of information and was almost immediately pronouncing whole sentences. No one in the family spoke baby talk to this serious child. It seemed inappropriate. "Adults in the family felt his wisdom," said his aunt Nellia, "and so they didn't bring him toys and games. They brought him books."

There are many stories about young Kasparov's intellectual precocity. His aunt Nellia recalled that once, when Garry was two, they were riding on a trolley bus and he noticed that the buildings on one side had odd numbers and on the other side even. At five, his father bought him a globe and he immediately began to study it. Within months he had the knowledge of geography of an adult. His favorite

early book was the encyclopedia. Overnight, it seemed to the family,
Garry knew everything about this country and that one, which were
the highest mountains, the longest rivers, the populations of countries. The young boy had a remarkable memory, to go along with an
insatiable appetite for knowledge.

When Garry was seven, his schoolteacher asked the children to
write something, recalled his grandmother. "Most of them wrote a
few words about mommy or daddy. Garry wrote three words:
'peace, people, party.'" The ideas he was beginning to discuss with
her husband were making a deep impression. "Garry was fond of
eating dinner with his grandfather," said Nellia. "They started to eat,
and soon they would be talking about politics and life. They would
begin to argue. His mother and grandmother would try to stop them,
because Garry would forget to eat."

Members of the family not only acknowledged Garry's serious
turn of mind, they cultivated it, and coddled him, as if they were all
involved in sculpting a masterpiece. "Everyone in the family worked
with him," his grandmother said. He was lavished with attention, his
needs carefully anticipated. Garry's father resisted the desire to visit
his close friends who lived in neighboring towns, because he was
concerned about Garry's schedule. He believed that the boy should
always have his own room in which to sleep. His cousin Eugene,
twenty-four, recalled with pride that Garry enjoyed riding his bike
with him. Though they spent considerable time together, they rarely
had conversations, Eugene said without resentment. "Garry wanted
more to communicate with adults." At first the family believed that
Garry would make his mark in mathematics or the sciences, but they
never doubted that there would be greatness in his life. And they
banded together like a little team, Garry's team, to support his
development.

Today the family lives in Moscow, and they are still, first and
foremost, Garry's team. Eugene frequently stops by Garry's sprawling offices in the center of Moscow. Though he has little in common
intellectually with his cousin, Garry is a big part of his life, and the
love for his famous cousin shines in his eyes. Eugene's mother, Nellia,
comes by her sister's apartment with cakes and pies that she knows
Garry likes with his tea after lunch. But she also knows that he likes

her to be around. The family seems to steady Garry. They are his foundation, his love, his talisman. He is more confident preparing to joust with Karpov, Gorbachev or Yeltsin, if he hears the faint voices of his aunt, grandmother and wife chatting with his mother in the kitchen.

While he plays his games against Karpov thousands of miles away, back in Moscow the family suffers for him. They agonize as he struggles over the board, and afterwards they are so distraught they take tranquilizers to calm down. His games are religious moments to them. They believe that if they root hard enough, feel enough pain, Garry will feel their energy, and it will help him win. They point out that Garry has frequently demonstrated feats that tested credulity. At the age of six, he was beating his father at chess. At the age of nine, he won the chess championship of Baku, competing against many excellent local players who had studied the game their entire lives. "It was considered a miracle," said his grandmother. "Everyone in the city knew him after this. There were magazine articles written about the miracle in Baku."

"You know, during the pogrom, Suzanne's house was not touched," added Nellia, "because everyone knew who was living there, the grandmother of Garry. He was loved by the whole city."

When he was little, Garry wanted to follow his father everywhere. But when Kim Weinstein became seriously ill, he decided not to see his son again, lest the impression of a dying man cause harm to the boy. "On the day of the funeral, Garry isolated himself in the bathroom and spent the whole day there," said his grandmother. Members of the family understood that he was crying, but Garry was left alone. They sensed that he needed to grieve by himself.

"Seven days after the funeral, Garry came to me and said that he would think his father was on a business trip and not dead," recalled his mother, Klara. "He said, 'For my life, I shall think of him on a business trip.' After our conversation, he spoke to everyone as if his father were still alive. His teacher in school said he told his friends that his father was away traveling." Seven-year-old Garry had decided upon this tactic to cope with his pain, and it is interesting that the family played along with his denial until Garry decided that he was ready to face his father's death. Two years later, when he signaled that it was time, the family began softly pronouncing the father's name and talking about the events of his life. Garry's school friends were surprised to learn that his father had passed away so long ago. "This was when Garry started to play a lot of chess," said Klara. "At the age of nine, he had switched to another life."

"You know, Garry's life has been marked by big losses," she continued. "His father, his grandfather, and now the loss of his home. After each loss there is deep mourning and then he acquires a new impulse, starts a new life. The more painful the loss, the more energy he has for the next phase of his life."

We had traveled to Lille for a simultaneous exhibition against twenty students selected from different engineering universities. For the three-and-a-half-hour event, advertised as a contest of intelligence and sponsored by Sollac, one of Europe's largest steel manufacturers, Kasparov would be paid the equivalent of about twenty thousand dollars, more than any chess player would earn in any tournament in 1990. Then, as now, the world champion was hugely popular throughout Europe, frequently in the papers and on television. He is asked to give many such exhibitions, but usually refuses because they are not serious chess.

Before the event and the spate of press conferences and TV interviews to follow, we were taken to a fine seafood restaurant by five student organizers and their girlfriends. Kasparov immediately launched into a political exegesis, as though he were addressing a symposium of newspaper editors. At some length he elucidated Zbigniew Brzezinski's faulty evaluation of European communism in his book, *The Grand Failure.* He indicated reservations about Boris Yeltsin, arguing that the man lacked a comprehensive political vision and, despite his recent political evolution, maintained deep roots in the Communist Party. Gesturing sharply with his hands, Kasparov framed his points with such irreproachable authority that his audience responded as if we were listening to a man Kissinger's or Gorbachev's age. The waiter interrupted and the world champion ordered small eels in butter sauce with the élan of someone who has been appreciating small eels for many years.

"The police in Moscow are no longer doing their job. They are out on the streets fighting democrats," he said. The student hosts kept trying to guide the conversation to chess, but Kasparov patiently explained that right now, chess was not important in his country; people were starving. The student hosts, all of them players, were a little confused. For months they had been looking forward to this once-in-a-lifetime opportunity to talk chess with the world champion. Two of the girls were looking Kasparov over in a way to suggest that their thoughts were not entirely political. Garry became a little shy. This was an unusual lunch for him. Normally, meals on the road were shared with celebrities, promoters, editors, politicians, people who were much older. He was clearly attracted to the students, who were only a few years younger than he, but at the same time he felt hopelessly at a remove. They were so much more casual, their mannerisms, posture, dress and language suggesting a carefree life that he could only imagine.

The young men persisted asking about chess and finally, when one of them brought up Dan-Antoine's tournament the following weekend in Paris, Garry relented. "After I beat Speelman," he said of the great English grandmaster Jonathan Speelman whom he would play in the first round, "I will face the winner of Korchnoi-Renet." In a few sentences, he predicted whom he would beat en route to taking first place in the tournament. "I should not have much trouble," Kasparov ventured uneasily. "But of course at speed there is luck as well as skill." Kasparov had taken first place in every serious competition he had entered for the past nine years (this did not include tournaments with rapid time controls such as Dan-Antoine's Immopar Trophée). A remarkable record, when one considered that virtually each "serious" tournament he had entered was a small round robin event consisting of the very strongest grandmasters in the world, often including Karpov. Only the very top players inspired his best efforts; but still, in his mind, his games were never a contest between two equals. In a sense, Kasparov played against himself. He believed that he could lose only if he was stupid or rusty, that the only one on earth who could beat Kasparov was Kasparov. He still thinks that.

One of the students asked what it had been like for him playing two games against Deep Thought, the world's strongest chess computer. The match had taken place seven months before in October, 1989, and was televised on the PBS show *Nova*. "It was uncomfortable because I didn't exactly have an opponent," he answered. "At first I tried to concentrate on the man who made the moves, the programmer. I tried to convince myself that I was playing this man. It's very odd to play the computer. I was playing against a force without a human dimension. I knew that I was stronger than that force—he or it, what should I call it? The computer was helpless from the beginning, but it didn't realize this. After I won the first game, I had this uncomfortable thought. It wouldn't be affected by the loss. It wouldn't care. I was affected by the win. You cannot isolate yourself from the previous game, unless you are a computer. I realized that sometime in the future, in a long match, this could be the computer's advantage; it wouldn't become discouraged, overconfident or tired.

"But even if chess computers become stronger than humans, so what? Humans will create the art." On this afternoon, perhaps inspired by the enthusiasm of the students and the ogling of the girls, opinions were flying out of Kasparov. "No one will care that this artificial intelligence can do it better." Asked about Jan Timman, one of the several strongest grandmasters in the world, and for years a big chess celebrity in Western Europe, Kasparov said simply, "He is not a serious player."

One of the students wondered about the potential of the Polgars, three Hungarian sisters who were chess prodigies and considered by some grandmasters to be extraordinarily talented; in 1991, at the age of fifteen, the youngest, Judit, would become the youngest grandmaster in chess history, and has often been written about as a potential world championship contender. "She is talented, but not greatly talented," Kasparov said somberly, as if the future of this teenager were already history. Garry leaned my way to inquire if I were going to try the eels. I answered, "I use the slimy things for bait to catch striped bass." With a quick grin he changed his order to lobster.

"Women by their nature are not exceptional chess players," he continued without missing a beat. "They are not great fighters. For that matter, not many of them have been great composers or novelists."

"Feminists would not like you for saying such things."

"The feeling is mutual."

I took advantage of this brief window of opportunity to ask his opinion about problems in the American chess world: Why was it that since Fischer we had not produced a single player who consistently ranked among the top dozen in the world? Why was it that with few exceptions, tournaments in the United States were dreary affairs offering pitifully small prize funds? Was he aware that the situation on the professional level seemed to be growing worse?

Kasparov rarely minces words. "The problem with the game in America is that the leaders of the U.S. Chess Federation are small-minded," he said immediately. "They are trying to hold onto power and won't give professional organizers room to build something new. They are trying to keep it an amateur game. They are caught in old habits." The remedy: members of the federation must be purged like entrenched communist bureaucrats.

One of the students inquired when I had first met Kasparov, and I told them about Josh's game at the simultaneous exhibition. Kasparov overheard, and surprised me by recalling that my son had played the Benoni Defense against him. "I had a good attack against Josh, but then I misplayed it," he said, and then recited the moves of the game. Then he described exactly where Josh had been sitting in the gymnasium packed with children, parents and journalists, and then the final position of another game which had also been a draw against K. K. Karanja, whose name Kasparov also recalled.

He said that his prodigious memory was only of limited use to him as a player, that ideas born from inspiration and intuition were far more important. One gets the feeling that his memory sometimes annoys him, like a tune that replays in the mind; it wars with his craving for the exhilaration which comes from breaking free of traditional constraints, to play moves which come to him like little miracles, unexpected and terrifying for his opponents. "I have so much coming into my head, it is difficult to keep it under control. Sometimes I have to clean up my brain, just to get rid of the rubbish, like erasing an old tape."

At one point during dinner, Dan-Antoine was trying to remember if he and Garry had visited a particular city during a whirlwind trip a year and a half before. At machine-gun pace, Kasparov, who is on the road constantly, described the itinerary of the fifty-day journey, rolling days, places and events past his eyes, until he came to the city in question. At the end of this feat, he spoke ruefully about all the cities he had visited over the years but had not had a chance to experience—a press conference, a speech, the mayor, a rich dinner, autographs and on to the airport. Mayor Koch once asked me if I appreciated his beautiful city and I answered that I had not seen it, except from the window of my hotel or the window of the plane."

And all this time, he continued to observe the students and their girlfriends with curiosity, as if he were learning about a younger generation, but also with a certain wistfulness. Around these young adults he would have liked to have been unrestrained, to fool around, but he couldn't let himself go, he didn't know how: "If you are world champion . . ." he said, with his voice trailing off.

At the age of twenty-seven, Kasparov was haunted by the idea that early success born of painful struggle had cost him a normal childhood, leaving him without the capacity to experience life's lighter side. While friends rode bikes, flirted with girls, played ball, he had studied chess books and had done rigorous analysis with coaches. The games themselves are a great strain on anyone who plays at a high level, but for young Kasparov there was the additional tension of playing against adults, of judging himself relative to men who had dedicated themselves to chess knowledge for decades.

"When I was ten, I was playing against fifteen- and sixteen-year-olds," recalls Kasparov. "When I was fourteen, I competed in adult competitions. Now it is normal, but then it was unusual. I was among the first. Fischer did it also. I was isolated from players my age. Though I was convinced that it was my destiny, I felt the pressure of trying to live up to adult standards.

"I entered into the big life much earlier than other kids. I was used to talking with older people and thinking their way. I felt lost being in the company of my generation. The loss of my childhood was the price for becoming the youngest world champion in history. When you have to fight every day from a young age, your soul can be contaminated. I lost my childhood. I never really had it. Today I have to be careful not to become cruel, because I became a soldier too early."

For that reason, he speaks against serious tournament competition for young children. "Can you imagine my feelings when I entered Disneyland a couple of months ago? I was very sad. I was with a child and his parents and everyone was happy. I knew with my mind that this was a great place, a funny place. I could analyze it. But I couldn't feel what that boy and his parents felt."

Still, for this child chess was an auspicious choice. Adults who analyzed with the little boy came away from the experience stunned. Typical was the recollection of Ashken Petrosovna, who worked at the department of mathematics in Baku and was a strong chess player, the woman's champion of Baku in 1964. She recalls her first meeting with Garry in 1971, when he was eight years old: "Several days before, I had played a game that was adjourned in a difficult position. I had studied this position for two days and still I wasn't sure of the correct move. On a Sunday morning, I had arranged to study the position with my coach at the Pioneer Palace. When I arrived that morning, there was no one there, so I set up the pieces and started to analyze. Soon a few little boys came into the room. One of them came over to the board and looked at the position. Almost immediately, he showed me variations that I had not considered. After this, I couldn't think about the chess. I was just looking at this boy, Garry, as if I had witnessed a miracle of nature."

According to Kasparov's childhood friend, grandmaster Lev Psakhis, a former Soviet national champion, by the time Garry was ten years old he understood the game at the grandmaster level. In Garry's generation, a number of boys in the Soviet Union, such as Psakhis himself, Sergey Dolmatov and Artur Yusupov, were considered to have great talent, possibly even world championship–level talent, but, according to Psakhis, they all knew that Garry's potential was much greater, that he was the true genius.

In 1975, at the age of twelve, Garry, along with a group of schoolchildren from Baku, played against the new world champion, Anatoly Karpov, in a simultaneous exhibition. Neither of them could have guessed that, before long, their lives would be joined in perennial battle, that their seemingly endless matches would come to have a mythic quality which spurred people to argue systems of government. Kasparov writes in his autobiography, *Unlimited Challenge*, "The other boys . . . were nervous, and went into the game looking rather lost. In the hotel lobby where the tournament was taking place I said to them: 'What's there to be afraid of? Karpov may be world champion, but he can still make mistakes.' This remark was evidently overheard, because the next day one of Karpov's backers, Anatoly Tupikin (then secretary of a Leningrad district Party committee), told my mother: 'Bear in mind that Karpov never forgets a slight.' "

In the exhibition, after all the other boys had resigned their games, Karpov sat down head to head with Garry, while photographers snapped the picture. For a time Kasparov was winning the game, but eventually he missed a combination and lost. Afterwards, many journalists speculated that young Kasparov would be Karpov's future rival for the world championship.

By the age of thirteen, Kasparov was working hard at chess and traveling abroad to represent the Soviet Union in various tournaments. By eighteen, he was Soviet champion, an amazing accomplishment.

However, not everyone was pleased by Kasparov's precocity. Karpov was one of the most influential men in the Soviet Union, with a close relationship to Brezhnev. According to Garry, the world champion was surrounded by a chess mafia, who Kasparov believed tried to block his chess progress. In 1982, to prepare for the elimination tournaments for the world championship, Kasparov applied for travel permits to a strong tournament in Bugojno, Yugoslavia, but instead was offered a second-class tournament in Dortmund, West Germany, an insult to such a promising player. More importantly, for an up-and-coming grandmaster, participation in the strongest events was essential to development. Kasparov writes, "Karpov ruled as the king of chess. As befits a reigning monarch, he was surrounded by a large retinue. His was the power to decide who should go abroad and who should not. All chess players found themselves divided into travelers and nontravelers, and the principle by which they were divided was no secret." Those who pandered to Karpov by offering him their best ideas were given privileges, Kasparov says; those who didn't were frozen out. When he asked Nikolai Krogius, head of the chess department of the USSR Sports Committee, why he had been refused permission to compete in the Bogojno tournament—he was Soviet champion, after all—Krogius replied, "We've got one world champion, we don't need another."

While still a teenager, Kasparov discovered that good chess moves alone would never give him the chance to win the world championship. He understood that to get his opportunity he would have to learn something of political infighting, lobbying and organizing, and so he tried some politicking of his own. He made contact with Geidar Aliev, first secretary of the Azerbaijan Communist Party. Kasparov acknowledges that it was heady for him at the time to be on speaking terms with a top communist. Aliev intervened for Kasparov, who was finally permitted to play in the Bogojno tournament—and Kasparov finished first.

The following year, after beating Alexander Beliavsky in the first round of the candidates match (a knock-out competition among the final eight candidates competing to face the world champion), Kasparov was next scheduled to play Victor Korchnoi, who had defected from the Soviet Union in 1976. For months before the players pushed a pawn, the match was shrouded in political intrigue, and the young Kasparov barely survived elimination by default. As Kasparov tells the story, he was tricked by a member of the Sports Committee into changing his order of preference for the venue of the match, which made his first choice different from Victor Korchnoi's. According to the rules of FIDE, the international governing body of chess, when two players disagree on the playing site, the choice is made by the FIDE president, who was Florencio Campomanes from the Philippines. Campomanes, who it later became clear was a close friend of Karpov's, chose Pasadena. Soviet authorities then promptly rejected Pasadena, claiming that the city could not provide proper security. To Kasparov, the maneuver had been clearly prearranged between Campomanes and the Soviet Sports Committee, working in the interest of Karpov. Stukalin, the head of the propaganda department of the CPSU Central Committee, told the increasingly suspicious Kasparov, "As a citizen you've got to understand that it's in the interest of our country . . . You're still young, you can afford to wait three years [for the next cycle]."

Kasparov again asked for the help of Aliev, by then a powerful member of the Politburo. But still, on the day appointed, Korchnoi went to the tournament site in Pasadena, started the clock, and Kasparov, half a world away, was declared the loser by default. Kasparov felt as though he were fighting for his life. He gave numerous interviews; he sought out fellow chess players for support. At a tournament in Yugoslavia he lobbied with the strongest players in the world to sign a petition, and, in the end, Victor Korchnoi was compensated and agreed to meet Kasparov in London. Kasparov won. Then, just twenty-one, he beat former world champion Vasily Smyslov in the finals for the right to face Karpov, in a match that would be remembered more for its political infighting and dirty tricks than for its chess strategy and tactics.

The simultaneous exhibition in Lille was held in a blue and white tent bulging with four to five hundred people. Before he appeared, there was a thrill in the air, hard rock blaring from big speakers, people nudging one another, whispering, "Kasparov." The champion entered, his arm in the air with a self-conscious smile that spurred a wave of cheering and applause. A couple of girls whispered, "It's him." Everyone crowded around the tables of the players, creeping over shoulders to get a glimpse of his moves. We're talking about chess here, not Bruce Springsteen.

Kasparov moved swiftly from board to board as if someone were pacing him in a race, pushing pawns and pieces ahead. He is beautiful when he plays, a wild creature. His body is tense, his face taut, punishing, at times fierce, as if he is about to physically attack. I have seen top grandmasters wither from his fury, becoming disheveled, alarmed (although others are caught in the jet stream of his energy and genius and play their inspired best against him). He paused at one board, his bottom lip stuck out, mirroring an inner churning.

As he thought, there was a sway to his body, a connection between the mind that created games brimming with complexity so deep that few in the world could fully understand them, and the long graceful sweep of his arm moving a bishop across a diagonal, the athletic move from board to board. Indeed, he said later, he is a rhythm player, making better and better moves when he is on the beat from game to game.

Suddenly, Dan-Antoine appeared, speaking into a microphone in mellifluous French, an arm around Kasparov's shoulder, asking Garry—who for a few seconds looked like a man emerging from a dream—to tell the audience who was giving him a hard time. I had never seen this before in any kind of formal chess event. Games are typically played in religious silence, but Kasparov wanted chess fans to feel the fear and excitement. He realized that for the game to succeed as a professional sport, fans had to identify with the players, as they do in other sports. In Dan-Antoine's tournament the following weekend in Paris, there would be close-ups of Kasparov's face projected on two large screens, so that the fan could feel his exhilaration and wonder, or his anger and mortification if he should lose. "Chess is a passionate game, but people don't know. The game can't exist in empty space—it needs a public."

Towards this end, from time to time in the exhibition, Kasparov had agreed to edify fans about why he was doing well or badly, which was a little bit like a general giving away his war plan in the middle of the battle. Then he was back to his games, whirling around the room, snatching pieces, calculating, grimacing, rocking on his heels. When games turned his way, he was relentless, pressing, pushing pieces ahead, his knuckles white with struggle. He was lusty to win, and the more he won the more the crowd cheered.

"He is a ferocious attacker, he keeps increasing the pressure," explained one young master, thrilled to be in the presence of his hero. "Top grandmasters flinch under the tension of his style and confidence. You can tell from their moves that these guys are scared. They don't play normally against him. Their attacks are either wild and hopeless or they play very timid moves."

Of course, Kasparov occasionally loses. When he makes a weak move in an exhibition, there is no attempt to conceal his emotions, to maintain a poker face as he would against Karpov. After a blunder, his jaw clenches tight and he shakes his head, no, no. The pain ripples through him. "When I make a mistake, I feel it earlier than my opponent. I feel vulnerable and angry at myself. Losing is a shock. I feel punished by the gods, because I've got this talent and I don't feel that any opponent should beat me."

In Lille, Garry won all twenty of his games and the fans were rapturous. "I feel happy but exhausted," he said afterwards. "If they get something, I must lose something."

Exhausted, to be sure. He had just overcome twenty players, and now his mind was flooded with calculations and scores of chess positions; a few of them, the most interesting, he would wrestle with in his head for months—searching for moves that might have been a little better, like figuring out a clever retort after the argument is over. "If only I had done it better. It's a pity," he said in Paris the next week, after losing a game in a simultaneous exhibition. Chess does not allow for revisions: no takebacks. The moment is lost forever, but still the scene plays over and over in your head and will not leave you in peace.

Kasparov's face looked drained. I shook his hand and the muscles in his arm were slack. It was time to give back-to-back press conferences. Where would he find the energy? We walked to a large trailer overfilled with photographers and journalists.

"Four years ago Margaret Thatcher made a comparison between interest in chess and politics," he began, his words full of snap and irony. "She said politicians and chess players are always in time trouble. Today I get scared when I see politicians playing chess. One is so easily tempted to sacrifice a pawn. Why not sacrifice a small Baltic pawn?" Of course. Kasparov had primed himself for the European press by invoking Gorbachev's disingenuousness. Gorbachev could nearly always be counted upon to bring him back to life.

Thirty or forty journalists sat ready with their questions about the exhibition and the coming match against Karpov, while Kasparov lectured to them about Gorbachev's treachery in the Baltics. Then he allowed a few questions about chess:

"I believe in human beings. That's why I believe I will be replaced by a human being, not a computer."

"For chess I devote less time than I want, and for leisure I devote less time also."

"Must you hate your opponent to win?" someone asked.
    "Sorry, I'd have to hate so many people."

"Have you ever been to Cuba?"

"I never visit communist countries, except my own."

You could see that Kasparov enjoyed lobbing his one-liners at the reporters, presenting firsthand evidence that chess players were not narrow, cerebral creatures. For the same reason, he relishes his regular visits on the David Letterman show, practicing his jokes beforehand, working to overcome his serious turn of mind. It is an occasion to demonstrate to millions that he can banter silliness with the best—who would expect it? But his performance in press conferences is often very crafty. One-liners and chess insights are all directed toward warming up his audience, preparing them for tough political talk. "My country is the kingdom of convex mirrors," he said to a reporter, who scribbled down each word. The world champion was determined to use his status as a sportsman to publicize his political point of view. When a reporter asked for his observations about the upcoming generation of chess players in the Soviet Union, he answered that with his country in chaos and misery, chess was simply not very important now; in fact many of the top players were leaving to live in other parts of the world, where they could live a normal life. He was impatient with questions about Karpov's style and stressed that the most significant aspect of the coming match would be its political overtones. "For years, Karpov has been the symbol of the system. I am known as the Soviet sportsman who fights to destroy this system, who is trying to organize democratic forces to build a normal society."

A few days later, we were eating in a restaurant in Paris, and Kasparov was speaking with great exhilaration. After lunch, he would give another simultaneous exhibition against selected students, most of them master strength, and then there would be a press conference and television interviews. If he lost two or three games, it would be written about in European newspapers and chess players would begin to wonder if the champ was slipping, if maybe Karpov would beat him in the fall. But while we talked about hockey (his political infighting at home had made it possible for the Soviet

Viacheslav Fetisov to play for the New Jersey Devils in the National Hockey League), Robert Penn Warren (*All the King's Men* was one of his favorite novels), Camus ("he is too wishy-washy") and Gorbachev (the criminal), the events of the afternoon did not exist for him. His concentration and passion for conversation was tactile. He held forth on one topic or another as if it was hugely important, and did not notice what was going on across the restaurant or at the other end of the table.

When Kasparov enters into a conversation, there is a sense of commitment and importance to the encounter, almost as if there has been a contractual arrangement. Whether speaking with a student or a famous movie actress, he seems to want to squeeze the moment for its possibilities, to complete it like the last pages of a book. Once, in New York, I watched him talking about a chess position with an amateur player while Mayor Dinkins stood by awkwardly, waiting to have a word with him. I think an hour would have passed this way if Andrew Page had not stepped in to make a smooth transition, and even at that, Kasparov appeared to be pained to break off the discussion.

A conversation with him is rarely casual. Kasparov's face is etched with purpose; he is out to learn or to teach. At times he was dogmatic, lecturing, and then for no apparent reason, accessible and open to suggestion. To hold his attention you must be intense and honest, at your best, or he will walk away—you sense this while you talk. Over the course of several hours with him, switching gears and trying to match his intensity can be exhausting.

About a half hour before it was time to leave for the exhibition, Kasparov became very quiet. He pinched his eyes and appeared to be distracted. After a time, he rested his head on the table. His silence was very loud, awkwardly loud. Although conversation went on around him and people looked at him from across the room, he remained perfectly still.

During my days with him in France, there were other moments like this when he fell into an uneasy repose, suddenly becoming silent and unapproachable. "He has bursts of tremendous energy and then becomes exhausted," said Andrew Page. But during some of these quiet times, Kasparov did not seem to be resting. Occasionally, his lips moved. He mumbled a little, as if conferring with another part of himself, and he appeared to be in pain. In France, I found his moodiness confusing. As I have said, I knew little about the events in Baku. I did not understand that he was grieving and depressed. At the time, perhaps he didn't fully appreciate what was wrong with himself. "I am not only a troublemaker. I'm a troubled soul," he told me, enigmatically. Under normal circumstances, Kasparov is an emotional man, but for at least a year after the loss of his home, his moodiness became more pronounced, good humor gave way inexplicably to painful awkward silences. Despair was Garry's ready companion, and he complained almost daily to friends of a lack of energy and wondered if he was physically ill.

While traveling through France, Kasparov gathered himself in his brooding way for the next public event, where more often than not he was outgoing, friendly and quick-witted. But sometimes he would appear before a group of journalists and simply have no energy to answer their questions. At a press conference in Lyon, where the second half of the championship would be played the following winter, Kasparov appeared exhausted and without color. Standing beside a smiling Michel Noir, mayor of the city and a leading political figure in France, Kasparov's answers to the press were often no more than a quiet word or two, and all the while he was looking at the door.

Occasionally protocol and small talk seemed to overwhelm him. One afternoon in Paris, he had been signing autographs and answering stale questions at an elegant cocktail party given in his honor. After forty-five minutes of this, he whispered, "I must leave." I chased him out the door and down a winding street. For all of his tactical and strategic ability, Kasparov has a terrible sense of direction, as I do, and I worried about how we would ever find our way back. Kasparov walks at the pace that most middle-aged men jog, so keeping up with him without running was very awkward. Nevertheless, I tried to do it, and at the same time to keep track of the heedless turns he was making. Kasparov increased his blistering pace, smiled, pumped his arms and like a kid playing hooky reveled in his escape into the fine sunny afternoon.

After not speaking for a while, he slowed down and said, "My wife Maria is twenty-six. We should have one or two children, but look at this life that I live. When would I see them? What do you think?" I told him that, for me at least, children were the most important thing, and he nodded. I had the feeling he was deciding right then. When we managed to find our way back, Kasparov neatened his tie and was ready to be world champion again.

Sometimes a reluctant world champion, though. Bridling against the constraints of his title, wishing to be other things as well, Kasparov cannot bear the idea that he is what he is and that's it. With energy and purpose that borders on greed, he strives to make himself better, smarter, broader. He is his own work in progress, constantly analyzing himself, working at a facet of his being, whether it be a political idea, a chess opening or a psychological frailty.

"Sometimes it strikes me that I could go back, I could change." He mused often about his lost youth. At times he spoke of it as if he were searching for a child who was lost and wandering somewhere. "I am trying to do something," he said, with a painful stutter. "To keep these childish corners of my mind. For example, I eat ice cream. It is sweet, you know. And sometimes I try to be involved in something silly."

One morning, at the exclusive St. James Club, where he stays in Paris, he ate an omelette, and with a draft of a political speech attacking Gorbachev and the editorials of a half-dozen newspapers strewn around, he watched cartoons on television. Watching this serious young man with graying hair watch cartoons was very moving. He was purposeful about enjoying himself, as if the diversion were a medicine prescribed for his soul.

A few days after I arrived, we began to have long talks without the tape recorder. "Leave it off, Fred," he would say to me. Talking was also self-prescribed medicine. For a time, it quieted the demons inside. Then, after hours of speaking about everything under the sun—nuclear arms, Hemingway, abortion, wives, sex, death—he would suddenly grow silent, and if I tried to say a word or two, he would mumble something, an impatient admonition from far off or an annoyed glance which said, Not now—can't you see that I am preoccupied? Then there were times when Garry stared at me for a response, but I had to guess the question. It was a disarming question, something like, so what do you think of me, of my politics, of my life? I would say a few words. Sometimes a smile was enough or a touch on the wrist. After dinner we would walk for miles, all the while talking, and afterwards he would make long distance phone calls around the world until one or two A.M., when he finally felt tired enough to sleep. He said to me that being alone for more than a few hours was unnerving, and this bothered him. He decided that he would have to tackle the problem head-on. But he had little time in his schedule to practice being alone.

Kasparov dined in only the finest restaurants in Paris. Dan-Antoine was a master of selection. One night we ate beside a lovely river, another at the edge of a forest. One night Le Grand Véfour, the next, Les Jardins de Bagatelle, the next, La Tour d'Argent. The food arrived looking more like a sculpture than lobster, or bass or duck. At an outdoor restaurant, with the air fragrant with spring flowers and peacocks strolling nearby, Kasparov looked at the gorgeous dishes before us and roared like a barbarian, "Food, food." But more often than not, Kasparov was wired with political insights and barely noticed the food growing cold before him. At more than a few of these fantastic meals, his face grew dark with fury over Gorbachev and with me for asking annoying questions. "Go away, Fred . . . go back to America. We will remember who were our friends." Then he would grow silent. It was hard for me to eat under such conditions. I became sorry I had ever heard of Gorbachev.

"In the West, Gorbachev is viewed as the man who wants to destroy the communist system," he told me frequently. "I believe that he is trying to save the system. He is the last communist dictator. Why else does he organize ethnic clashes within the various republics? Russians against Moldavians, Georgians against Abkhazians."

One fantastic course after the next grew cold while he talked and then he threw down his food in seconds. "Now is the time when we must defeat communism. We must do it now. History does not often give a second chance." Kasparov was in such a rush to get his ideas out, as if the ideas would fly away, the moment would be lost. I had rarely in my life had a chance to sample food like this, but Kasparov spoke with such fervor that picking up a fork felt rude and inappropriate. And then, when I tried to scarf down the langouste, côtelette or canard at his pace, my stomach was in a knot.

Throughout France, Garry was rushing—rushing to eat, rushing to walk, rushing to drive. For all that, he was always late. If he was due somewhere across Paris at eight, that was the time he might think about getting dressed. He left late for exhibitions, fancy dinners and even appointments on television, which gave his publicists heart failure and promoters headaches. I think he warmed up that way, prepared himself by allowing the tension to build, forestalled leaving until he felt purpose and fire. I also think he believed that being world champion, being Kasparov, gave him the right to be spoiled and even outrageous. Lateness was his calling card. He was never guilty about it. Why? He was busy doing something else. Then, when everyone was irritated, he came striding into the press conference or the three-star restaurant at a walk that was nearly a sprint, radiating energy, smiling, a modern hero.

In chess, as in life, Garry knew that his colossal energy was his most effective ally. When he was inspired and vigorous, his expression was fixed and impenetrable, his body hard, bridling itself back and bursting to begin, like a runner before a race; he had no doubt that he would win. Without his energy, Garry felt nervous about playing chess or meeting an important business contact or giving an interview. Kasparov searched for energy, mined it in strange ways, such as arriving late, or allowing his anger to build and then transforming it into inspired moves or passionate ideas.

One afternoon, he reluctantly agreed to talk a little about chess. We began walking through Paris to find the right place to talk. He decided that we would find a bench to sit on. We passed many benches along broad tree-lined avenues. Each was not quite right. One was in the sun. One was in the shade. One had old bird droppings. He was becoming a little tense, rejecting benches. We returned to his suite at the St. James Club, walked past a half-dozen people seated formally on leather couches in the lobby waiting to see Kasparov as if he were a head of state. He walked briskly past them without noticing.

The St. James Club, in the center of Paris, is a small exclusive hotel built within a courtyard. Garry's room was decorated in an art deco style and had a view of the rear of the courtyard, which is landscaped to duplicate a peaceful country scene. Garry wanted to raise the curtain, but didn't know how, which surprised me, for he had been living there a week. I found a hidden button and showed him. He paced a little and then asked sharply if I was ready. He was a little angry and wired.

Then finally, for the first time, Kasparov and I were talking about chess, but it hardly seemed like chess at all. No variations. No chess moves. To hear him, chess was an abstract struggle, a psychological and philosophical confrontation more than a game. At its center was a grappling against dark forces. "When you understand the essence of chess, the hidden mechanisms, you can make something brilliant from what might appear really stupid. Some positions are so complex that you cannot calculate two moves ahead. You must use your intuition. Sometimes I play by my hand, by my smell."

At one point, I said that he sounded like a captain trying to navigate his ship through a blinding storm. He took that in for a minute. "It is like comparing different dimensions. It takes imagination. At the highest level, chess is a talent to control unrelated things. It is like controlling chaos." At this he sat up from his chair. He had never thought of chess this way before. "It is like controlling chaos," he repeated.

About this time, the doorbell rang. It was a reporter from the newspaper *Figaro*, who had been waiting for an hour in the lobby. She was thin and beautiful. Garry invited her in and then gave me a high five in the manner of Magic Johnson complimenting James Worthy after a sensational slam dunk. "We did great," he said. We nailed it, baby. He was very excited about controlling the chaos. I was tired. Usually after he talked, I felt tired. After a minute or two, Garry was speaking with great passion about Gorbachev and Azerbaijan to the woman, who nodded and smoked a cigarette. Kasparov builds upon his energy, gearing himself up from a good interview to a better one, constantly revising his best ideas. The lady journalist was nodding to the cadence of his sentences, getting high on this chess champion with a troubled soul. I overheard Garry talking about

controlling the chaos in his country, as if the two of them had just
come upon the idea.

Before the Immopar Trophée it was a foregone conclusion among
grandmasters and fans that Kasparov would win. He always won.
Yet, considering him the odds-on favorite was probably more a
function of the man's reputation and growing mythology than an
accurate assessment of his current playing strength. First of all, games
played with only twenty-five minutes on each player's clock are full
of peril. At this speed, anyone can blunder. Second, at the highest
level, success in chess, as in basketball, swimming or track and field,
depends to a significant degree on conditioning and practice, which
for a chess player translates into high-level study and competition.
The most talented miler in the world would have little chance to win
a top-level race if he had not trained seriously for several months
before. In May of 1990, Kasparov had neither studied nor played a
serious game of chess in months. When I asked Garry if he were
looking forward to Dan-Antoine's tournament, he answered, "Fred,
how could I?" as if I had accused him of insensitivity or questioned
his values. It was as if Kasparov were fasting from chess, demonstrating to people back home: Look what I am willing to risk. This is the
time for men to take a stand. History does not often give a second
chance.

It occurred to me then, and I think it is still true, that it had become
difficult for Kasparov to enjoy playing chess. As a youth, it was the
burning passion of his life, and now, when he plays a world championship match or a serious tournament, the game absorbs him
fully—each move is hugely important to him, as though history
were sitting as his judge—but liking it is something else. He can be
cheerful and a little silly playing geography, cards or video games,
but for him, chess is too serious, too filled with portent, fear and
consequences for light-hearted enjoyment. What if he were to lose
a game or two? Would chess commentators begin to speculate that
he is no longer the greatest of all time? Could he continue to find the
motivation to play if he were no longer considered the greatest? If
he were to lose a championship match, what would happen to his life,

to the lives of his family? In the spring of 1990, he was surely worrying: If he were to lose against Karpov, would he still have political clout? In some small way, would a Karpov victory set back the cause of democracy in his country?

A few hours before the first round of the Immopar Trophée, Garry and I were sitting in his living room at the St. James Club. He was waiting for a phone call from his mother in Moscow. He wanted to ask her about his grandmother, who had not been in good spirits. He paced for a few minutes and then said to me. "I had to convince my grandmother to leave Baku. She left her life behind, the graves of her relatives. We lost everything we had. I lost twenty-six years. It doesn't exist for me anymore."

4

IMMOPAR TROPHÉE

Before the start of Dan-Antoine's Immopar Trophée, the lovely Théâtre des Champs Elysées was drenched in libidinous music. On gigantic screens, grandmasters faced off with the determined expressions of outsized road warriors. While a huge display board blinked in a light show of purples, greens and reds, revved-up fans hung over the balcony, wired for chess. Then a master of ceremonies called the first two grandmasters to the stage with the epic cant of a Nevada ring announcer introducing heavyweights to fight for the title. By traditional chess standards, this production was blaring and gaudy, but the audience was swept into it.

Dan-Antoine had imported the strongest group of grandmasters ever assembled for an "action" tournament, and they were competing for a record purse. But the river of passion running beneath the Immopar Trophée was the opportunity to watch the best in the world gun for Kasparov. Kasparov's fame and charisma packed the theater; his participation had convinced Immopar to put up the prize fund and was the reason this chess event was attended by scores of journalists and photographers, and was appearing on French television.

In this format, each player had only twenty-five minutes to make all of his moves, which was about six times faster than grandmaster chess was usually played. When a player ran out of time, regardless of the position on the board, he would lose the game. Many chess purists don't like action chess, claiming that even top players have to make mistakes at this speed and don't have time to develop deep and beautiful ideas, but Dan-Antoine pointed out that five- and six-hour games, however rich in art, are not audience-friendly. The fan goes to sleep long before the thrilling moments at the end.

All great chess games develop toward a crisis, a moment of truth, which may not come for many moves, many hours. At one point in the unraveling of scholarly openings or during the imaginative feints and counterfeints, attacks, sacrifices and complexities of the middlegame or in the austere and puzzling standoff of a few pieces at the end, it becomes apparent that the game will result in a breakthrough and victory for one side, or will fizzle out into a draw. After hours of trading cerebral blows, such moments are highly emotional.

In action chess, paced by the clock, players and fans feel crisis from the opening move. Playing at this speed, grandmasters have some time to calculate deep variations, but they also make more blunders than in slower games. It's painful for them, to be sure, but thrilling to watch, like game-turning fumbles in football. These chess fumbles are concrete proof to patzers that, despite the encyclopedic knowledge and mental gifts of grandmasters, we all play more or less the same game. In addition, when chess is played at action pace, the pieces are on the move rather than sitting for an eternity on one square, and consequently, even a relatively unsophisticated chess fan can maintain a feel for the flow of the game by watching the display board and listening to the animated commentary on earphones.

It is daunting to observe how a man you know quietly disappears in the theater of hype and reputation. While the popular French prodigy Joel Lautier was beating the former world champion Boris Spassky in the first two-game match, the standing room crowd was already awaiting the chess fury of Kasparov, and so was I. As the smiling Lautier made his exit, pulsing music summoned the powerhouse

Russian on stage. The Garry whom I had come to know during the past two weeks had little to do with the fierce warrior face on the huge television screen overhead. "Kasparov never loses," someone beside me said. "He's a chess machine. He never smiles. He's all chess."

Kasparov walked to the table in the center of the stage, waved quickly to his fans and loosened his tie. Jonathan Speelman, a thin man with long disheveled black hair, was a head taller than the world champion. Kasparov was clearly impatient to begin, tapping his foot while the announcer said a few words.

Within a minute or two, the chessmen were spread all over the board and it was apparent to everyone in the theater that the world champion was attacking. With a sneer on his face, Kasparov pushed his pieces forward. He placed them on squares where, progressively, they had more range and attacking potential. Meanwhile, Speelman's pieces were maneuvering defensively in their own terrain. "Speelman knew Kasparov has incredible knowledge in the opening, so he tried something original. It didn't work," said the Siberian grandmaster Anatoly Viser, who was visiting Paris and hoping to immigrate from the Soviet Union. Speelman had tried to trick Kasparov by varying the move order of a standard opening, but the world champion had understood immediately that Speelman's variation held little threat. Sitting next to me, grandmaster Viser was enraptured with Kasparov's aggressive play. "His pieces are always moving ahead and they have a crazy attacking harmony," he said. While Kasparov stared bullets at the chessboard, Speelman appeared to be disconcerted, his pieces cramped together, hunkered down for a siege.

In high-level chess, players attempt to improve their positions incrementally. It is extremely rare for a great player to overlook a simple threat to a rook or knight or to get checkmated from a position that is roughly equal, although this happens to amateurs all the time. Grandmasters spar for tiny advantages, to create a weakness in an opponent's pawn structure which will be exploited thirty moves later in the endgame, for example, or to maneuver for the chance to play the middlegame with two bishops against an opponent's two knights, or to gain an open file or diagonal which will increase the play of a rook or bishop. Crushing combinations, resulting in the winning of material, usually evolve from an accretion of subtle positional advantages. Afterwards, in chess journals and books, master analysts demonstrate the inexorable development of these powerful moves, like meteorologists charting the growth of small storms over warm oceans.

The world champion is a fantastic positional player, but what thrills chess fans is his penchant to do the unexpected. When he sacrifices material for attacking initiative, the move frequently comes like a bolt out of the blue. It seems to have little basis in standard chess logic. Even when not entirely unexpected, his sacrifices often appear to be premature, as though the world champion had not fully and carefully laid the groundwork for his attack. Invariably in each of his tournaments, there are games in which Kasparov sacrifices a rook or queen, and the analyst, often a grandmaster, cannot find justification for the move, other than in the fact that it was Kasparov's creation and therefore brilliant and possibly even decisive. But afterwards, in analysis, Kasparov demonstrates that the stunning move or series of moves was well within the logic of the game. The catch is that to find it, one must be able to calculate as deeply as the world champion and at the same time possess his uncanny feel for the intangible elements of chess. For even the world's greatest players, it can be terrifying to play against him, worrying from the opening move where and when the gauntlet will fall.

Speelman acknowledged that he had to overcome a psychological disadvantage to play effectively against Kasparov. "He is intimidating," said the three-time English champion. "He has remarkable energy, and he sometimes finds moves that somebody else wouldn't find. He does this rather consistently. His style is very forcing. He likes to do things and doesn't like his opponent to do things to him. When you are playing against him, you feel that you're playing somebody very good at chess and almost everybody else is pretty bad at chess."

The incremental buildup of pressure upon an opposing position has a teasing and arousing effect upon fans; they sit on the edge of their seats waiting for the final blow. Such was the expectation of the audience in the Théâtre des Champs Elysées as Kasparov tightened the noose on Speelman's kingside. But then, much to their surprise,

Kasparov traded queens and, with a bored expression, took the first game by quietly exploiting a small endgame advantage. Normally, when a player suffers under a powerful attack he attempts to defuse it by trying to lure his opponent into an exchange of pieces. Likewise, the attacker attempts to avoid exchanges, unless they lead to concrete advantages that are likely to assure a victory later on. But great players do not need to hold material in their hands to feel confident of victory. Against Speelman, an endgame specialist, the world champion was so confident in his assessment of the endgame position that would evolve six or eight moves down the road, and in his technique to exploit it, that he was willing to trade a larger but more diffuse advantage for a smaller one that eliminated all chances of his opponent's counterplay.

Perhaps Kasparov's easy handling of the ending took something out of Speelman, who offered little resistance in the second game. Playing the black pieces with the same aggression that he had shown with the white, Kasparov attacked Speelman's kingside, and the Englishman's own queenside attack was feeble and slow-developing. After gaining a pawn advantage, the world champion was content to settle for a draw, which gave him the first match and knocked Speelman out of the competition.

Kasparov's next opponent was the grandmaster Victor Korchnoi. As the announcer said a few words, Kasparov, sitting at the board, smiled and raised a hand to his cheering audience. Kasparov was living up to his billing: dazzling, untouchable, unpredictable. French girls who didn't know a rook from a pawn were adoring him. The fifty-nine-year-old Korchnoi was hardly a proper test. Korchnoi was haggard and tense. His long weird face rippled through different emotions—charm, suspicion, modesty, anger, arrogance—as the announcer recounted a brief history.

Although their relationship had from time to time been strained, Korchnoi was Kasparov's older brother politically. In the seventies, while developing into one of the several strongest grandmasters in the world, Korchnoi had gained a reputation in the USSR for being a troublemaker. At a time when public criticism of the Soviet state was dangerous, Korchnoi complained that it was absurd for teams of KGB agents to shepherd Soviet grandmasters when they traveled abroad.

In 1974, he narrowly lost a final candidates match to Karpov to determine the next challenger for the world championship. In effect, this contest turned out to be the world championship match itself, when Bobby Fischer refused to defend his title. In his autobiography, *Chess Is My Life*, Korchnoi claimed that Soviet authorities wanted Karpov to win and offered him all possible advantages, such as the best trainers and his choice of venue and hours of play. "Karpov had been chosen as the favorite, and it was clear why," he wrote. "One hundred percent Russian, he compared favorably with me, Russian by passport, but Jewish in appearance. He was a typical representative of the working class, the rulers of the country according to the Soviet Constitution, whereas I had spent my life in the cultural center of Leningrad, and was contrasted to him as a representative of the intelligentsia. Besides, Karpov was younger and more promising, the future was his, whereas I would not be playing much longer. Karpov was showered with endearments and he had become a member of the Central Committee of the USSR Communist Youth Organization, the chairman of which was his friend. Karpov well understood what he represented." He had become the symbol of Soviet Communism. The frail, fair-skinned man had quickly washed away the bitter taste of Bobby Fischer, the first non-Soviet world champion in twenty-four years. Karpov was proof, once again, that communism produced the best minds.

During the 1974 candidates match against Korchnoi, Karpov had the full support of the Soviet state. Top grandmasters were ordered to give him their best ideas and advice. Korchnoi worried incessantly that his own trainers, much weaker than Karpov's, would be ordered by Party members to betray him. He received hate mail, and intuited that if he evened the score against Karpov, then something might happen to him in the street.

Following the match, Korchnoi was outspoken in his criticism of Karpov, and particularly of the brazen manner in which Karpov had been favored in the match. Consequently, Korchnoi was stripped of his income and privileges, including the right to play for a year in international tournaments abroad. In 1976, he defected from the Soviet Union. Subsequently, playing his best chess as a forty- and fifty-year-old man, when grandmasters are usually past their prime, he earned the right to meet Karpov twice for the world champion-

ship. He lost both matches under scandalous and bizarre circumstances.

In Baguio in the Philippines, Korchnoi was thrown off-balance by
Karpov's psychologist, Dr. Zukhar, who sat in the fourth row staring
at the challenger, apparently trying to hypnotize him. Also, Korchnoi's delegation claimed that Karpov's team of crack grandmasters
was sending him coded messages by varying the color of the yogurt
being handed to the world champion while the game was in progress.
Whatever the reason, Korchnoi lost. After the victory, Karpov sent
a telegram to Leonid Brezhnev: "I am happy to report that the world
chess championship match has ended in victory. Please accept, dear
Leonid Ilyich, my heartfelt gratitude for the fatherly concern and
consideration you have shown me and my delegation during the
preparation period." Brezhnev responded that Karpov's victory
demonstrated the embodiment of "our Soviet character."

By the time of Korchnoi and Karpov's second championship
match, in Merano, 1981, politics had become far more important than
chess. Backers of Karpov argued that the world champion was defending his country and system of government. For his part, in press
conferences before and after the games, Korchnoi pleaded repeatedly
to the press for the release of his family, who were, in effect, being
held hostage in Leningrad. "The two opponents found themselves in
totally different circumstances," wrote Kasparov in his autobiography. "Whereas Korchnoi was ill-prepared . . . , Karpov had received
help from all our best grandmasters. We'd been obliged to furnish
him with information about our opening lines and variations, to
reveal all our professional secrets. We were given clearly to understand that this was our patriotic duty, since the 'traitor' had to be
routed at all cost." (The youthful Kasparov had refused this order.)
Korchnoi lost again.

Still, as if fueled by his old battles against the Soviet system, in the
years following, Korchnoi continued to compete successfully in the
highest-level tournaments against grandmasters less than half his
age. To be sure, he had paid a price. His long face was permanently
creased with suffering and suspicion. Although he had lived in the
West for many years, he continued to look over his shoulder while
playing the game. When he lost, he was apt to complain that someone had tainted his food or that a hypnotist was in the hall.

Against Kasparov, the old grandmaster played in a rage, as if the title that had escaped him for three decades were finally within his grasp. He made his moves quickly, and dramatically tossed his head when he sensed that the world champion was off-balance. Korchnoi was known as a tireless student of chess, and it was clear that he was well-prepared for this match. He had anticipated Kasparov's opening setups and had planned sharp, tricky replies. From the start of the first game, Korchnoi took the initiative by developing an intricate attacking formation while brazenly ignoring Kasparov's threat. Korchnoi built the tension of the position, as Kasparov had against Speelman. His pieces found the best squares and roamed ahead. To save the first game required Kasparov's most careful defense. The game was a draw.

The second game was a carbon copy of the first, with Kasparov's kingside attack crumbling and the world champion forced to defend very carefully on the queenside to hold the game to another draw. For two games in a row, Kasparov had been back on his heels, just holding on. This had rarely happened to him before.

In these games, Korchnoi had played very aggressively, but when a grandmaster plays wide-open chess, he leaves himself vulnerable to counterattack. Grandmasters in the audience speculated that if he hadn't been rusty, Kasparov would have punished Korchnoi for his boldness.

Since the score was tied, the match would be decided by a single blitz game. Each man would be given only five minutes on his clock for all his moves. For those unaccustomed to blitz, attacks and parries follow so quickly that there is hardly a moment to evaluate the position or anticipate the outcome. Pieces come on and off the board at sleight-of-hand speed, and yet grandmasters can play at this pace with remarkable precision. It was Kasparov's choice to play the white pieces, and by the rules of this tournament, the player with white needed to win the game to win the match. To take the tiebreaker—and the match—Korchnoi, playing black, only needed to draw.

We watched close-ups of Korchnoi and Kasparov on the huge television screens as they fidgeted with the pieces until they were centered on their squares. Their faces were wet and strained. Kasparov's hands were shaking. Later he would tell me that he kept seeing mistakes the moment he played them. The world champion no longer played with the helpmate of intimidation. Korchnoi had faced down the KGB and had no fear of Kasparov. Still, blitz is a young man's game. Rusty or not, Kasparov was still the favorite to win.

But again the older man played sharply. This time, the world champion did not back off, and soon the position was double-edged. There were threats all over, and no time to calculate them. Both men were visibly shaking. Neither was sure who had the edge. Then they began trading pieces. The tension came out of the position like air from a balloon. Kasparov looked desperate. Trading was a mistake on his part. There was no winning endgame here. He should have kept attacking, avoided exchanges, but now there were few pieces on the board, and the ones left were faced off against one another symmetrically. There was little time left on each man's clock, maybe twenty seconds. Kasparov tried pressing ahead, but his army was too small, and each diagonal and file was blocked by Korchnoi's crafty defense. The older grandmaster was playing for a draw. He had created a fortresslike position. Each man had no more than six or seven seconds on his clock. Maybe Kasparov had a second or two less.

Then an incredible thing happened: Korchnoi inadvertently knocked one of Kasparov's pieces off the board. Kasparov replaced it at the cost of a second or two. Moved. Then Korchnoi moved a piece, only a couple of seconds left, and, with his arm shaking, he belted the clock so hard that it flew off the table, while it clicked off the last of Kasparov's seconds. Close-up of Kasparov's incredulous face. The game was over. Fans were bewildered. Kasparov's face was now red and furious. The arbiter quickly decided that the position was technically drawn: Kasparov would not have been able to win it even if he had had the last of his time. Victor Korchnoi won the match. Kasparov had lost. He had actually lost. He stormed off the stage and immediately left the theater.

Again and again, instant replays showed the two men playing the last moves with arms flailing and shaking, Victor Korchnoi knocking Kasparov's piece off the table, then belting the clock, which tumbled to the floor. Then Kasparov's bewildered face, trying to win with no way to stop his clock from running out of time at his feet. With all of this high-tech paraphernalia, the match had ended on a note of absurdity and incompetence. No one had thought to anchor the clock.

The old warrior, Victor Korchnoi, would play the Englishman, Nigel Short, for the title. Grandmasters in the audience seemed pleased that the older man was getting a chance, and also that Kasparov had been beaten. In that moment, perhaps, the world championship felt more attainable for them than it had a few hours before.

Then, after a thirty-minute delay, there was an announcement. On further review, the arbiter had decided to change his decision. He reasoned that the world champion had been deprived of his chance to win when Korchnoi had knocked the clock onto the floor. The men would play two more blitz games to decide the winner.

A big furor immediately erupted, with fans booing and hissing. Some said that Korchnoi had been robbed once again. His whole life he had been robbed. Some grandmasters, among then Lautier from France, said that the decision was just, but most pronounced it unfair, or worse. "The world champion can do anything he wants," said one of them. "It was a totally unjustified decision," said Jonathan Speelman, who muttered something about the power of Kasparov. "How could he do that to Korchnoi?" said Olivier Renet of France, who had lost to Korchnoi in the first round. "It's a disgrace. It smells like a payoff."

After walking off the stage, Garry Kasparov had left the theater, followed by Bob Burkett, an associate of Ted Field, the producer of the New York half of the upcoming Karpov match. According to Burkett, Kasparov had been angry and dejected. He had felt that Korchnoi might have blundered or lost on time if not for the clock fiasco, but while they had walked the half-hour back to the St. James Club, Kasparov had come to terms with the decision, and the two of them had talked about where they would go for dinner that evening. When they arrived at the hotel, both men were surprised to find a message from Dan-Antoine, saying that they must come back immediately to the theater, the arbiter had reversed his ruling.

In the Théâtre des Champs Elysées, Victor Korchnoi came on stage to say that he agreed with the arbiter's decision—it was fair—but fans and players continued to speculate that Kasparov had spent the last half-hour sitting in a backroom lambasting the poor arbiter. "You never know what they agreed to behind closed doors," said the grandmaster Boris Gulko, who had been eliminated earlier. "One thing for sure. This was good for French television."

As the men prepared to play their last two games, journalists, fans and players were talking scandal and rooting wildly for Korchnoi. Garry looked yellow, and there was an expression on his face: What can I do? What can I do? He appeared to be a man in crisis.

The last two games were very different from the first three. The world champion did not play in the style of Kasparov. He was no longer the wide-open attacking world champion, pieces coming forward like Marines. Kasparov recognized that Korchnoi had studied his most recently published opening ideas and was jumping all over them. He had to change his style. So he played his last two games as if he were Karpov. He played quietly, calmly, apparently trying to hold the position rather than win it. He gave Korchnoi the attack, almost indifferently. He absorbed the energy of the older man's moves by defending ingeniously, frustrating Korchnoi by anticipating threats before the older man thought of them. He allowed Korchnoi his attack, but in doing so recognized that if he could survive it, Korchnoi would have to play the endgame with a weakened pawn structure and misplaced pieces. The world champion was playing prophylactically—defending, luring Korchnoi ahead, all the while strengthening his own position little by little. Kasparov drew the fourth game, though he stood better at the end. Then, milking a tiny endgame advantage, he won the fifth. Korchnoi had lost again.

At the end of the match, Kasparov looked sick. Perhaps he did not like playing this way, in the beguiling, defensive style of his nemesis, Karpov. Perhaps he simply couldn't bear the hissing, and the chanting of "Victor, Victor," even when Kasparov had won and was trying to smile as he shook Korchnoi's hand.

The final match against Nigel Short was something of an anticlimax. Kasparov played grimly, like a survivor. He seemed punch-drunk from too much chess. Short sensed Kasparov's vulnerability; everyone in the theater sensed it. Short attacked, and Kasparov tried to hold him off, but both men were making mistakes. Short erred in the first game, and Kasparov won. In the second game, Kasparov had the superior ending, but somehow lost the thread of it and lost. He shook his head no, no, what's wrong with you, Kasparov? And then it came down to a blitz game for the title. Eighteen thousand dollars, not to mention the prestige, coming down to one five-minute game. With lightning moves, Short completely outplayed the world champion, gained a winning position—and then blundered horribly at the end and lost.

Kasparov had survived, barely, but he looked terrible, defeated. The crowd cheered. He had won some of them back, perhaps because they had seen him bleed and felt his depletion and misery. The theater was again drowned in devouring, prurient music, and the huge screens played close-ups of Kasparov's petulant expressions, which in the moment seemed ludicrous.

A few minutes later, he was standing backstage, enveloped in a crowd of two hundred admiring fans, a few dozen of them wiggling programs and pens in front of him.

My plane was leaving in a couple of hours, and I needed to speak to him. We walked together to the back of the theater and escaped into a dark storage room with plaster falling from the walls and electrical wires dangling. "I feel devastated," said Garry. The crowd began pressing against the door, and Dan-Antoine was calling "Garry, Garry."

"I could see my mistakes, but somehow I couldn't prevent them. I kept making bad moves." Kasparov had won the tournament, but he had nearly lost a half-dozen times. He was mortified. He was also worried. This would be the last tournament before Karpov-Kasparov V, and Kasparov in this form would lose the title.

Then Dan-Antoine managed to push the door open a couple of inches. He was annoyed, he couldn't figure out what Kasparov was doing in the back room. There were postmortem interviews to come. "And, Garry, I want to remind you that we have a press conference scheduled for nine-thirty tomorrow morning," he said.

Kasparov seemed dumbfounded. "I can't," he said, with an unusual shrillness.

"Please, Garry. We've set it up. I told you yesterday. All the top papers. Television crews are coming."

"Don't you understand, I can't. I can't."

5

GATA AND
RUSTAM—FOOTSTEPS

"Fred, I've been told that your life may be in danger," said Allen Kaufman on the phone. It was about a month after I had returned from Paris. Kaufman, the executive director of the American Chess Foundation, was normally an unflappable man, but on this occasion he sounded agitated. He had received a phone call that morning from Eugenia Dumbadze, the business agent of Gata Kamsky, the fifteen-year-old chess prodigy, and his father, Rustam. She had said that Rustam was incensed by an article I had written about him and his son for *The New York Times* Sunday magazine. He had made threats. Kaufman told me that the woman sounded frightened, and he urged me to take precautions. I dialed Eugenia Dumbadze, a Russian emigré whom I had met and spoken to numerous times during the past half year, and she was indeed extremely upset. Rustam had told her he was coming to my apartment building and would wait for me outside and then stab me to death. Rustam wasn't worried about going to jail, she said, because he had already spent a great deal of his life behind bars and believed that, given the American system of law, he would be sent away for only a few weeks.

*   *   *

I had first met Gata Kamsky and his father in the summer of 1988, in Timisoara, Rumania, where Gata was competing in the under-14 division of the youth world chess championship. "He is the most gifted chess prodigy of all time—the next world champion," said a Rumanian journalist, who was shaking with excitement as he led me to a solemn boy with bangs and owl eyes, who moved the chess pieces against another great prodigy, Zsofia Polgar from Hungary. The lithe, porcelain-pretty Zsofia had been fighting off Gata's attacking pieces for hours, and with a wounded expression that might melt any adolescent boy's heart, she whispered her offer of a draw. Gata refused, and with only the slightest trace of a smile, he pushed his pawns ahead and snuffed out Zsofia's championship dreams with endgame technique so punishing and precise that it gave me goosebumps.

That summer, Timisoara was swarming with prodigies and their pampering parents who craved the world championship as though it conferred immortality. I was one of those anxiety-ridden parents; Josh was playing for America in the under-12 division. Among the young international stars were the brilliant twelve-year-old Judit Polgar, Zsofia's little sister; the cherubic Gabriel Schwartzman from Bucharest; and Ilya Gurevich from Worcester, Massachusetts, who withered his opponents in the under-18 section with a brutal glare while pummeling them with sharp tactics. Though just kids, all of these players had international reputations. Their careers were closely watched by chess lovers, who wondered which of them might someday grow powerful enough to threaten Garry Kasparov. But insiders said that Kamsky was the most gifted of all. As a twelve-year-old, Gata had won the Soviet under-18 championship, an astounding achievement matched only by Kasparov.

In the dining room of the players' hotel, nationalistic rivalries were in the air. Over watery soup and inedible mystery meats, American parents and coaches complained that the Russians were always served first—somehow this was construed to be an edge. Each country was assigned a table, but Gata Kamsky and his father, Rustam, ate apart from the other Russians, a country unto themselves. Rustam believed that the Russian coaches were of little help to his son, as they were either not strong enough to give him sound advice or secretly conspiring against him. Gata never mingled with the other children, who played soccer and whiffleball in a nearby park and met each evening in the lobby to become friends despite language difficulties. Except for Rustam's conversations with a few Americans, during which he conceived a plan to defect, the Kamskys kept to themselves, a picture of growing unhappiness. Rustam had expected his son to win the tournament and, as a consequence, to be invited to the prestigious New York Open, and then to stay. In spite of his win against Zsofia Polgar, Gata was not in top form, and each time he tipped his king, Rustam yelled at him with unrestrained anger. "We all saw the awful expression on Gata's face after he lost," recalled the American coach, Victor Frias, an international master. "He knew what was coming during his training sessions with daddy." On several nights in the Hotel International, players and parents heard the sound of furniture crashing against the wall and Gata's weeping. In this championship quest, he had failed.

Nevertheless, eight months later, Gata Kamsky's name was on the front page of *The New York Times*. Friends in the chess world had arranged an invitation to the New York Open, and he and his father had announced their defection at a news conference during the annual event. American players had grumbled that the newspaper articles had focused on this talented kid while hardly a word had been written about all the thrilling games played at this annual showpiece of American chess at the Penta Hotel; it was barely noticed that the international event had been won by an American grandmaster, John Fedorowicz.

The Kamskys settled into a sparsely-furnished apartment in Brooklyn, and methodically mounted an attack against the American chess elite. In tournament after tournament, Gata placed among the winners, who were usually decades older than he.

Still, I was taken aback in October, 1989, to find him a finalist in the sixteen-player elimination tournament to choose an American contender to face Garry Kasparov. It would be the first serious match against a reigning world champion on American soil since 1907.

Our country's most distinguished players had been invited to participate in this historic event at the Manhattan Chess Club, then located in Carnegie Hall. Gata Kamsky had not been invited to play—his published rating of 2345 was not high enough to qualify (numerical ratings, such as Kasparov's 2800, the highest in chess history, are estimates of skill based on tournament results), but at the last moment, when one of the players had failed to appear, Gata's father had persuaded the organizer to give his son a chance.

To the surprise of spectators and the other players, the boy won his first three two-game rounds against highly regarded grandmasters, including Roman Dzindzichashvili, the 1989 United States national co-champion, considered by many the most talented player in America. From the point of view of this bystander, there was an inevitability about Kamsky's victories. The boy's more seasoned and learned opponents moved their bishops and knights with trembling fingers, spooked by his age, by his almost unearthly calm, by his ability to defend delicate positions quickly and accurately. They lost with a grimace, shaking their heads. While Gata played with detachment, Rustam, the father, paced around the periphery of the room, his war-torn prizefighter's face—he had been a boxer in the Soviet Union—showing first sadness, and then inexplicable fury. A child's prodigious chess talent can be both a joy and a trap for his parents, who sometimes become so intoxicated by the child's magical accomplishments, so overwrought during games, that little else seems important.

After each win the boy barely smiled, although his accomplishment that day in November might be compared to knocking out heavyweight contenders one after another to win the chance to step into the ring with the world champion.

In the fourth and final elimination round at the Manhattan Chess Club, Gata, wearing the drab pants, skimpy sweater and close-cropped haircut of an Eastern European schoolboy and possessing only limited knowledge of English, faced Alexander Ivanov, then thirty-three, also Russian-born and one of the highest-rated players in the United States. To win the right to represent America against Kasparov, one of them needed either two victories or a victory and a draw.

The first game was a draw, so the winner of the second game

would face the champion. Ivanov played creatively in the opening moves and won the boy's knight, a decisive advantage. However, Gata defended with great resourcefulness and tenacity.

Most chess prodigies are distinguished by their daring and sometimes injudicious piece sacrifices, by sparkling attacks; but Kamsky had gained a reputation for his staunch defense and intricate counterattacks. His conservative style was often compared to that of Anatoly Karpov.

While Ivanov squirmed in his chair, trying to capitalize on his advantage, Rustam glared at his son across the room, as though he were projecting the will to win. The older player was becoming frustrated, pressing too hard, making little mistakes. Ivanov's tiny errors had become windows of opportunity. Gata's defending pieces were suddenly poised for attack; and after barely holding on by a thread, the game was suddenly his.

Then a chilling moment. The older player extended his hand, no eye contact, his face twisted unhappily. The room was silent. No one clapped or cheered or raced forward to embrace the young winner of an event that would be written about in chess periodicals around the world. Gata would be the youngest player in chess history to face a world champion in a formal match. He looked around furtively, as if wondering what he had done wrong.

A few minutes later, in the next room, masters chatted in small groups. "He's not very good, just lucky," said one American master. "I hate Russians," said another.

During the last decade, the problems of American-born players had been compounded by the influx of highly-trained Soviet masters who emigrated for political reasons, often with the naive assumption that the wealth of America extended to its chess players, and who did, in fact, win a considerable share of the meager cash prizes available in our domestic tournaments. It's a joke in the chess world that in international events our Russians often compete against their Russians.

"I am envious that Gata Kamsky gets so much attention and money," admitted twenty-two-year-old Patrick Wolff, a loser in the third round of the tournament. "It makes me angry. It makes everyone here angry. In America, Kamsky is a more interesting prospect than an equally talented American." At the time, Wolff, who became U.S. champion in 1992, was on a leave from Yale and was living on a stipend as the winner of the 1989 Sanford Fellowship, which provides the United States' most promising player funds to study and play chess full-time. Many American-born masters complained that Soviet emigrés and defectors such as Kamsky were hired guns, lured to the United States by grant money not as readily available to our home-grown players, who competed against natives for coveted positions on teams traveling abroad and for cash prizes in tournaments.* "Passing over local talent to pour money into foreign players would be inadmissible in almost any other country in the world," said Victor Frias, Wolff's trainer.

"I understand the resentment of American professionals," said Allen Kaufman, whose American Chess Foundation to a significant degree keeps the American chess world afloat by distributing three to four hundred thousand dollars a year to promote the game—less than one percent of what the Soviet Union spent on chess before the political upheaval of the summer of 1991. The ACF has frequently been criticized by American players for what they regard as preferential treatment given to Russian defectors and emigrés, and particularly for arranging temporary stipends for two famous Soviet masters, the grandmaster Boris Gulko, and more recently, Gata Kamsky. "There has to be resentment when a foreigner comes in here, and all of a sudden an American is one notch lower and earning hundreds or even thousands less," said Kaufman. "But I have the responsibility of looking at the long term instead of the short term. And bringing someone like Kamsky into American chess is eventually going to strengthen it." Alluding obliquely to Patrick Wolff's criticism, Kaufman delicately pointed out that there was simply no native-born American who possessed Gata's gift for chess. Kaufman believed that, given his

---

*Competition from Soviet-trained chess professionals has increased since the collapse of the Soviet Union because so many players have been lured to the States by the prospect of the good life. Under communism, chess professionals were among the most privileged and highly-paid, but today top chess trainers and players in the former Soviet republics are paid virtually nothing, and travel to the West to earn hard currencies for the support of their families.

talent and dedication to study, Gata had a good chance to become world champion.

The Kamskys lived in a three-room apartment in the Brighton Beach section of Brooklyn. I visited them in November of 1989 in connection with the article I was writing for *The New York Times Magazine*, and soon after arriving I had an opportunity to speak with Gata alone while his father was out parking their car. Through his thick glasses, Gata was studying a game between two august grandmasters published in one of the many chess books that lined the walls of his sunny bedroom. I asked him if he ever thought about his mother, who had left the family when he was a little boy.

"No," he said, moving the chess pieces. I inquired about whether he had made friends with any of the Russian-speaking boys in the neighborhood. "No." I asked if he had friends back in Leningrad, and Gata answered that boys there had been envious of him. At the age of fifteen, Gata apparently had never had a friend.

I inquired about the things in his life that made him happy, and about his dreams for the future. With a slightly bewildered expression, he looked up from the game and answered in his halting English. "I dream about chess."

When he was not traveling around the world to tournaments, Gata spent twelve hours a day in his room studying games in books or on his computer—the specifics of his training regimen were classified information. Gata ate some of his meals as he studied. He never watched television or read anything other than chess books. He didn't play sports with other boys, but he jogged for thirty-five minutes in the evening, which his father said was good for chess endurance. He didn't go to school—he had the equivalent of a high-school education in the Soviet Union by the age of thirteen, his father said, although various people who had known them in the Soviet Union, as well as administrators in the school he had attended, said that he had left school without finishing his studies. At the time, Gata didn't seem to want an American education, but added that his father would not allow it.

Gata giggled a little.

"What?"

"It's very funny," he said, pointing to a highly technical endgame position in front of him.

As I thought about Gata's short, detached, but provocative answers, I felt the austerity of his childhood and his isolation; but I also felt jealous. Like Gata, Joshua was a chess master, to be sure a much weaker master than Gata, but nonetheless, at thirteen, a scholastic national champion. For me, it was very strange entering into the world of Gata and Rustam, for with different details and textures their life had been my wicked fantasy. Like the parents of other chess-talented American children, I often wondered how well Josh would play if he studied chess for five or six hours a day, like the top Eastern European kids, instead of attending a very demanding school, playing sports in the afternoon and pursuing an active social life. Like Rustam, I had also fantasized about my kid winning the world championship, and it frustrated me that in our middle-class life there wasn't room to make a proper run at it. The American ideal of the well-rounded child stood in opposition to the idea of bold sacrifices for excellence.

Gata did not study chess for five or six hours a day, however—he studied virtually all the time. After our lunch, Gata lingered for a few minutes, but his father gestured sharply with a finger: Back to the books. There was hardly a moment I was with Gata that he wasn't going through chess books, pondering or smiling over ingenious moves, memorizing variations. He seemed more complete, more content with the pieces beneath his hand, and stiff, somehow fragmented without them.

"The life you are leading is highly unusual," I said to Gata. "Probably there is not another fifteen-year-old in the world living like this. Don't you sometimes wish you could play on a soccer team or go out with a girl?"

A flicker of a smile at the mention of girls.

"On his own, he would never have managed this," answered Gata's father. "Not any child in the world could, unless he had someone by his side all the time."

I addressed my questions to Gata, but except for the few minutes when we were alone, his father almost always answered, in the manner of a lecture to mankind. Indeed, Rustam, who did not have a job, referred to himself vaguely as his new wife's teacher and as Gata's teacher (I took that to mean "of all things") and chess coach, although his own knowledge of chess was far less sophisticated than his son's. Rustam gave his lengthy answers in Russian, his voice often baleful, and my translator provided the English. "Gata didn't become interested in chess," Rustam said pridefully. "At eight years old, I made him play. I am the person that deserves the credit for my son being a champion. It is not Gata's doing. Talent is not important. Any child can become a world champion. He has to work a lot and someone has to work with him. The coach has to put his soul into it. To give up his social life. Not watch television, no theater, no beach. The coach must completely forget about himself. There are few people like that."

"Do you believe that?" the boy was asked. "That anyone can become world champion by working hard with the right coach?"

"Sure."

"Good, good," Rustam answered impatiently. "I work twelve hours a day helping Gata, trying to make every second count. He has bad eyesight, so I read to him for hours and hours."

While his father talked, Gata sat in front of the chess set, moving the pieces. Occasionally he smiled a little. When I asked him why, he answered, "Because I listen to my father, and he is right."

"In the Soviet Union, I was paid as a coach," said Rustam. "Here I am not paid anything. Often I eat only once every two days, because we need the money for Gata to eat three times a day. We are treated like two hungry dogs," he pontificated, as if they were living in a gulag instead of an apartment in Brooklyn, supported comfortably by a wealthy financier. At the time, the Kamskys were given a living allowance of $35,000 a year by chess lover James Cayne, president of the investment-banking firm of Bear, Stearns. Several months later, Cayne withdrew his support, apparently due to reservations about Rustam's character and the nature of his relationship with Gata.

Rustam complained incessantly about money, and spoke of himself and Gata as global free agents. In the fall of 1989, he was lobbying for someone to pay him a coach's salary on top of the stipend from Cayne. If he was not paid what he wanted, Rustam threatened to leave the United States and win the world championship for another country.

Later, Gata received a lucrative five-year grant from Immopar. Combined with his tournament winnings and appearance fees, young Kamsky was probably earning better than $150,000 a year, a dazzling sum for a chess player. Still, in interviews, Rustam, who continued to use the United States as his home base, complained about the family's poverty. One area of frustration in particular was the failure of the American Chess Foundation to award Gata the Sanford Fellowship, which would give the family an additional $30,000 a year for two years. Rustam has made the point again and again that his young son is the highest-rated player in America, and that other Americans who have received it instead were lower-rated. One requirement for the Sanford fellowship, however, is that a player must first have completed his high-school education. As noted before, Rustam claims Gata did finish the Soviet equivalent of his high school education, and eventually, in the spring of 1991, he produced the long-awaited proof: Gata's diploma. When the diploma was sent to the Soviet Union for verification, however, it was immediately identified as a forgery. Despite his lower rating, Ilya Gurevich won the 1991 fellowship.

"American players have been jealous of Gata from day one," said Rustam, who often referred to Gata's opponents as enemies, and who couldn't find a teacher in the United States whom he trusted not to steal his son's ideas. "The Russian players and the Americans conspire to beat him. They all hate Gata."

A few months after arriving here, Gata took a lesson with a respected theoretician, the grandmaster Leonid Shamkovich. "He visited me for two hours," recalled Shamkovich. "It was impossible teaching Gata with Rustam standing over us. He was trying to tell me things that he knew nothing about. Gata is a very passive person. He never ventures his own opinion. He always says, 'You must ask my father.' Having such a dictator for a father is not the best way for a chess player. No one would teach him in the Soviet Union because of his father."

Trainers and chess journalists interviewed in the Soviet Union discussed the Kamskys as a single package, brilliant to be sure, but impossible to deal with, the father answering, complaining, pushing for his son. Some trainers turned Gata down as a student because of the reputation of Rustam, who had spent a considerable portion of his early adulthood in jail for petty crimes. Viacheslav Osnos, for years the trainer of grandmaster Victor Korchnoi, was one who refused to train Gata. "His father interfered in everything. Rustam would give advice that he was incompetent to give."

During their first year here, numerous masters, including Shamkovich and another grandmaster, Maxim Dlugy, observed episodes of verbal abuse following the boy's occasional defeats. When we were together, Rustam angrily showed me Soviet magazine articles accusing him of beating his son when he lost games, but Rustam said that they were lies spread by Soviet chess officials who were embarrassed by their defection. In the Soviet Union, many chess professionals said that the father's abuse of his son was common knowledge. Gata denied that his father hit him, however; he said that after he lost "he might get angry like normal people. He might scream or yell."

"The whole Soviet Union was against us," said Rustam. He contended that coaches were always stealing Gata's ideas and gave the boy "psychological poison."

Most curious was Rustam's belief that the world champion, Garry Kasparov, had been the single largest impediment in the development of his son's career. Rustam accused Kasparov of having used his considerable influence to keep Gata out of the Soviet Union's best chess schools and tournaments, so that the boy's development would be stunted. "Kasparov has been conspiring for many years now [against Gata], that's for sure. Gata is like a bone in his throat. Kasparov is afraid of Gata."

In Rustam's view, Kasparov's power was global, insidious and lethal, like that of the old KGB, and the world champion was preoccupied with his son. It was Rustam's belief—dismissed by all of the American and Soviet-born players whom I interviewed—that Kasparov had grandmaster cronies here, who somehow lobbied within the United States Chess Federation to prevent Gata from getting his proper share of publicity and to keep his international rating lower than it should be by suppressing the results of his best tournaments.

"Gata, do you agree with your dad that Kasparov is afraid of you?"

"I think so. Why else does he try to prevent me?"

Late in October, 1989, Gata Kamsky played his two-game match against Garry Kasparov in the stately Bates Forum at the New York Public Library, in front of a standing-room crowd of chess lovers. Sitting across from Gata, Kasparov, in a stylish tweed jacket, scratched his curly black hair, twisted in his chair and appeared nervous. Gata, wearing the same boyish sweater and pants as in the elimination matches, seemed relaxed and oblivious to the photographers crowded around their table.

Kasparov, playing with the white pieces, immediately attacked. His face became bulldoggish with sneers and grimaces, and someone in the audience remarked, "He must hate the kid." The world champion brooded and suffered over the board as he played, scratched his head and looked up to the heavens for inspiration. Each gesture seemed to have great weight. He won the first game easily.

In the second game, Kasparov, again attacking, rocked in his chair and tapped his teeth with his finger. He seemed to grow larger as his pawns moved relentlessly ahead, taking a stranglehold on Gata's kingside. As in the first game, Kamsky made mistakes but methodically defended, never looking ruffled. Though he was nearly Kasparov's size physically, he appeared to be a mere boy across from the champion, who leaned lustily over the position, almost physically pushing Gata back. When Kasparov's advantage was overwhelming, the champion picked up a queen from the side of the table and shook it at the admiring crowd.

After the match, when Kasparov and I spoke at Olga Capablanca's party, he was extremely blunt about Gata: "He plays strong moves. Very professional moves. But he has no potential to be world champion. There are many strong grandmasters, but to be world champion you need that last component. I don't think Kamsky has it."

He reflected upon Gata's singularity of purpose. "My life has been much wider," he said. "I can't live only with chess. If you love only your profession, it could damage you. If I didn't spend time on politics and athletics and other things, I couldn't be Kasparov."

Gata Kamsky's defeat by Kasparov did not slow his astonishing assault on the international chess world. After tying for first in a prestigious tournament in California, he and Rustam flew to the beautiful Spanish seaside resort of Palma de Majorca. Kamsky finished ahead of 152 grandmasters, tying for second place—perhaps the greatest tournament result ever achieved by a fifteen-year-old. In the New York Open, he again tied for second, defeating the legendary former world champion Mikhail Tal. Since then, young Kamsky has been at or near the top in some of the world's strongest tournaments. At the age of sixteen, he tied for first place in the superpowerful round robin Interpolis tournament in Tilburg, Netherlands, to earn his GM title. In 1991, Gata placed first in the World Open, and a month later won the U.S. championship. At seventeen, he was the youngest player to accomplish that feat other than Bobby Fischer, who first won the title at the age of fourteen. By the end of 1992, Gata's rating of 2655 placed him twelfth in the world.

But for virtually every Gata victory, there has been a scandal involving Rustam. In the crucial second-to-last round of the World Open, while Gata was playing against Patrick Wolff, Rustam boisterously accused Wolff's trainer, Victor Frias, of signaling moves to his player. While Wolff struggled to concentrate, Rustam challenged Frias to walk outside and fight. In the U.S. championship, Gata was losing the decisive game to grandmaster Joel Benjamin, when Rustam claimed that grandmasters Patrick Wolff and John Fedorowicz and international master Ilya Gurevich were signaling Benjamin moves. Benjamin, clearly distracted by the row taking place a few feet away, soon blundered and lost the game and the championship. Perhaps he would have blundered without Rustam's help. Nonetheless, Rustam and Gata demonstrated a kind of smooth razzle-dazzle teamwork never before seen in the chess world. While Rustam fumed and glared at opponents, made claims of cheating, and challenged players and coaches to fights, Gata played brilliantly, calmly, seemingly without distraction. Indeed, he seemed to gain strength and determination from his father's histrionics and claims of dark conspiracies.

*   *   *

In retrospect, Rustam partially attributed Gata's loss to Kasparov in 1989 to a jealous American grandmaster, a supposed friend, who revealed to the world champion all of Gata's opening secrets. As Rustam described the event, the tendons in his powerful neck bulged. He blazed with menace and ambition. It was Rustam, not Gata, who reminded me of Kasparov over the board. Gata, who was suffering with a cold, sat even more quietly than usual, his eyes glazed, perhaps a little happy that because he was sick he didn't have to study. "Not only will Gata win," Rustam said, looking forward to his son's next encounter with Kasparov, "but he will crush him like a fly."

Gata could never deliver a line like that.

"Bobby Fischer was lonely, and now Gata is going to have to be lonely," said Rustam, recalling that during his career Fischer often feuded with world chess organizations. "He is going to have to go against the Chess Federation and everyone else on his own."

Well, not exactly on his own. Gata has Rustam. Rustam has Gata. The father's energy and appetite for battle have spurred his gifted and reserved son to victories that are already memorable in chess history. But what a lonely and confusing life this father has carved out for his son—so much early success stirring crazily with the envy and enmity of contemporaries and the institutions that they must depend upon, and Gata hearing all of it as from the bottom of a deep well as he monkishly studies chess positions. "You must ask my father; I am only the player," he said.

I was thinking about Garry Kasparov's harsh assessment of Gata's play, that a component of greatness was missing. Of course, saying that Gata doesn't have it may have been the damning prophecy of a world champion who hears footsteps. But if Kasparov is right, and some in the chess world say that he is, one must appraise the coach's game plan, to shut out the world and study harder than anyone. Maybe there has to be air and outside experiences, as Kasparov suggests, for a creative mind to reach its full potential. Maybe a girlfriend and a soccer game make for a better chess player.

"It is hard to believe that someone of that mentality could ever become world champion," said the young grandmaster Patrick Wolff, who has absorbed more than his share of pummeling from the

Kamsky team. "As much as I envy him, you couldn't pay me enough to trade places with him."

"We've gone to England, France, Germany, Spain, and we have not seen anything really," said Rustam with fire and pride. "No sightseeing. When Gata is not playing, he is studying."

"Studying, playing, sleeping. That's it?" I asked him.

"Da."

Much of the above was published in *The New York Times* Sunday magazine in May, 1990, while I was in France with Kasparov. About a month later, the Kamskys' business agent urged me to be careful for my life. She spoke of Rustam's violent nature, and when I pressed her for examples, she recalled that earlier in the spring he had badly beaten up a visiting Russian player after some dispute. Dumbadze continued to represent the Kamskys, she said, because she was frightened that Rustam might harm her if she quit, and also because she cared for the boy.

Following this, I went with my lawyer to the police, and was subsequently told that the Kamskys received warnings from Kaufman, from the police and then from an FBI agent who had been instrumental in arranging details relating to their defection one year earlier. I suspect that the agent told Rustam that, even in crime-weary New York City, a man was likely to get more than a few weeks for premeditated murder.

I had virtually no contact with the Kamskys for the next nine months, until I traveled to Spain with my son for the Linares tournament—which I will write about later—where Kasparov next met young Gata over the board. During the intervening months, indeed to this day, Gata's uncomfortable expression continues to adorn the covers of our chess magazines, and some of our top players, chess administrators and ardent fans argue that he is a boon for American chess. It does not seem to offend his fans that the father produces forged documents and physically intimidates Gata's opponents. In the chess world the great moves of geniuses have always eclipsed any weaknesses of character or even the most reprehensible behavior. When Bobby Fischer was making his immortal moves against

Spassky in Reykjavik, the chess world ignored his affection for Adolf Hitler. I asked one American grandmaster why the Kamskys were tolerated here, and the man answered simply, "He may be the next world champion."

6

MIND GAMES

September, 1990—I was lost in the woods, somewhere on the south side of Martha's Vineyard Island. I was trying to find Kasparov's training camp and I felt absolutely ridiculous. I had been coming to this island off the coast of Massachusetts for thirty years. Garry had decided to train here at my suggestion and Andrew Page and I had selected the enormous beachhouse he had rented eight weeks earlier. But where was it? Clearly, I had taken a wrong turn and had no idea which way to head. I recalled that it was a couple of miles from the South Road to the house—actually there were a few houses on the property, providing privacy for Garry, his wife and mother, and a half-dozen trainers. I should have gone back to the South Road and started again, but after driving winding dirt roads for fifteen minutes in the moonless night, I had no idea which way to turn to get back. Everywhere I looked, there were more oak trees. I had called to say that I would be right over. It was already past eight o'clock at night, and Kasparov, whom I had not seen for some weeks, was waiting for me for dinner. He would be angry, drumming his fingers on the table. I would feel silly explaining that I got lost: Don't I know this island like the back of my hand? On his face would be a mixture of amusement and disdain, or perhaps only disinterest.

100

Such bad timing. Tonight I had planned to describe the book that I wanted to write about him. While I pulled into the driveway of a darkened house—not his, much too small—and then struggled to back out without hitting a tree, I imagined Kasparov's face when I asked him what he thought about my book idea. When people make demands upon his time, Garry's eyes narrow and one can almost hear him thinking, Why should I do it? Am I being taken advantage of? Or, can't you see that I'm too tired for this? To write the book I wanted to write, Garry had to agree to have private dinners with me once or twice a week while he played against Karpov. I would need to talk with him about the strategy of the match while it was unfolding. We would need to take long walks and talk about what he had been feeling while he played the night before. I would have to be with him after the wins, and particularly after the losses. I would need to talk with his trainers about what he was like to work for.

I wanted to watch the games sitting next to his fretting mother and his nervous wife. I wanted to sit in the kitchen with Klara while she cooked for Garry and worried about the game coming up in three hours, to talk to her about how we rooted and suffered for our children while they played their games, to gauge if the suffering of the mother of the world champion was any different from mine. Garry would have to convince his mother to allow me into their camp, their home. Klara would be suspicious. She would fear treachery. For a chess champion, our relationship would be virtually without precedent. During all the lengthy championship matches in the past, the world champions—both players, for that matter—kept themselves largely unavailable to the press, living hermetic, clandestine lives. They worried about spies divulging secrets. For months, they played, trained and saved their energy for the games.

I dreaded asking him about the book, fielding his suspicion and possibly his anger: "Fred, this is absurd—to play against Karpov while living in a fishbowl. How can you ask me?" It *was* hard for me to ask him. In truth, I wanted him to like me almost more than I wanted to write the book. I was like a kid who wants to be friends with Michael Jordan. That's only part of it.

An inspiration: I turned off the engine, got out of the car and listened for the ocean. I could hear the surf. I turned the car around to head that way. For the past few weeks, I had been thinking about why I was drawn to Garry. At times he was like my father. The idea made me uneasy and also a little giddy—Garry was twenty years younger than I! My father could be intimidating without saying a word, anger pouring from his green eyes while he contemplated the world's injustice. His weathered face naturally assumed attitudes of revenge, but grew soft when we talked together; he was unashamed of his affection for friends and family, he could cry in front of me—such shifts of mood, confusing but intoxicating for a son. My father was a sickly man, and it often fell to me to take care of him when he was ill. Kasparov, to be sure, was a physical powerhouse, but I think those who know him well sense that his life is dominated by his frailties. When he talked to me of his own father, tears rolled down his cheeks and he put his head on my shoulder. When I was with Garry, I felt the responsibility of shoring him up.

I walked onto the beach and looked east and west. About a quarter mile to the east, I spotted the lights of a cluster of houses—it looked like a small village. Garry's training camp. My father, who would spend his last dollars eating in a fancy restaurant or renting the most expensive motel room in town, would have loved this place that Page and I had selected: ten or twelve outsized rooms in the main house, towering windows offering the grandest views of sunsets and fishing boats plying the Atlantic, a fireplace the size of a van, twenty-foot ceilings, a state-of-the-art kitchen the size of half a basketball court—a house for little chess players big enough for a family of Wilt Chamberlains. Thirty thousand a month in the off season. Next door to it was a Ping-Pong and game house the size of most middle-class homes. It was the newest, most sumptuous, and, some would say, the gaudiest estate on this lovely island. Andrew knew that Garry would love it (even while he urbanely commented on its ungainliness). The boy from Baku would train for Karpov feeling rich and special, a winner. The following summer in Malibu, to train for a tournament in Europe, Andrew would select the enormous house where Madonna had gotten married to Sean Penn, at a cost of forty thousand for the month, considerably more than Kasparov would get for winning the tournament.

I looked through a window and could see Garry inside, leaning over a chessboard and writing in a notebook. He looked much younger than he had in Europe. His hair was long and bushy, his face set in naive purpose, like my son's when he writes his chess ideas in little notebooks, studiously preparing to become a great player like Garry. I watched him for a few minutes. His face was clear, no anger, no suspicion. Almost a schoolboy. Now I wondered if it was some resemblance to Josh that drew me to Garry. Like any superstar, Kasparov is a repository for a fan's dreams and projections. Even for friends, it is hard to know him truly for all the daydreams and opportunities for secondary gain. This probably makes Garry lonely.

I knocked on the kitchen door and Klara greeted me with a hug, "Ah, Fred Waitzkin," she said in her deep, emotional voice. I soon found out that everything about Klara rang with implication, portent and often dread, even my name. A full-bodied woman with a sensuous Sophia Loren face, she made most of the decisions relating to Garry's training—for that matter, many of the decisions relating to other facets of his life. Almost instantly, one could perceive that she was guided mainly by her intuitions. As she held my hand, she was deciding about me.

Garry walked into the kitchen to greet me. As he shook my hand, asked about New York, inquired about Josh, he leaned back toward the living room and his work, some chess variation tugging at him. Of course I was not late for dinner at all. This was Kasparov time. We would eat after he finished working and then finished relaxing.

"Are you going to leave it this way?" I asked, about his long hair.

"Do you like it?" A broad warm smile.

"It looks great long."

"No, I will cut it. My mother thinks that when it is short I look fierce. She wants me to be fierce for Karpov." He pursed his mouth: what can you do, my mother?

After a minute of two, he made a little gesture with his hand, a gesture which said, Will you forgive me? I have to study for a while longer. Garry's wife, Maria—friends and family call her "Masha"—led me into the living room. She was thin, pale and lovely, with the carriage of a ballerina. We sat in two rocking chairs and began to get acquainted. Garry was sitting on a leather couch a few feet away, leaning over a chessboard, pausing every two or three minutes to write in his notebook. The television played, and although the volume was turned up, he appeared to be entirely engrossed in his study. I have argued with Josh that he cannot do his best work with the TV on. Could I have been wrong about that?

Masha pointed to an article on the front page of *The New York Times*, and we began to talk about the predicament of blacks living in the inner cities of the Northeast, of kids trapped in a cycle of poverty and crime. She flushed with pain for the children. I mentioned that Josh and a number of his friends had been repeatedly mugged, one friend badly hurt, by roving bands of black and Hispanic teenagers who came to the Upper East Side of New York City to prey on privileged white kids after school. "When your kid has been beaten by one of these gangs, it tends to put a dent in your idealism," I said. She nodded. I was half making these points for Garry, thinking it was a subject that would interest him, but I couldn't tell if he was listening. He didn't look up.

It was Masha's first visit to the States, but she seemed to know a great deal about the country, our books, movies, current events. She spoke English with delicacy and near-perfect diction. Within minutes we were speaking intimately, as if we were old friends. At twenty-six, she worried about what she should do with her life. She had studied English in Moscow and for a time she thought she would be a translator, but years had passed and she no longer felt confident enough to do this professionally. I asked about her options, and she shook her head. She didn't know what to do. Her brow wrinkled with concern. She looked very beautiful this way. She said that doing nothing except helping Garry be world champion would not be satisfying. Over time she would feel empty.

Discussing these questions with Garry sitting within earshot was titillating. I had a sense that Masha was teasing Garry a little. Within minutes I had a crush on her. Without saying a word, we were both playing a game, getting to know each other and trying to get Garry to notice. "So far I have chosen to be with him, to help him. Maybe in the future I will find something for myself." I thought Garry knew about our game and used it for leverage, to push deeper into his ideas; for the next hour or so he never took his eyes from the chessboard, except to write in the notebook.

Then, when Garry looked up from his work, he was in mid-thought. "Fred, do you know that the USSR had a thousand advisors in Iraq? I hope you don't believe that Gorbachev supports Bush in Iraq because he is a good guy. Gorbachev goes along with the U.S. because he has no other choice. He barely holds onto power today and only because he has the full support of the West, because he demonstrates his close relations with Bush. But soon he will be gone."

Masha was off to the kitchen. She covered for Garry. Whenever Garry broke off conversation in mid-sentence to study or to call someone on the phone, she rushed to fill the space, entertained, soothed a bruised ego. She was light where he was heavy, faultlessly polite where he could be rude. She was the one to call from Europe filled with warmth and good cheer to wish the family a happy new year. When Garry returned, with his combative smile and confrontational ideas, Masha retired to the edges.

"In Paris, I said that in nineteen ninety-one there won't be a Soviet Union. Maybe I made a mistake. It could happen earlier." In his voice there was the familiar scorn for American liberals, for Bush and for the editors of *The New York Times*, who continued to write glowingly of Gorbachev as if he were a Messiah adored by his people and destined to rule his country long into the twenty-first century. "But let's be conservative and leave it nineteen ninety-one."

Kadzhar, Garry's old friend from Azerbaijan, cooked the dinner, a typical training meal: well-done steak, potatoes, cucumbers in a sour cream sauce. Garry ate with relish, and talked, his thick bottom lip glazed with sour cream. At one point he scanned the table for bread, and, seeing none, reached onto my plate, broke my roll in half, a quick smile, took a bite, kept talking. Conversation coursed from the morality of using nuclear arms to the chess potential of the young Soviet grandmasters Vassily Ivanchuk and Boris Gelfand. Kasparov felt that nuclear arms were an acceptable alternative against a tyrant such as Hussein, and that both Ivanchuk and Gelfand were "big" talents but lacked the psychological stability to become world champion. There were allusions to a disturbing problem concerning the match, but Garry shook his head, no, he didn't want to talk about it tonight. Tonight he was in good spirits. Unlike in France, Kasparov was struggling to be the master of his moods. A few times during dinner, he thought of something, and spoke sharply in Russian to one of his trainers, an idea that nagged at him from the day's study—they must look at this tomorrow. Kasparov was no longer fasting from chess. Chess was stage front. Karpov was coming in less than two weeks.

After dinner, Garry walked back to the living room, sat on the sofa, and I joined him. The sounds of Klara and Masha working in the kitchen were warm and wholesome. We joked about the immensity of the living room. Giraffes could graze in this room. He loved it. After a few minutes, I said that I was considering writing a book about him and the forthcoming match. His jaw tightened a little, and he nodded, as if he had known that I had something on my mind. He suggested that we talk about it tomorrow. I thought glumly that if I never mentioned it again, he would never bring it up. He was staring at the chessboard and pieces in an irritated way. He hadn't intended to study chess after dinner, but the pieces, still arranged in a variation, triggered a concern. He looked up at the ceiling, lips moving, calculating, envisioning what would happen six moves ahead. He began to make moves. After each one for black, he tapped the piece into place, a kind of exclamation mark. Kasparov's hands were delicate and oddly small on his heavily muscled body, hands perfectly made for moving little wooden pieces. For all the things we talked about, I sometimes forgot that chess was what he did the best.

Even without trying objectively to understand what he was doing, it was pleasing to watch Kasparov take apart a variation he had played many times, jiggle it around while searching for a tempo, for a slightly better square for a piece, some little improvement. It was not unlike watching a master mechanic take apart an engine that is less than perfect, spill all of its parts into a large tray of oil, and then put them back together.

It occurred to me that whenever I came to visit Kasparov, I brought my own agenda. I worried that I would feel like an idiot surrounded by so much world-class chess, or that I would become bored. I worried that I wouldn't like him or that he wouldn't like me. I wondered if he would ask about my life. But minutes after my arrival, I was swept away by his pace, by the freshness or outrageousness of his ideas, by his appetite for new worlds to conquer, by the thrill of watching him play blitz chess with his trainers or the silence in the room when he moved the pieces by himself. All of Kasparov's visitors are pulled into his orbit, walking at his furious pace, eating at his odd hours, attentive to his timing, gravely concerned about his concerns, as if they had been thinking about them for years. ("Fred, did you read Mayor Popov's speech yesterday. Here it is, take a look . . . No, we'll talk about that later. First, read Popov's speech.") This happens very naturally. I've seen him with wealthy business-men, well-known political figures, top grandmasters, editors, ac-tresses, hockey players, novelists: they quickly began to function in his world—he rarely crossed over.

In the variation that Kasparov practiced now with the black pieces, he sacrificed a pawn for the beginnings of an attack. His opponent had more material, but Kasparov's pieces controlled more space on the board. The world champion favors variations that lead to dy-namic imbalances, double-edged positions where the possibilities are vast, the chess terrain best suited for flights of imagination. Through-out his career he has been inspired by the abstract and paradoxical nature of chess; that, for example, depending upon the position, a pawn may be worth more than a rook, a knight more than a queen, that more does not necessarily mean better. Again and again he replayed the variation, his smaller but more aggressive army swoop-ing down on his opponent's queenside knight, trying to force it from the middle of the board back onto a square where it would be more passive and perhaps vulnerable in a few more moves. Against Kas-parov, who is relentless when he has the initiative, little weaknesses quickly become fatal weaknesses. He is a killer with his foot in the door. While he works at a position, Kasparov is not studying moves so much as power, the dynamics of power.

"In chess you have general rules," he said to me, "to find the best position for a piece, to fight for the open line, to have a strong center, to attack the opponent's king. The real art in chess is to evaluate the factors because they are so different. What is more important, one pawn or the open line? What's more important, the weak position of your king or some initiative on the queenside?

"Material," he continued, meaning the number and kinds of pieces still on the board, "must be compared against time—how long it will take for one's attack to crystallize, relative to an opponent's. Material and time must be evaluated against quality—whether the pieces are located on squares that are tactically and strategically strong. It takes imagination to control unrelated things," Kasparov said with a big smile, no doubt recalling our conversation in Paris. "It is like controlling chaos.

"People think of chess as a logical game, and, yes, there is logic, but at the highest level the logic is often hidden. In some positions where calculation is almost impossible, you are navigating by your imagination and feelings, playing with your fingers. For weaker players, great moves often appear to be stupid. But if you feel the unity, you can do what nobody understands.

"Have you seen my game against Lajos Portisch in 1983?" Kasparov set up the pieces and quickly moved them to a position in the middle of the game. "You can see that Portisch had a strong and logical defense. But I had something. I felt it," Kasparov sniffed the air like a hunter divining clues in the fresh early morning breeze. "I was playing by smell, by feel. All of my pieces were closing in. It was very sensual. I didn't spend very much time thinking. I just looked at one line and said to myself, this is great. Portisch spent a great deal of time on his moves. He was not upset, because his position was solid enough. He found good moves. He found a way to exchange some of my more dangerous pieces. He remained under attack, but his position appeared to be defensible. But I looked at the position, and the factors that we have been talking about, they seemed positive for me. His king position was weak, his knight was to the side and couldn't get back to the center of the game. The coordination of his pieces was bad. You recall, a few minutes ago we were talking about the quality of the pieces. A knight away from the action is worth less than a knight poised to attack. When pieces are working in harmony, they are worth more than the same pieces in disunity. The quality of his pieces was bad, but still we kept making normal moves. I didn't appear to have any concrete threats. More and more, it looked like a draw.

"Then we came to the critical position. Look at it, Fred. In the center my bishop blocks my knight from the central square, where it would be most effective in the attack. Many players in this position would retreat the bishop. But if you withdraw the bishop, it slows down the attack by a move, it wastes a tempo, which gives Portisch an extra move to defend. Only one decision. I sacrificed it for one pawn. Portisch couldn't believe his eyes. I had no concrete threat. I didn't even have any checks afterwards, just quiet moves. I needed my knight in the center where it would have great value, and the bishop meant little in this game. Portisch was forced to spend a move taking the bishop back. I sacrificed my bishop for a tempo, for time, as well as for the increased quality of the knight."

"But if you are wrong about the attacking potential of your knight or the timing of your attack, you're down a bishop against a great player. You're probably lost."

"Of course."

"Do you ever think that you need to feel danger to play your best, that you like to live on the edge?"

"I cannot describe the feeling when I play this way, hanging by a thread. I can feel it all through me."

"I'll never forget the twenty-fourth game in Seville," I said, referring to the last game of the 1987 title match against Karpov. "Josh, he was eleven then, was playing in a tournament in Connecticut. One of the wire services was sending the moves of your game to the tournament hall."

Kasparov had been playing poorly in the fourth match, as if he had become bored with playing marathons against Karpov every year. He kept missing wins. When Karpov won the twenty-third game, Kasparov's situation was suddenly grave. Karpov needed only a draw in the final game to win back the championship. When a grandmaster with Karpov's defensive genius is playing only to draw, it is extraordinarily difficult to defeat him. The twenty-fourth game had the makings of a great storybook finish: the champ down on points needed a knockout punch in the final round. Virtually everyone in the Connecticut tournament was rooting for Kasparov. There was a feeling in the air that the chess world would suffer a setback if Karpov won.

"Some Russian emigrés playing in Connecticut were saying that your life would become very difficult if he won," I continued. "Everyone was following the moves of the game. Josh was beside himself. He couldn't concentrate on his own game for checking your position."

"It was terrible for me as well," recalled Kasparov. "When I lost the twenty-third game I didn't believe that I would recover. In the night, I went to the hotel where my coaches lived and spent three hours playing cards, just to relax. My future was on the line in this game. I began thinking about what the plan should be. I remembered that Karpov was down twelve to eleven in '85 and had to win the last game to draw the match and retain the title. In that game, he started to play very risky aggressive chess and he lost. As I recalled, his strategy had made my task simpler. By attacking with all his force, he had given me concrete problems to solve and removed elements of doubt. Before that game, I had been really afraid that he would play quietly and slowly, trying to postpone my celebration. I had envisioned him having a slight edge and playing on and on. Okay, maybe my position wasn't dangerous, but it was very unpleasant, and Karpov would be waiting patiently for my mistakes.

"I decided that maybe that was the chance. I knew that Karpov expected me to play risky chess. Instead, I played quietly. But when you play this quiet way with white, nursing a slight edge, you present black a choice and a dilemma: to make the best move or the safest move. Karpov is a great player, and normally he would play the best move, but the best move sometimes involves some risk. This quiet style can have a narcotic effect. The position does not seem dangerous to him. And so he chooses the safest move. But the safest move is not always the best move.

"Now the position is slightly worse, a little worse, and he must play with the psychological discomfort of knowing that he did not make the best moves. Karpov understood this very well, but he could not change his psychology. I remember the moment when he could play a move fighting for initiative. But this would break the symmetry of the game, make the position unclear, unpredictable. He felt it was the best move, but he couldn't, you know. It was against the logic of the game. And now the position was getting worse for him, worse. I had a big advantage and if he made the final mistake, I could win. Then, when we were in time trouble, he made it—but I answered with another mistake. Now he could draw, but he didn't play accurately. After exchanging several mistakes, the position was adjourned.

"Even today, I don't believe that the adjourned position was won for me. It was fifty-fifty. During the night, we couldn't find a way to win. But, also, we couldn't find a certain way to draw. A couple of hours before the resumption of play, we found an interesting idea. Still, there was no obvious win: Chances, but who knows? When I went to the tournament hall, however, I looked at his eyes and I knew that he would lose. I could see that he didn't believe that he could save the game. In three moves he made the decisive mistake, a horrible positional mistake. Incredible. He couldn't sustain the tension. In this game he was defeated by psychology more than chess moves.

"Of course, the loss of this game would have been a disaster for me. The Sports Committee, Karpov, they would have tried to smash me as a person. Maybe they couldn't keep me rotting somewhere, as they did Gulko five years earlier—things had changed in the country and I was not as vulnerable as I would have been in '84 if I had lost—but they would have made my life a misery. I might have been forced to leave the country, and I didn't want to do that."

In 1984, when Kasparov finally had his chance to challenge for the championship, the five-month, forty-eight-game marathon against Karpov was dominated more by politics, elements of the bizarre, and dirty tricks than by brilliant chess. At the start of Karpov-Kasparov I, a story circulated that Karpov had used his considerable political clout to have one of Kasparov's top aides, grandmaster Gennady Timoshchenko, drafted into the army, and that this unexpected and disconcerting event accounted in part for Kasparov's bad start. Whatever the reason (perhaps at the time Karpov was simply a much stronger player), the nervous challenger could not have begun much worse, and was losing the encounter 5–0, with Karpov needing only one more victory to retain the title.

After Karpov's pummeling of young Kasparov in the early rounds, however, the match fell into a rut of endless draws: at one point, seventeen in a row. There are various theories about them. Some said that Kasparov had come upon a clever strategy similar to Muhammed Ali's rope-a-dope against George Foreman in Zaire, to frustrate and exhaust Karpov. Others in the chess world, such as the prominent chess coach Mark Dvoretsky, claimed that Kasparov, humiliated at the prospect of losing the match 6–0, was playing like a coward, again and again running away from promising positions in order to force draws, because bold play carried a measure of risk. In his autobiography, Kasparov makes it clear that his poise and self-esteem were very shaky. In those dark days, he was seeking counsel and confidence from Tofik Dadashev, a psychologist and mystic who had predicted that, despite the score, Garry would not lose. Kasparov was not proud of the draws, and explained simply, "I was not yet ready, psychologically, to take the initiative."

Be that as it may, after months of mostly draws, a kind of stressful and exhausting running-in-place, Karpov, a physically frail man, began to falter, and despite unexplained official time-outs that infuriated Kasparov and gave the champion time to rest, Kasparov won three games. Suddenly, he seemed to have Karpov on the ropes.

The world press was heralding the match as one of the great sporting comebacks of all time—when, incredibly, Florencio Campomanes, president of the Fédération Internationale des Echecs (FIDE) and a close friend of Karpov's, suddenly declared the match canceled, due to the "exhaustion of both players." Canceled! The enraged challenger told journalists, who were already interpreting the decision as a fix, that his health was fine, thank you, and that the decision had been made at the behest of the Soviet chess federation in order to save Karpov's title, but there was nothing to be done.

Months later, Kasparov won a rematch, and this time nothing could save Karpov. Kasparov became world champion, and subsequently won two more closely-contested encounters with his nemesis. All the while, though, swirling around their chess wars were bizarre rumors: Karpov's seconds were sending him messages during the games in color-coded snacks and drinks; the former world champion was getting through demanding games with the aid of amphetamines. During the third match, Kasparov lost several games after his opening novelties were easily outplayed by Karpov—Kasparov claimed that one of his most trusted trainers, Evgeny Vladimirov, who had been acting suspiciously in camp, had been discovered copying the world champion's newest opening ideas into a notebook. Kasparov was convinced that Vladimirov had been bribed by Karpov. Another Kasparov trainer, grandmaster Mikhail Gurevich, has said that before the Seville match in 1987 he was offered a $30,000 bribe to reveal Kasparov's opening secrets.

Despite the new liberalism in the Soviet Union and the apparent security of the New York–Lyon venue, there were some in the chess world who cautioned that the cloak-and-dagger side of the world championship was still an ongoing reality in the summer of 1990. "Many forces in the Soviet Union want Karpov to win," said Lev Alburt, a grandmaster who had defected from the Soviet Union in 1979 and had just won the United States national championship for the third time. "Kasparov is an enemy to Gorbachev. If I were Kasparov, I would hire some expert to check my rooms. I would never discuss an opening novelty with my trainers in my room and never on the phone." He added, somewhat paradoxically, "Of course, he must not become too paranoid."

When Kasparov recalled Karpov's machinations away from the board, his manner became tight, his mind Byzantine and flexible, as though he were trying to shadow Karpov through a complex variation, trying to fathom his infinitely tricky opponent even while he spoke. "Dirty tricks are not as likely now," he mused during a conversation in June, "but nothing is clear. The state is losing power. If I could be patient and wait until it is dead, I would feel completely safe. Of course something could happen, because I am an important problem for the state and Karpov has always had strong connections with the KGB. The question is, will he use them? Karpov is quite clever and he knows that his long-term interest is in the West, not with a dying communist regime. Of course, it might be useful for him to employ the KGB in some manner for the match, but if it is revealed, his reputation would be destroyed here forever.

"Right now in the Soviet Union, he has supporters among our Russian fascists and anti-Semites. But their support makes him uneasy. If they make a big campaign using anti-Semitic ideas in articles favoring him, he would immediately read about it in the American press. He knows this. Karpov would like to attack me in the Soviet press, but it is uncomfortable for him, because I am known by everyone as the anticommunist. Many people who have spent their lives connected with the communist regime are now afraid to be touched by the contamination. Karpov's attacks against me must be indirect, so as to not bring a shadow to him and to his new image in the West. He has had to change his image, even his personality, to prepare for the future.

"It is important to understand that these dirty tricks played by Karpov in the past were based upon the Soviet life. A man could not live a normal life without having good relations with the *apparat.* You couldn't travel, leave the country without permission. In America you don't understand such things. When he was world champion, Karpov had enormous power. He was the country's leading sportsman and the symbol of the communist system. He had full state support. It was dangerous to say no to Karpov. He had the power to make a man's life much better or much worse. When I discuss my history with Karpov, I know that some people say, 'They hate one another,' which is a way of not listening. People quickly forget. When he was the world champion, Karpov used the state to crush Korchnoi, Gulko, Nikitan and many others. Everyone who didn't behave. Before our matches, Karpov's people tried to bribe my trainers. Or someone was sent to my camp to spread the rumor that one of my trainers had been bribed. The problem with these stories is that they sound so outrageous, people don't want to believe them."

"He can't prove these things," said Anatoly Karpov, one night over dinner. "He's just talking. If I lived in the United States, I think I would invite him into the courts." Karpov dismissed Kasparov's allegations of dirty tricks in previous matches with congenial distaste and suggested that Kasparov made up such stories to gain sympathy and to annoy him before the next match. "He tries to get an extra bonus. He is trying to exploit everything which is not true. His normal behavior is that when he tells something, he tells fifty percent truth and to this he adds a lot of legends."

Karpov had delicate features, a fair complexion and straight, dark blond hair. As we ate Chinese food, he seemed vastly different from the sickly-thin, stressed-out thirty-three-year-old I had observed in Moscow during the first match with Kasparov. The thirty-nine-year-old former world champion sitting before me was relaxed and growing thick around the middle. He was pleased to be in New York, optimistic about the coming match and generally sanguine about life's prospects. When I asked if he was a millionaire (for years there has been speculation about his wealth), he folded his hands on his chest and smiled like a middle-aged capitalist who is proud of his years of material success. "I am a wealthy man," he answered. As we spoke about embarrassing subjects (Have you ever tried to bribe Kasparov's assistants? "No." Have you ever taken drugs to sustain yourself through matches? "Of course not."), his manner remained kindly and intimate. He seemed like a man entirely at peace with himself.

"After losing the world championship, life didn't change too much for me," he said in his high-pitched voice. "Probably this is because I love playing chess. I played tournaments when I was world champion, and I play tournaments now when I'm fighting for the championship again. I feel almost the same. I have put on weight because of age, but also it is necessary for me to put on weight because there is so much tension during a championship and normally I lose ten percent of my weight. At the end, I expect to be thin."

When I pressed him on the question of whether life was less interesting without the championship, he smiled a little, as if to say, glad you asked. "I have my peace movement," he said. "I have been involved in this for many years. For eight years I am president of Soviet Peace Foundation. So now we became more active under new conditions. Also, I am president of the organizing committee for telethon for Chernobyl. I was in the United Nations, Washington, Turkey, Belgium and France trying to collect money for these people."

For more than an hour, he described his political life and disaffection with the communist system. "Before, they had crazy plans. Everything was planned, planned badly, but planned. For example, before, you needed approval from immigration authorities to send schoolchildren on a visit. Now we don't need this approval, so we just make a decision." Karpov said that he was in favor of a multi-party system. "That way you have more chance to protect democracy and not go back to the previous situation, to dictatorship and cult of personality like Stalin and Brezhnev." This hardly sounded like the Karpov who had said that the two great loves in his life were chess and Marxism and who had been awarded the Order of Lenin. I mentioned that many chess fans in the West had heard that he had a close personal relationship with Brezhnev. "This is a lie," he answered, with a shy and engaging smile. "People in the West think this is true due to Kasparov. [He spreads] this type of information." In his understated manner, Karpov made it clear that he was critical of Gorbachev, whom he considered too much of a communist and too slow to accept change. He faulted Gorbachev for difficulties in the Baltics and for resisting general elections for the presidency, such as we have in the United States. His message was a more moderate version of Kasparov's. "I always had the idea that people should be free," he said. He added that as his country seemed to be rocketing toward a new day, he was so busy with his political work that there was hardly enough time to study chess, even with the world championship approaching. "It takes a lot of my time. Much more now than in nineteen eighty-five, because the situation has been changed and we have more possibilities."

After listening to Kasparov and others, I had been expecting to meet Swamp Thing for dinner, and instead, Karpov came across as a regular down-to-earth fellow. His political message was similar to Kasparov's, but his style was very different. Karpov's rendering of himself was even, low-keyed and friendly. He was open to suggestion. There was no huge anger here, at least none that he showed. No core of angst rippling the surface. No ominous silences. No hurricane of passion. No long-spoken paragraphs of hurt and poetry. Karpov politely inquired about the routine of my life and the chess education of my son. When he spoke of his distaste for Kasparov, he did so in an even-keeled, almost generous manner. "Personally, I can't accept him. We have different characters."

Karpov had trained for the match at home in the Soviet Union. When I inquired about his training regimen and how he planned to exploit Kasparov's weaknesses, he smiled faintly and shook his head, no. "No, I can't tell you. Not even in general."

"Let's pretend you were about to play against someone other than Kasparov," I asked, attempting a sly move against the master of the game. "What kinds of things would you focus on? Would questions of this opponent's personality give you clues about how to beat him over the board?"

"If I described to you weaknesses in general, I would reveal my own view. You would learn how I work, how I see other people. I would open myself up." As always, Karpov's manner remained friendly, but his circumspection on the subject of chess preparation and Kasparov's weaknesses was daunting. He had something in mind and did not want to show even a glimmer of it.

But addressing the subject of Kasparov, the player, had changed Karpov's demeanor. His cheeks reddened a little, he tensed as though realizing that the contest of his life was again close at hand. He was most eager to describe Kasparov's gifts: "Despite his age he is a deep psychologist on the chessboard. He is good at sensing what his opponent is feeling. Because of this, he knows whether to take a risk or not. And sometimes you must take a risk to win. His sense of the initiative is fantastic. [Despite what people say] he controls himself very well. He is quite cool inside."

At the chessboard, unlike the flamboyant Kasparov, Karpov strives to improve his position little by little, maneuvering subtly, masking his threats. Karpov avoids weaknesses and waits for his opponent to make mistakes. Mark Taimanov, the great Russian grandmaster and theoretician, said, "He can rearrange the pieces without violating the internal life of the position. It is a hypnotic style that sometimes makes his opponent fall asleep." Karpov works to neutralize threats and to gain control of certain squares and files, so that with his superior technique he will be able to win in the endgame. "When he is in top form, he is taking away your energy, like a spider," said Kasparov, who has seen many of his most creative and apparently overwhelming attacks immobilized by Karpov. "It is very difficult to get to him, to catch him, but he is also a very heavy hitter. If you make a mistake, he will put you out."

My conversation with Karpov wandered here and there, but the challenger always maneuvered it back to politics. "Many people mix up democracy and anarchy," he said, alluding to Kasparov's call for the immediate overthrow of communism. "I hate anarchy." Perhaps six or eight times during the evening, he referred to himself as a democrat, and stressed that when he had been world champion he had sympathized with refuseniks such as grandmaster Boris Gulko. In a speech at Howard University, Karpov said that he had tried to help Gulko during the early eighties, when the Soviet champion had been held under house arrest. Why, I asked Karpov, if he had been in sympathy with the political views of refuseniks and their desire for freedom, had he refused to shake hands with grandmaster defectors from the Soviet Union, such as Lev Alburt, when he met them at international tournaments? "Only with Korchnoi, I didn't shake hands because we had personal problems," he answered. "I always shook hands with them. I shook hands with Alburt."

Karpov explained that his poor image in the West had had its inception in Bobby Fischer's refusal to defend his title against him in 1975, as if somehow Fischer's madness had been Karpov's fault. Then, while he had held the world championship title, it was Brezhnev's time, and the closed nature of Soviet society had prevented him from properly introducing himself to a Western public that more and more thought of him as a communist bad guy. When Kasparov came on the scene, he said, Kasparov had further distorted this negative image for his own ends.

Could it be that Anatoly Karpov had always been misunderstood? Could he in truth have been a freedom fighter and democrat, trying to do the best he could while constrained by the shackles of an evil regime? There were many such stories in history. The literature of World War II abounds with stories of supposed Nazi sympathizers who worked quietly and effectively to help save Jews. I began to question the many Soviet chess luminaries I met during my visits to Europe and Russia about Karpov's life and political heart. What about it? I asked, referring to Karpov's description of himself as a democrat and of his efforts in the early eighties to help refuseniks.

The initial response of his colleagues was often laughter. When I proposed this scenario to Boris Gulko, his face seemed to be caught for a moment between a smile and a sneer.

"Only people who don't know him can believe this nonsense," said Gulko, who is now one of the top grandmasters in the United States and lives with his wife and son in New Jersey. "Karpov spoke at Howard University and people asked him about relations with me and he said that he helped me when I was a refusenik. It's bullshit. It is impossible to create a bigger lie, because he took part in making the decision to keep me imprisoned in the Soviet Union."

In 1978, when Boris Gulko and his wife, Anna Akhsharumova, a former Soviet woman chess champion, made public their desire to emigrate to Israel, they were stripped of all state support and barred from playing in chess tournaments. For several years, they lived under virtual house arrest, unable to work, entirely dependent on friends for food and the necessities of life. To publicize his plight, Gulko went on two lengthy hunger strikes, and at one point he was badly beaten by KGB thugs. When I visited him in his Moscow apartment in 1983, his hair was pure white and he had the aged face of a sixty-year-old. I was dumbfounded when he told me that he was thirty-seven. "If you don't eat for forty-two days, you too will look sixty," he said during our lengthy conversation in his flat, while I worried about the repercussions if our talk was monitored by the KGB. In fact, on the following day, Gulko was pulled into KGB headquarters for a grilling.

"I will tell you how Karpov helped me," Gulko said eight years later. "He sent his manager to my apartment. It was about the time that the authorities were going to make the decision about our case, whether they would let us leave for Israel or force us to stay. The manager said to me, 'Mr. Karpov likes your ideas. He would like to work with you.' He said that if I would change my mind about emigration, Karpov would become my patron and help me to occupy a normal position in the Soviet Union. I knew that it was a lie. This arrangement would have left me completely dependent on him. I answered Karpov's manager that I also like my ideas and wouldn't like to work with Karpov.

"Karpov is a very great chess player away from the board. At the time, he forced all strong players to work for him. If you refused to help Karpov, he made sure that you did not go abroad. He was the tsar of chess, the Brezhnev of chess. When Karpov was the world champion, it was black days for Soviet chess. Because of his great power, there was born a new kind of chess literature. When they published Karpov's games and the commentaries to his games, nobody could mention anything about his mistakes. It was very strange. In one game against Korchnoi, Korchnoi missed the opportunity to mate in four. In the commentary, all that was mentioned was that Korchnoi could have played better, but the game was a draw.

"A few days after the visit from Karpov's manager, I was invited to come into the KGB office, and a powerful man in the agency repeated the proposal. They thought I would change my mind. It was obvious that Karpov and the KGB were working hand in hand."

"Karpov is a total cynic," said Lev Alburt, who referred to a photograph which appeared in *Chess Life* in the spring of 1981, showing Karpov refusing to shake Alburt's hand at the Malta Olympiad about one year after Alburt's defection from the Soviet Union. Alburt had spent considerable time with Karpov studying chess when they were both promising young players in the Soviet Union. He said that young Anatoly was the ultimate pragmatist, to whom communism was attractive only insofar as it could be used to further his career. "Karpov took life as a game and he played it very well. He considered someone who did not use the communist system to his advantage an idiot. It would be like playing chess without castling because one happened not to like castling. In 1975, he said that the two major events in his life were joining the Communist Party and having a son. But privately he would tell anticommunist jokes like the rest of us."

It was disquieting to hear Karpov's political life and character described by these men who had known him for decades. A journalist develops a nose for duplicity. But I had dined with Karpov twice and each time come away impressed by his sincerity and charm. He had seemed to answer the most difficult questions candidly. He was saddened by his dark reputation in the West and admitted honestly that he didn't know what to do about it. He asked almost meekly for advice. Could this be the same person who had ruthlessly blackmailed the Soviet chess world for a decade? Could he be such a brilliant illusionist? But why had he told me that he had shaken hands

with Alburt, that he had been Gulko's benefactor? Had he thought
that I wouldn't ask them? Or did he have some compelling refutation
prepared for their answers? What was the truth? Like a great attorney
for the defense, Karpov had created doubt despite overwhelming
evidence by the other side. Despite mounds of slimy anecdotal
material, Karpov seemed decent and reasonable. It was tempting to
compare this puzzling man to the way in which he played the game;
if indeed, Karpov's nature was cleverly veiled, there was a similar
elusiveness about his unique chess style. Like a great martial artist,
he had the bewildering ability to deflect the power of lethal blows
back upon his opponent. He was a defensive genius, who often won
by absorbing his opponent's power, as Kasparov said, like a spider.
For decades over the board, he had defended the indefensible, wrig-
gling out of mortal predicaments to come out on top. He had done
this, in part, through an ability to appear cool and confident even
while under heavy attack. Kasparov had said that Karpov was difficult to hit. How can you hit an opponent if you cannot find him?

"It is senseless to speak of Karpov's beliefs, because he has never
had any," said Boris Gulko. "He changes as animals change in the
winter and summer. When communism was the ruling ideal in the
Soviet Union, Karpov used it to help him. He was a great communist
success story, an example of what communism can achieve. When
communism began to break down, he moved in other directions.
When anti-Semitism seemed to be gaining strength in the country,
he tried to use it, not because he is an anti-Semite, but because it
could be useful to him. In interviews he said that he is a real Russian,
and that Jews like Gulko, Kasparov and Korchnoi don't like him
because he is a strong player. Now when it is clear that communism
is finished, Karpov says he is a democrat."

"I recall a simultaneous interview given by Korchnoi and Karpov
at the time of one of their matches," said Mark Taimanov. "They
were asked to name a favorite book and movie. Karpov named a
communist propaganda novel. Korchnoi, a great French novel. Your
favorite movie? Karpov, *The Battle of Stalingrad*. Korchnoi, *Nights of
Cabiria*. Karpov was out to prove to communists that he was very
reliable. He always stressed his patriotism and adherence to socialist
ideals. Everyone knew how close he was to Brezhnev. For years there

was a large portrait of Brezhnev embracing Karpov, which hung in the Moscow Central Chess Club. Then there was the question of Karpov's fantastic wealth. There was an article in *Der Spiegel* magazine during the second match, which reported that he had made millions outside the country endorsing computers, and that this money had been deposited in the name of another man and had not been reported to the Central Committee so that he would not have to pay taxes. Karpov is certainly the greatest defensive player in chess history, and in this instance he made the most fantastic defense. He said to friends that he had never concealed the income. He explained that it was Brezhnev himself who allowed him to take the money without paying taxes. At this time Brezhnev had already died, so no one could know for sure."

For the past five weeks on Martha's Vineyard, Kasparov's days had been more or less the same. Each morning he arose at nine-thirty or ten, had breakfast and then did physical training. On the beach in front of the house, he ran for two and a half miles and then swam for a half-hour in the cold ocean and rode a few waves on his boogie board. If the Atlantic was too rough for swimming, he played tennis with Kadzhar on a court nestled in the forest a couple of hundred yards north of the house. These two old friends were well-matched, big on hustle and short on style. Their beef stew tennis was peppered with taunts and side bets.

After the morning of physical exertion, Kasparov slept for an hour and had lunch. Around four in the afternoon, he worked with his trainers for four or five hours. They analyzed Karpov's games, particularly the most recent ones, looking for tendencies and weaknesses to exploit, and tried to develop an overall strategy for the match. Most of the time was devoted to opening preparation, coming up with new ideas to spring on Karpov. Often his four grandmaster trainers worked in pairs in separate rooms, checking specific variations at Kasparov's direction. He walked from one room to the other, analyzing for a while, making comments, giving orders, occasionally walking to the mammoth alcove near the kitchen to ask Shakarov, who manned the computers, to find games in the large data base, called ChessBase, developed by Kasparov's friend Fred Friedel, that were germane to the opening variations they were studying. In past matches, Kasparov had depended on his old trainer, Alexander Sergeyevich Nikitan, to direct the daily work of the team, but this time he had decided to do it himself.

As much as finding new lines and moves, training for the world championship was about becoming mentally tough, preparing to concentrate for months on end by spending months of long hours exercising and concentrating. Short cuts were dangerous. It would be like a great marathon runner abandoning his distance training, and then attempting to maintain a near–world record pace for twenty-six miles. "You must be prepared not to lose the theme of the match, which is difficult because it goes on and on," said Kasparov. "This is especially difficult if you have not been playing or studying for a long time. You can become bored by the games and that is very dangerous."

Prior to the events in Baku the previous January, it had been Kasparov's intention to train for about a hundred days, more or less what he had devoted to other matches. As it turned out, he managed only a little more than half that amount.

"Two months before the match, I was finally ready to start the serious preparation. Unbelievable." For nearly ten years, he had had regular training sessions every three or four months, but except for a few weeks in Spain earlier in the summer, before coming to Martha's Vineyard, he had not trained seriously for almost a year. Kasparov was out of practice and it was hard for him to begin. As he sat at the board during the first days, feeling bored and fidgety, Gorbachev, Baku, and political disputes in the chess world competed with chess variations for space in his thoughts. Klara sat at a desk nearby, reading a magazine or knitting. Her face was severe and sometimes fierce. She was willing Garry to stay in place, waiting for his love of chess to take hold. If the maid came into the room to dust, Klara drove her out. For his whole adult life, Klara had waited and worried while her son did his thinking. Klara was afraid of this match. She knew that Garry's banter about crushing Karpov was empty, and it made her feel frantic. He had not studied enough.

Kasparov became inspired during his last month on the island.

"We had a fantastic session," he said. The sea air and ocean sounds had softened the urgency of Soviet politics. "I had phone calls from Moscow every day, but the advantage of being on this island thousands of miles away was that I was not obliged to react. I knew that life was going on, but I wasn't anymore an active player." Running on the soft sand at the water's edge had made him physically strong. He had lost a few pounds that had been gathering around his middle, and his chest looked as hard as a wrestler's. Kasparov had come up with some sharp ideas, particularly with the white pieces, and for the first time in a year was beginning to feel his strength as a player.

But after the day's work was over, the island evoked moments of sadness. "The view from my window is almost exactly the same as from my training camp at Baku overlooking the Caspian Sea," he said. "The angle of the house to the ocean is almost the same. The sound of the waves . . . maybe it was a little softer there. It is very strange, because this island gives me a feeling of stability but also there is much sadness. At dinner my mother and I look out at the ocean and listen to the surf. We remember everything that we lost."

September 28: On this day the routine of training was broken. When I arrived at the house for breakfast, Garry was on the phone with the assistant to the organizer of the match. He was shouting, and his face was red. "No. I have made my decision. I will not change my mind."

Several weeks before, Kasparov had resolved to use the match as a public forum to demonstrate his solidarity with freedom fighters in his country. He had decided not to play under the communist flag, but instead under the prerevolutionary flag of the Russian Republic, which during recent months had come to be a symbol of protest against Gorbachev's regime. But the organizer of the New York half of the championship, who had invested millions of dollars to host the first twelve games, was upset with Garry's decision, as were his public relations people. They were convinced that politicizing the match would confuse and ultimately turn off an American public that liked to take its sports straight up, Frank Gifford–style.

"Here, speak to Andrew." Page took the phone and began mollifying, while looking up to Garry for clues. "No, Andrew. No," said

Kasparov from across the room. Kasparov expected Page to smooth things over, to present his positions more palatably than he did himself, but at the same time he found it irritating—it was a dance they did. "No, Andrew, the match isn't worth it to me," he said irritably, while Page spoke into the phone in his soothing voice.

"I'm sorry, but Garry doesn't sound like he is going to change his mind," said Andrew cheerfully. "But, yes, I will talk to him."

The phone had been ringing all morning. A lawyer representing the organizer called from Paris to say that if Karpov protested Kasparov's use of an unofficial flag, they would probably be forced to go along with the challenger. What then? Would Kasparov refuse to play at all? The advertising agency hired to promote the match had called four times that morning, urging Kasparov to forget about his protest or, at the very least, to delay it. They were afraid that Karpov might refuse to play. A friend from Europe had called Garry to say that such a public affront to Gorbachev might be dangerous. Andrew fretted that as usual Garry wasn't thinking about chess.

Garry and I walked on the beach. He wanted me to read a draft of a statement that he would fax later that day to the wire services. "How could I play under the red flag at this point?" he said while we walked. "Now when there are just a few months left, I don't want to be represented by a red flag." It was easy to understand the organizer's dismay. Beside politicizing the match in the newspapers, which would relegate chess itself to a sidebar, Kasparov might come across as a political extremist kook, rather than as a cerebral sports hero. In the fall of 1990, there were no serious political pundits in the United States, liberal or conservative, predicting the immediate dismantling of the Soviet Union.

I read the statement. He had written it in Russian, and Masha had done the translation. It was passionate and also repetitious and in places awkward. He asked me to work on it with him. We walked back to the house. Kasparov began looking at a chess position, while I sat beside him, cleaning up the paragraphs. It was clear that his heart wasn't in chess. Every five minutes or so, he would think of something to add or ask me to read a few sentences. "Karpov will be shocked," Kasparov said, without trying to hide his glee. "He can make a protest. But he cannot attack too much, because he also knows that in one year the country is finished." He laughed like a child who had played a good trick.

I recalled another afternoon in Lyon in the spring. He had come to select from a number of possible venues for the second half of the match and also to choose a training site for the work period in August—he had not yet decided upon Martha's Vineyard. We looked at the most wonderful villas, one placed on a hill with a breathtaking view of the city. It had every possible convenience. "Fred, what do you think?" He appeared to be weighing, musing— was this the very best place to study for Karpov?—but he also knew how ridiculous it was. In Moscow he lived with his in-laws in a claustrophobic three-room flat with laundry hanging in the bath- room. He looked up at the ceiling of the villa, some little imperfec- tion. He wrinkled his nose—not just right.

An assistant to the mayor of Lyon brought us to a number of possible playing sites. "What do you think of this, Fred?" Garry asked.

"Garry, it doesn't feel right. It's too big. Too impersonal."

"I think you're right." There was amusement around his eyes. He had drawn me into it. Two kids pretending to rule the land. Which villa to choose? Which fantastic stadium? The boy from Baku pre- tending to be King Kasparov. Do you see how I live? Can you believe it?

The mayor's assistant drove Garry, Andrew and me in a matching fleet of Renault sedans from one possible playing site to the next, and responded gravely and immediately to each small sign of Kasparov's displeasure. He drove us to one that appeared to be the ruins of a Roman amphitheater which the city was willing to enclose at a considerable cost. I whispered to Garry that I could see him and Karpov rushing on stage each night dressed in leathers and holding tridents. Garry tried to hide his smile.

The mayor's assistant was a nervous wreck. Karpov had been here the week before making his choices. The assistant told me that trying to satisfy both men was nearly impossible. He was fearful, for exam- ple, that if Kasparov were to catch wind of the fact that Karpov favored the Roman amphitheater, it would be rejected out of hand. When we traveled back to Paris that evening in the train, I couldn't resist and said to Kasparov that I had learned that Karpov's preference was the outdoor amphitheater.

"I know Karpov a little," Kasparov said, his voice devoid of the playfulness of the afternoon. "He doesn't like the Roman amphitheater at all, but assumes that I will discover this preference and automatically choose another—possibly the one he secretly wants." Karpov had a sobering effect on Kasparov. His hair wouldn't be gray if it weren't for Karpov.

"You see, in a way, he is trapped," Kasparov mused, as I edited his statement. Karpov was likely to protest. If he didn't, and he sat in his custom-made, leather-cushioned chair playing chess beside a little red flag, while Kasparov sat beside the flag of revolution and democracy, that would tell a story to many people. Karpov might win his protest—Kasparov was demanding to represent a country that did not legally exist—but this victory would be pyrrhic. "He knows that if he attacks me too strongly it will blow up in his face." The match was suddenly in a state of absolute chaos—it wasn't entirely certain that there would be a match, but Kasparov was feeling pleased. He had devised a way to politicize the games, but just as importantly he had come upon a tactic with which to inspire himself. At this stage in his life, chess alone had become an unreliable stimulant. He needed bigger stakes. He needed to make chess bigger than chess. "The match against Karpov will have black-and-white symbolism—old versus new, communist versus anticommunist."

"This is a matter of conscience to me, more important than a chess match," he said, but at the same time, Kasparov was admiring his own foreplay. When Karpov read the statement in *The New York Times*, he would be shocked and off-balance as he saw himself cast anew in the role of old-time communist in opposition to Kasparov's anticommunism. At the moment, Kasparov had seized the advantage in the games that these two played, even before the games began. "Tell him that it is impossible, Andrew," Kasparov called to Page, who was holding the phone. Someone from the organizer's office was pleading for Kasparov to hold off his announcement until after the first game or two. "I already have my

statement," he said, as though these paragraphs we had been craft-
ing were engraved in stone.

Later that afternoon, while Garry was taking his nap, Klara received
a phone call from Moscow. It was the grandmaster Zurab Azmaiparashvili, a trainer of Kasparov's who had worked with Garry in
Spain earlier in the summer and had been resting in Moscow for a
few weeks before coming to New York for the match. Klara spoke
in Russian in a raised voice, very upset, while Andrew stood nearby
with a troubled expression. "Zurab was offered a hundred-thousand-
dollar bribe to turn over Garry's opening novelties," Andrew said a
few minutes later. Andrew and Klara tried to figure out what to do.
Should they tell Garry? He would be upset, nervous. They decided
that they had to tell him. He would begin the match on this disquieting note. Advantage to Karpov.
    At the time, Page knew few details about the Azmaiparashvili
incident in Moscow or how it was likely to be resolved. I spoke with
the world-class grandmaster from Georgia some time later. "A neighbor of mine in Moscow told me that a man had been looking for me,"
began Azmaiparashvili. "This man said to my neighbor that he
wanted to talk to me about the possibility of participating in a joint
[business] venture with some French people, and he identified himself
as a close friend of grandmaster Iosif Dorfman, a member of the
Kasparov training team in the past. I was busy, preparing to leave for
New York, and forgot about it. Then, this man called on the phone.
He said he wanted to take me and my family to dinner at the Hotel
Continental, where we would meet these potential French partners.
We were picked up and driven to the hotel in a limousine. The driver
said that my family should walk around while I talked to the man.
The guy was nice enough, tall and blond, with a relaxed manner, but
from the start, things looked strange. We were the only ones in the
restaurant, no Frenchmen. 'We need some chess information from
you,' he said. He spoke Russian with a Baltic accent. Immediately, I
knew what he was getting at and I told him that I couldn't help him.
    " 'Maybe you misunderstand me. I need some specific information
relating to the match.' He wanted information about Kasparov's

openings. Now, I wanted to get out of there. I stood up to shake his hand. But he kept talking, 'Look, everyone plays games. Karpov plays them and Kasparov plays them. It is beneficial to us for Karpov to win this match. We need your help. . . . Zurab, how much do you make in a year?'

"I told him that I make about twenty thousand dollars, which is more than enough in the USSR. The man said, 'We're offering you a hundred thousand dollars if Karpov wins and half if he doesn't. You only have to give us the information.'

"When he could see that I wasn't going to go along, he began threatening me. 'You know, you have a family.' This made me frightened, because they weren't in the restaurant. Maybe someone had them.

"I said to the man, 'Look, I won't help either side. That's all I can do.' I was very frightened. I was prepared to remain neutral in the match if he would leave me alone. But this didn't satisfy the guy. He said, 'Take this seven thousand. It's a deposit. We'll talk again. Take the money and think about it.' I couldn't take the money. Maybe he was a KGB agent. I could have been arrested on the spot.

"For the next two nights, I couldn't sleep. I was terrified. Then two days later someone threw a bomb or Molotov cocktail at my house in Georgia. I had sent my family there to be safe. My aunt's hair caught on fire trying to put it out. That's when I called Martha's Vineyard and spoke to Klara. She told me to call the Russian Chess Federation for protection. I called them and another agency as well. I recalled some of the numbers on the license plate of the limousine and told them. But no one would do anything. They were holding their hands behind their backs. It seemed clear to me that this bribe was either the work of Karpov or the KGB. It is well known in my country that Karpov's guys are very friendly with the KGB."

Bombs, bribes, and chess. Probably the most unnerving part of this for me was how matter-of-factly Page and Kasparov took in this turn of events—some disgusted expressions, nothing to be done about it. Masha and Klara packed mounds of books, clothes and knicknacks in suitcases and boxes. Klara was irritable. Garry read the *Times*, didn't want to talk. Kadzhar cooked steaks and lamb chops and didn't make any jokes. I didn't understand. Nothing like this happens before the Bulls play the Lakers. "These things always happen when we play Karpov," said Page, the evening before we left Martha's Vineyard for New York for the start of the match.

7

NEW YORK

The world championship brought about a renaissance of spirit in the New York chess scene. In the days before the match, everywhere one went in chess circles—clubs, local tournaments, coffee shops, parks where there were clusters of chess tables—the talk was about how Karpov and Kasparov hated one another or whether or not Karpov was over the hill or what Kasparov had up his sleeve against Karpov's Zaitsev variation of the Ruy Lopez. The world-famous but physically worn out Marshall and Manhattan chess clubs, which had been barely hanging on financially since the Fischer days, were suddenly getting phone calls from prospective new members, from fans seeking information about the match, as well as from poor chess players trying to wrangle free tickets.

According to Bruce Pandolfini, chess teachers around town who had been virtually out of work were suddenly getting calls each day from prospective students. Some of the callers were the well-to-do parents of kids attending private schools such as Dalton, Trinity and Browning, middle-aged men who had rooted fervently for Bobby nearly two decades before and had just seen Kasparov on the David Letterman show or read an article in the newspaper saying that he was the best ever. "How could it be? Better than Bobby Fischer?" Not that these parents cared about chess skill *per se*, but recalling Bobby and those heady afternoons in front of the television in '72 brought a flood of emotion, like hearing *Sergeant Pepper's Lonely Hearts Club Band* when you hadn't heard it for years, and they were prepared to lay out fifty or sixty dollars an hour for their little kids to learn to play the elite game in a way that they themselves never quite managed. So their brilliant little ones came to Pandolfini and to other chess masters for their first lessons, primed with the knowledge that Bobby Fischer was better—daddy had said so—than this Russian guy, what's his name?

In the southwest corner of Washington Square Park, half a dozen blocks from our apartment, regulars were buzzing about the match, and pronouncing the names "Anatoly" and "Garry" with the familiarity of members of their families. The match seemed to invest park games with a new crispness and sense of purpose, and I found myself going in the evening to watch for an hour or two. From the age of six to nine or ten, Josh had lived a considerable portion of his life in this section of the park. Each afternoon after school, he had come here to hone his tactics in speed games against retired workers, drop-out chess masters, failed lawyers, alcoholics, hustlers of various commodities, a rag-tag crew bonded together by a sense for the huge importance of chess and of the park itself, particularly this little corner that was a circle of nineteen marble chess tables set into the pavement to prevent their being stolen in the night.

There were many like Josh and me, who stopped by each day for a few hours of thrills and sporting conversation, but some lived the park life, playing intense games from the late morning into the night, sweating over tough positions through the stifling summer while looking forward to fall, when the wind whipped through the trees overhead, driving the pace of money games. Park regulars ate Greek and Chinese takeout on the grimy tables where Fischer had played when he was a kid, while staring at a position from Robert Byrne's column in *The New York Times*. Even in the winter, a down-and-out master might be found sitting in front of his pieces, hoping for a customer, and occasionally this poor fellow with no money and no place else to go would have to sleep on one of the benches partially sheltered by his table. During the cold months, chess hustlers marked time until the spring, when college students, businessmen, whoever (if they were weak players they were known as "fish" to the hustlers), began showing up in front of the tables with renewed optimism.

To a significant degree, in the park a man's self-worth was determined by how well he played the game. When Josh and I used to come here every day, players were improving or losing their edge, reputations were rising and falling, but the professionals, the men who made their living playing against passersby, gauged themselves relative to the sheriff. Israel Zilber, a Latvian international master with a winning record against the immortal Mikhail Tal, was the sheriff, the top gun in the park. A man of fifty-odd years, Zilber appeared to be in his seventies. He was mad and played his games while singing Latvian lullabies to the squirrels in the trees overhead, and sometimes while he moved the pieces he reminisced about imagined games he had won against Karpov and Kasparov. When he had been the champion of Latvia thirty years before, Zilber had been a natty dresser, and now he wore the layered clothing of the homeless, adorned with a sheriff's badge and cap and clumps of costume jewelry which bent his fingers into the shape of talons. The international chess community is very tight, and players around the world knew about Zilber's park residence. Often top players visiting New York would come to the park to test their endgame technique against him. One afternoon, Josh and I watched him play for hours against the great sixteen-year-old prodigy, Zsuzsa Polgar from Hungary. Zilber was a great endgame player and this lovely, well-mannered girl did not seem to be offended by his odor or that he sang to the squirrels while waiting for her to move.

During those years, second-best in the park was Vinnie the hustler, a man who played better the more he rapped and razzed his opponents. Vinnie's games were always a circus and he gave many chess fans joy. But like all the park players, other than Zilber, Vinnie played the game with a sense for his limitations. Showman that he was, Vinnie was not in Zilber's class, and he knew that he would play out his years as the deputy, second-best draw in this community of ceaseless shootouts, except for those rare times when the sheriff mysteriously hobbled away from his table for a few days.

The sheriff disappeared from Washington Square when Josh was about ten, and after a few months, park regulars said that he had frozen to death sleeping in a hallway somewhere in the city. Within a year or so, many of the guys whom Josh had sparred against were gone. A couple of the best players had died. Vinnie had spent considerable time in the hospital, and some in the park were saying that Vinnie was very sick. Years of tough games, taking drugs, no money, living the outdoor life, did not make for longevity. A few other park players we knew were in jail doing long stretches. For a time, cards, backgammon, checkers and drugs became the games of choice in the park, and Josh and I stopped coming. The sad state of affairs there seemed to mirror the perilous condition of professional chess in this country, where even our top grandmasters could not make a living and were beginning to turn away from the game to find ways to support themselves.

But during crisp October afternoons in 1990, with the match about to begin, chess players reclaimed the territory from the card players and drug pushers. With Garry living just fifty blocks uptown at the Regency Hotel, patzers and masters alike were feeling more respectable about spending their days toiling over the Coca-Cola– and fast-food–stained marble tables. Groups of titled players (grand-masters and international masters) in town for the match made their way south to this corner, and were soon offering park hustlers delicious time odds in blitz. But Ilya Gurevich, junior world champion and a breathtaking tactician, took odds from no one. He was a freshman at NYU and he spent each afternoon taking scalps, building a reputation while he earned spending money. Ilya was the new sheriff. Vinnie was out of the hospital, watching Ilya's games while he sipped white wine and made side bets. He was telling the guys that soon he would be back at one of the tables, taking care of business.

"Garry's going to bust him," said Al, a tall, handsome man Josh used to play, who had sweet tactics but knew little opening theory. I hadn't seen Al for three years and he confided to me that he had just come out of the joint, where for the last months he had imagined sitting in the park in the morning with a cup of coffee and the paper, playing over Garry's game against Karpov from the night before. I loved the way the guys in the park called him "Garry." When an assistant to the organizer of the championship gave me some complimentary tickets for opening night, I gave a few of them to guys in the park. They promised to dress up.

"I don't feel like playing," Garry told me a day or two before the first game. Despite Al's prediction, which was the prevailing match assessment in the park, Garry didn't feel as though he were about to bust up Karpov. "I'm not ready," he said, in a thin voice. "I'm not in good shape right now. I'm not prepared." Garry had rented the seventeenth floor of the Regency Hotel on East 61st Street for his family and the team of trainers, and although he had stayed here many times before, with the match about to begin the luxurious suite seemed claustrophobic. The ceilings were too low and the smell of Kadzhar's last high-cholesterol meal always hung in the air. When Garry looked out the window, the view was of rising acres of concrete and glass. No more breaking surf and sweet sea air and visions of squashing Karpov like an insect. Garry had left his confidence on Martha's Vineyard. Perhaps the Azmaiparashvili episode had thrown him off-center. He was reluctant to talk about it, but from New York he had hired bodyguards for Zurab's family in Georgia. Maybe the incident had jolted him into recalling Karpov's suffocating strategies over the board as distinct from the daydream of winning easily. Maybe he was just nervous because the match was about to begin. The great world champion Mikhail Botvinnik, an early mentor to Kasparov, had preached that in the days before an important tournament, and especially before a world championship match, a player must keep his mind off chess, take walks in the country, relax, allow his energy to build and his mind to freshen. Kasparov felt as though he couldn't allow himself this interlude. In the last days, he played practice games against his trainers, cramming. If a door opened or someone said a word while he thought, Kasparov snapped at him. After drawing a game against one of his trainers, Mikhail Gurevich, a world-class grandmaster, Kasparov appeared to be down in the dumps. Pacing from room to room, he was irritable and jumpy. "He's always this way when he goes into a tournament without enough preparation," said Masha.

At the press conference Kasparov explained his decision to play

beneath the banner of the prerevolutionary Russian flag, and Karpov
seemed unruffled. He responded glibly that if Kasparov were truly a
democrat, he would disavow the imperious drawing-odds that world
chess champions have held as their edge for more than forty years.
Drawing-odds gave Kasparov the advantage of retaining his title if
the twenty-four-game match ended in a 12–12 tie. Karpov smiled,
while Kasparov appeared awkward and unprepared while declining
this proposal.

Each Monday, Wednesday and Friday evening at 5:30, unless a
player took one of his three sick days, Karpov and Kasparov squared
off in the intimate three-tiered Hudson Theater in midtown Manhattan, where the best tickets went for a hundred dollars. The production, staged by Dan-Antoine Blanc-Shapira, was similar to the one in
Paris at the Théâtre des Champs Elysées. Above the stage, mammoth
video screens were mounted on each side of a fifteen-foot computerized chessboard. The cameras picked up each nuance of a player's
mood. They magnified twitches of anxiety or the face of feigned
tranquility, so that a viewer might catch Kasparov's mood shift even
before Karpov sensed it. Reading the two outsized faces while watching the ebb and flow of attacks on the colorized display board, and
listening to Bruce Pandolfini's smart commentary over cordless earphones, was powerful theater. Even very weak players found themselves drawn into the illusion that they were understanding the game
the way the big boys played it.
    On opening night, the first moves were delayed a few minutes by
a minor fiasco. As the standing room crowd of about 650 filed into
the Hudson Theater, it became apparent that the first rows of chairs
were too close to the stage: the rustling and whisperings of fans
would be a distraction to the players. At the last moment, the first
three rows were roped off. The complimentary tickets I had been
given were in this section, and when I arrived at the theater I noticed
that several of my friends—a lawyer, a magazine publisher, an editor
and three guys from the park dressed in dark suits (I had an uneasy
feeling about how they might have laid claim to these outfits)—were
standing in a line behind an assistant to the organizer, who was

exchanging their tickets for others in the first balcony, apologizing profusely and giving each of them a fifty-dollar bill. My more affluent friends pocketed the money sheepishly, but the park guys did not conceal their satisfaction. Soon, the weather would turn bad, and a park hustler wouldn't be able to earn that much in a week. From their point of view, Kasparov was already making good on his promise to help American chess professionals.

Kasparov is extremely attuned to his moods, and before the start of the first game his confidence played upon him like a teasing, inconstant woman. I asked him why he worried so much about it. He was the same player, after all; he had his memory and ideas, his unequaled ability to calculate deep variations. Garry answered that having a positive state of mind was like having extra material on the board. Since coming to New York, he had been making Andrew Page and his mother feel desperate with his expressions of ennui. Around me, he was more controlled and analytic. "Confidence helps you to make the decision faster," he said. "If the position is complicated, and you lack confidence, you hesitate. Maybe it's a good move, maybe bad. If you are confident, you use less time and then you don't worry about your decision. But also, there is another factor. You affect your opponent with your confidence. He feels it and maybe he backs off. It helps you to gain the initiative."

"And now, what will be your strategy when you are feeling shaky?" I asked.

"Try to play bold chess. Take risks. Pretend that I am confident."

In the first game, playing the black pieces, Kasparov surprised commentators at the match by choosing an aggressive line in the King's Indian defense instead of a more staid and solid variation in the Grunfeld that he had used in earlier matches. At the world championship level, players normally push to win with the white pieces, trying to build upon the small but tangible advantage of moving first, while the player with black is usually satisfied to draw. Playing black, a grandmaster will often try to create an ironclad position, anticipating threats and avoiding crucial weaknesses in his own position, while he counterattacks enough to keep some of White's big guns bogged down defending and unable to join ranks with the forward troops in a lethal attack. Certain lines of the King's Indian lead to dizzying and unpredictable complications, in which Black may gain the initiative, but to play such attacking lines entails considerable risk—especially so against Karpov, who might be history's greatest counterpuncher.

For the first five minutes of the games at the Hudson Theater, the players made their moves surrounded by scores of photographers. On opening night, they were also swarmed by television crews. On the huge screens, Karpov's angled face was focused, inscrutable. Kasparov's expressions were metallic and haughty—he seemed to be establishing terms: I will give you no quarter. Whether I am playing white or black, I will play to win.

Respected chess journalist and international master Jonathan Tisdall, who had covered all of their championship encounters, commented that Kasparov's demeanor and choice of openings suggested a kind of confidence and overaggression that had hurt him in the last match in Seville. Indeed, for much of the game, Kasparov appeared to be unconcerned about the little man in front of him, as though he himself operated on a higher plane. By the seventeenth move, Kasparov, playing with black, had equalized the game. This was something of a victory for the world champion. White had lost the little advantage that comes with moving first.

In the King's Indian, jagged pawn configurations sometimes pinwheel into complex and promising attacks for Black. But to gain equality, Kasparov had traded off a few pawns and pieces, which had the effect of smoothing the position. Instead of wading into a double-edge melée, Kasparov had reduced the tension. The pieces and pawns were now more or less symmetrical. There were no apparent imbalances to exploit for either side. The position seemed lifeless, likely to wind down into a draw—when Kasparov abruptly muddled things by moving his dark-squared bishop to a long open diagonal. Was there an attack here? Was Kasparov about to manufacture something out of nothing?

As a player, Kasparov stretches to make complications, to create profound confusion. Then, with a mind which sees farther and faster, he works his way through the dense chess jungle, as he likes to call it, until, bleeding and exhausted, he discovers the winning way. Karpov's style is dominated by prophylaxis, stopping the play of the other side. Karpov's genius is more difficult to appreciate. His is the style of constraint, of undoing, of denial. Working apparently without emotion, his strategy in some games is nothing more than to expose the weaknesses in his opponent's strategy. Each attack, each bold movement forward in chess, creates something of a void, a weakness, a lessening of what was there before. When troops rush ahead to assail the king, there are fewer left behind to defend the fort; when a knight bounds forward to initiate a queenside attack, it may leave a pawn vulnerable to attack, or a weak square where a strong enemy piece can eventually lodge itself. Each attack creates some measure of risk. Grandmasters are continually weighing potential initiatives against weaknesses and risk. The element of timing is crucial. Will the attack succeed before the weakness can be exploited?

With hardly a pause, Karpov countered Kasparov's bishop by sliding his rook back to its original square at the opposite side of the board. After a few more moves, it became clear that Kasparov had underestimated this move, or even missed it altogether. Unwittingly, Kasparov had improved the quality of Karpov's pieces. After two pawn exchanges, Karpov's bishops were suddenly controlling more squares than before, and his queenside rook was no longer hemmed in by pawns. Pieces expand and shrink in power relative to their ability to move around the board and the number of squares that they control. Karpov had gained a positional advantage and was now threatening to win a pawn. On the big screen, Garry was disgusted with himself. A weak player sitting in the audience commented, "It looks as though Kasparov forced Karpov into a good position." Yes, but the distance between a stunning attack and a clumsy failure can be very tiny—a miscalculation of one square in a variation that might extend eight or ten moves deep, traversing hundreds of squares. Garry had said that because of his lack of play during the past year, he had been having difficulty calculating accurately, that he had been unable consistently to back up his intuitive assessments with precise tactical analysis.

But then Karpov missed his chance. He played several inaccurate moves. After Kasparov sacrificed a pawn which he knew that he would eventually win back, he was out of danger. Perhaps Karpov had been thrown off by Kasparov's demeanor and aggressive opening play, and hadn't fully appreciated his advantage. When a player is a little back on his heels, it is sometimes difficult for him to seize the day. On Kasparov's face, then, came an expression that was derisive and chiding. I had seen it before, when he was analyzing with a trainer who persisted in arguing a point that Kasparov considered incorrect. It was the expression of an impatient pedagogue: Why are we wasting our time here; the position is clearly drawn. Then Kasparov's eyes glazed over with boredom, or perhaps feigned boredom. He hardly looked at the board as they played out the last few moves, until Karpov agreed that the position was drawn.

All and all, a lively and suggestive game. In championship matches, games impact upon succeeding games. They are evocative, send messages, establish patterns. After game 1, Karpov would be annoyed with himself for missing a real chance. For his part, though he had played inaccurately, Kasparov would feel steadied. He had needed to remind himself that he was Kasparov. He had shown that, even against Karpov, he wouldn't hesitate to take risks and that he could survive mistakes.

In addition to the Hudson Theater on the street level of the swanky black-and-chrome Macklowe complex on West 44th Street, there were two other floors devoted to the match hosted by California billionaire movie producer Ted Field. On the eighth floor, some seven hundred journalists from around the world tapped on laptops, while studying closed-circuit monitors showing close-ups of the players or their current position. Others roamed what seemed like acres of chess tables foraging opinions from groups of grandmasters huddled over the latest move. On the fifth floor was the chess book store, as crammed as Dalton's when Tom Clancy is signing his newest techno-thriller, except the buyers standing on line were hefting abstruse tomes on the King's Indian and Ruy Lopez. Nearby were three commentary rooms, where a fan could ask naive questions of grandmaster lecturers. There were also two VIP suites.

For decades, the American public couldn't have cared less about the sagest opinions of grandmasters, but all of a sudden television crews were competing to get players to give their spur-of-the-moment hunches. Chess was featured in the press and on network news. Of course, some reporters assigned to cover the event wrote as if the match were a tea party, and used the old chess-nut, "These games are about as exciting as watching grass grow," but there were others, like Manny Topol, *New York Newsday* crime and sports writer, who knew little about high-level chess but became captivated by the building drama of Karpov and Kasparov trying to take each other out. Topol camped out at the Macklowe for five weeks, catching the flavor and doggedly pursuing the leads of grandmasters, delivering the goods each day to his million-plus readers in the terse hard-hitting prose with which he had written stories on murder and sports corruption.

For the first week, reporters were asking all the top players who would win. Most grandmasters at the Macklowe picked Kasparov in a tight contest, but seventeen-year-old grandmaster Joel Lautier, covering the match for a French newspaper, said that Kasparov's lack of preparation and overconfidence made him a slight underdog. Lev Alburt, who considered Kasparov the most creative player of all time, expected the world champion to win, but suggested that the very qualities of mind that made Kasparov unique might lead to his undoing. "He has one flaw, in character as well as in chess," said Alburt. "Garry has an internal urge to create wonders, to put himself in lost situations and then make a Houdini-like escape. He does this because he has learned that he can make a miracle at the last moment, and this is dangerous, because miracles don't always happen."

One of the VIP rooms was hosted by Ted Field. Here, while keeping track of the game on the monitor or a demonstration board, one might overhear two pint-sized prodigies debate the technicalities of the current position, or observe a wealthy lady in a strapless gown raise a knowing eyebrow as a tipsy ex–world champion commented upon Karpov's weak squares. When he was in town, the reclusive Field, a strong amateur player himself, sat in a corner analyzing with his close friend, writer Jerzy Kosinski, whose face during the last months of his life was gaunt and spooky.

Vinnie and other guys from Washington Square, as well as hustlers who worked chess tables in midtown and on Wall Street, could not afford tickets to the games. They took an elevator to the fifth floor, where they could watch on a monitor in the hall or in the book store. Although there was supposed to be someone in charge of the guest list at the door of Field's suite, party-crashers were tolerated, particularly if they were known players, and no one said anything when one of the park guys, looking self-conscious in makeshift finery, wandered into the line behind Jerzy Kosinski, Mikhail Tal or some CEO, for a glass of champagne and a plate of cheese, veggies, shrimp and fruit.

Next door was another VIP room, this one hosted by Belgian entrepreneur Bessel Kok. At the time, Kok, forty-nine, was CEO of the SWIFT corporation and the executive director of the Grandmasters Association (GMA), a trade union of grandmasters which Kasparov had created in 1987 to improve the working conditions of professional chess players and, according to Kasparov, to redress the corrupt practices of FIDE. Headed since 1982 by Kasparov's nemesis Florencio Campomanes, FIDE had controlled the chess world for more than forty years.

The fall of 1990 was a critical time in the young life of the GMA. During recent months, the organization had become philosophically split between the points of view of Kasparov, its president, and Bessel Kok. In the early summer, despite Kasparov's fervent lobbying, the grandmasters had voted to enter into an agreement with FIDE—in effect, a treaty of peace between the two organizations which conceded to FIDE a share of revenue from the world championship match, as well as a measure of the organizational control that the GMA had wrested away from FIDE during the past three years. The grandmasters were tired of war, and they also feared that if Bessel Kok did not get his way he would withdraw his considerable financial support, and that of his corporation, from the elite tournaments he had been sponsoring. Kasparov had been so incensed that he had resigned from the executive board.

Not everyone minded that. As the games commenced, influential members of the organization, such as grandmasters Yasser Seirawan from the States, Jan Timman from the Netherlands, and ex–world champion Boris Spassky, were outwardly festive, and perhaps even a little heady about being able to conduct their chess business without the abrasive Kasparov, who they said made life miserable when he did not get his way. The more sparsely populated GMA/SWIFT suite clearly favored Karpov, while Field's cram-packed place seemed to lean toward the world champion. Though they sat side by side, there was little seepage between the two rooms. From the door of the GMA room, one could hear the pop of champagne bottles and the mellifluous voices of Seirawan and Spassky, both cultured men with a flair for showmanship, as they stood in front of a display board ad-libbing erudite and entertaining analysis. Any chess lover would have found their act memorable, but this was a very tight club. To get in, your name had to be on a list, and to get on the list you needed to be famous, rich or a very strong chess player. Kok, a man eloquent in many languages, often stood beside the door with an icy drink in hand. As he turned away the poor and untitled, he had a slightly bemused expression, as though these decisions weren't really his doing, but rather some ancient and incontrovertible law.

Karpov and Kasparov played the first seventeen moves of game 2 very quickly. The position they arrived at, developing out of the venerable king pawn opening known as the Ruy Lopez, was something of a modern classic. Many recent games have evolved from this setup and it has been much studied.

"I believe the position is very good for White and he always plays it for Black," said Kasparov later. "We have the beginning of a genuine chess fight here, two opposite views competing." In return for an active queenside knight and bishop, Karpov had conceded Kasparov the middle of the board for his two center pawns. In the Ruy Lopez, such a concession is dangerous because those slightly advanced pawns frequently serve as a staging area for a kingside attack. Then again, Karpov had made a career out of turning such smart-looking attacks into mincemeat. On the earphones, Pandolfini explained that White had to be patient while trying to exploit his slight positional advantage. "It's like milking a cow," he said. For this game he was joined in the booth by Yasser Seirawan, arguably

America's strongest grandmaster, and by my son Josh, who had recently won his fourth scholastic national championship. As Karpov and Kasparov played through this well-known opening variation, the talk in the broadcast booth was relaxed and chatty.

"Then I made an innovation, a strange-looking move. I pushed my pawn to f3," said Kasparov. Grandmasters usually identify their moves in a jargon called algebraic notation.* Each of the sixty-four squares on the chess board has a name consisting of a letter and a number. To arrive at f3, Kasparov pushed the pawn sitting ahead of his kingside bishop forward one square, from the second rank to the third. A quiet move. A move that doesn't bring fans out of their chairs. In fact, at first glance it seemed to shut down lines of attack. Before this move, Kasparov's rook, sitting on the third rank—the third horizontal row—had been poised to shift over to the kingside to participate in an attack. Now the rook was blocked off by the pawn. Still, Josh loved this new move. In his next tournament game, the following weekend, Josh played f3, and my hunch is that, around the world, other young players intoxicated with Kasparov's chess made the same move without beginning to understand its nuances.

"F3 doesn't look great," said Kasparov, implying that you have to study the position a long time to get an inkling of its strength. With f3, Kasparov had protected his central pawn, but there was more to it than that. The move transformed Karpov's Zaitsev defense into an old friend who had come upon bad times. Karpov stared at it for fifteen minutes. His knuckles grew white while he stared.

Early piece placement in chess is based upon long-term strategy. Three of Karpov's pieces, his queenside bishop and his kingside rook and knight, were fighting for the center, pressuring Kasparov's king pawn. The novelty, f3, had not only increased White's control of the center, but in doing so it had dynamically readjusted the position, so that Karpov's three pieces were now strategically misplaced. Imagine a defending football team that has lined up tight in its best short-yardage defense, linebackers socked in close to fill all the gaps, only

---

*Each of the sixty-four squares on the chessboard has a name consisting of a letter and a number. From the perspective of White's side of the board, vertical files from left to right are lettered "a" through "h." Horizontal rows or "ranks" from bottom to top are numbered one through eight.

to discover one or two beats from hike that the opposition's tight ends are flaring wide and the quarterback is probably about to throw long. Similarly, Karpov's key defenders were in in the wrong places.

For months, Karpov had concocted intricate countermeasures against each known attacking line in the Zaitsev. It was his meat-and-potato defense against Kasparov's king pawn opening. Who knew the Zaitsev better than Karpov, other than perhaps Zaitsev himself, who was working for Karpov as a trainer? F3 was a stunner. This seemingly innocuous move would give Karpov sleepless nights, he would see it in his dreams. "The move changed the shape of the position," said the world champion. "I spent days on Martha's Vineyard analyzing this, preparing this move."

But at the time, Karpov didn't appear to understand fully the depths of his predicament, or perhaps the move had numbed him. He answered by moving his queen up a square, in what is known as a developing move, a move that has little specific purpose other than to take the piece off the back rank and bring it to a square where, in a general sense, it might be useful later on. It was Kasparov's habit to pace behind the stage while Karpov thought, and when he returned to the board there was an expression of incredulity on his face, and he held out the palm of his hand, as though he were about to say to Karpov, you must be kidding. "This move was very bad," said the world champion. "It's from another planet. He needed to attack the center, but this move did nothing. Then with each of his next four moves, he worsened his position."

While Karpov played several aimless moves, Kasparov brought both knights ahead and moved his bishop toward the center of the board. On the display screen, it looked as though all the big guns for White had been wheeled forward in preparation for a crunching assault. Black's position was riddled with weaknesses. Pieces were out of position. Pawns looked vulnerable.

Watching chess, like playing, is passionate and very personal. The fan, even under the best of circumstances and even if he is a very strong grandmaster, can drift so far into his own fantasy of the game that it comes to have very little to do with the choices that are being made by the players. In the heart of a complicated middlegame, a player will consider a number of possibilities leading ahead in time and space from the position in front of him. Each choice suggests a different landscape and a different degree of risk; some routes may wind their way to victory while others may lead into an ambush. When a grandmaster on the sidelines gives his instantaneous analysis to the press with the sure-handed confidence of a TV sports color man, funny things sometimes happen. Often his cocksure prediction of victory overlooks the very trap that one player has set for the other. Off-the-cuff analysis is often little more than a test of a man's aesthetic preferences or his rooting interest.

On the twenty-fifth move of the game, Kasparov surprised virtually every chess player in the house by initiating a thrilling combination in which he sacrificed his queen bishop for Karpov's kingside rook pawn. A powerful bishop in exchange for a lowly pawn? What on earth was he thinking of? "I felt it," Garry said, about his bishop sacrifice. "I didn't calculate, I played it by intuition." If Kasparov's hunch was wrong, he would probably lose the game. "This is vintage Kasparov, a leap into the darkness," said Pandolfini. This was the kind of chess that had won Garry millions of fans, and chess lovers at the Macklowe were on the edges of their seats. All over the hotel, masters offered vastly differing interpretations of this unexpected move. In the booth, Seirawan said that the sacrifice was one of the worst oversights of Kasparov's career. Josh strongly disagreed, arguing that Karpov's kingside was now busted, and that if there were not some precise defense, Karpov would get mated. It occurred to me, while listening to Pandolfini, Seirawan and young Waitzkin bat out opinions with each move, that an entirely different—and just as interesting—game was taking place in the analysis booth.

According to past world champion Mikhail Botvinnik, a "combination" is a forced sequence of moves involving a sacrifice. At the conclusion of Kasparov's six-move combination, the position was still being debated as hotly as on the very first move. He had exchanged two minor pieces—two knights—for a rook and a pawn. In purely materialistic terms, Karpov had come out the better. Seirawan said that Kasparov's position was lost. Josh said that he was winning.

By now, other grandmasters in the Macklowe were beginning to favor Kasparov's position. Grandmaster Patrick Wolff came into the booth and reported to the audience that analysts on the fifth floor were now giving a big advantage to Garry. Seirawan insisted this was ridiculous, and struck an eighty-dollar bet that Karpov would win. Bruce pointed out that the exchange of pieces had cleared the queen file—one of the center vertical rows—for Kasparov's rook, and that Black's forces were scattered. Kasparov saw it Pandolfini's way: "At the conclusion of the combination, there was no harmony to Black's pieces," he said. "Of course, a grandmaster would usually prefer to play with two knights rather than with a rook and a pawn, but Karpov's two knights weren't working together. The quality of my pieces gave me an edge. White had a huge initiative. My attack was coming much faster than his."

Now, Karpov had less time on his clock than he would have liked. He calculated variations with sharp little nods of his head, while he held his arms with his hands, as if to contain his jumpiness and restrain the impulse to move prematurely. Garry sat motionless, but under his chair his feet were dug in as though he were about to push off. Josh and Seirawan continued to squabble, like fans of opposing teams. Josh, a lover of Kasparov's attacking style, could hardly bear to consider Karpov's defensive resources, and as for Yasser, Garry could do nothing right in this game. A few moves later, Garry continued his assault by pushing his bishop pawn. Almost instantly, Seirawan called the move a blunder. Later, Garry would say that this, in fact, had been the winning move, because it had led to the rending of Black's kingside, and set up the quiet attacking moves which soon broke Karpov's back. Kasparov speculated that Seirawan's commentary had been an attempt to humiliate him, but I think Yasser simply could not let go of his vision of the game, and like most others at the Macklowe, his judgment was impaired by his fan's heart. Even after Karpov had resigned and the two men had left the stage, Seirawan continued to insist that Garry had played poorly. "Garry is a perfectionist," said Yasser. "And despite winning, I think he will feel badly about this game."

A few months before, Seirawan and Kasparov had been friends and had often spent time together when they were playing in the same tournament. They were about the same age and both had diverse interests to go along with their love for chess. In June, when Kasparov had begun his lobbying effort against the proposed GMA agreement with FIDE, he had assumed that he would have Seirawan's support, and that Yasser would try to convince other grandmasters from North America to vote for the proposal. Kasparov was convinced that backroom deals had been struck between Kok and FIDE officials that would eventually give Kok dictatorial powers over both organizations. Yasser believed that Kok's motivation was simply to help professional chess, and according to him, when he told Garry that he intended to support the FIDE agreement, Kasparov became enraged, and threatened to use his clout with the organizer to prevent Seirawan from having any part in the 1990 championship. Yasser was furious. During the ensuing months, he repeatedly lambasted Kasparov, calling him corrupt, and proposed that in response to the world champion's resignation from the executive board of the GMA, grandmasters in the West should consider refusing to play against *him*. "If he doesn't play against Western grandmasters," said Seirawan in an interview with chess journalist Cathy Forbes, "we can say to Kasparov, 'You're not the world champion, you're the Soviet champion,' or the Azerbaijan champion, depending what crowd of fans he wants. . . . The GMA can then elect one of our own members to be world champion. I'll recognize him, and Garry can go eat chicken Kiev."

And so Yasser Seirawan rooted for Karpov.

When Josh and I visited Garry the afternoon after game 2, he was wearing jeans and a black sweatshirt, he hadn't shaved and his broad smile was ecstatic against the darkness of his clothing and beard.

"So what did you think of my opening, Josh?" he asked immediately.

"I loved it, but will you try it in the next game when you have white?"

"Why not? He had all summer to prepare. He showed his best defense against my king pawn opening and look what happened. Right now he has no defense to e4!"

This was a very funny idea, that the ex–world champion might be feeling defenseless against White's first move of the game, but there was also some truth in it. Karpov had taken one of his sick days to try to figure out what to do about his seriously weakened Zaitsev, and analysts who the day before had been predicting a long tough match, were now speaking of Kasparov's winning in a blowout. While we chatted, Klara passed Garry a piece of chocolate and he took a bite. Then after a minute she passed him a seedless grape. "Mama, please," he said, with a trace of exasperation. She held it in her hand until he put it into his mouth. Klara was forever placing delectables before him. She calmed herself by feeding Garry the most shapely chicken breast, the loveliest red apple.

We had planned to take a walk that afternoon in Central Park. Garry asked if Josh and I would mind waiting for a few minutes while he spoke with his trainers. When he left the room, I said to Klara, "You look very happy today." Immediately, her expression slid into guardedness. "I will be happy after twenty-two more games," she said gravely. And then, after a long pause, "You can have no idea what it's been like, four championships in three years. We have been through all of the emotions." She gestured with her hands to show that the family had become bloated from so much winning and losing. "You will be happy when he is finished with his chess life," I said. She nodded, as though trying to imagine it. It was painful for Klara to attend these championships, but for Garry it was a necessity. His mother was a spiritual advisor and he relied upon her intuitions. He has said that his mother has powers that he cannot explain; her presence gives him confidence and a feeling of well-being.

For ten minutes or so, Garry walked in and out of rooms down the hall, presumably looking in on the analysis of his little team of grandmasters. Then he settled in a room directly across from us, where we could see him reading *The New York Times*. After a few minutes, I walked over to him and said something. He was annoyed that I had interrupted him and burrowed into the paper. More time passed. Garry did this and that. Made a phone call. Read an article in a Russian newspaper. He passed me the op-ed section of the *Times* and asked me to read a column by Abe Rosenthal. Soon he would feel like walking in the park and we would go. His sense of timing bordered on the superstitious; life's little harmonies must always be considered, or else. He ministered to himself by doing things precisely when they felt right to him, not only big things, such as leaving the GMA, but many little things. A day was like a chess game. The advantages built upon one another. The walk would be better for leaving at precisely the right instant. The evening's training would be better for an invigorating walk spiced by good political conversation. Then, with his appetite piqued by this day of perfectly-timed moments, he would enjoy a late hearty meal, followed by an absorbing movie, a Western maybe. He would play better tomorrow for this close attention to his inner timing.

Grandmaster Mikhail Gurevich came into the room to make a phone call. Afterwards, he asked me questions about what he had to do to apply for credit cards, and we spoke at some length about credit references. He knew little about such things, but, like Kasparov, he felt that communism was finished in his country and he was preparing himself. Preparing for a new life of paying off the bank, I couldn't help thinking. I asked him how he would describe the work of the team. "We are a small but very productive factory of ideas," he answered, in his deep soulful voice. Gurevich was a very brilliant chess player, at the time ranking number seven in the world. Working for Kasparov for six months was a double-edged proposition. The money was good and Kasparov's ideas were often inspiring, but all of Gurevich's energy went into the preparation of the other man. "Too much analysis and not enough playing," complained another grandmaster, Sergey Dolmatov, who also worked for Garry through the training period and the match. "The problem with all this analyzing is that you make mistakes and don't get punished, as you do in games." In Thomas Mann's novel The Beloved Returns, characters who live in close proximity to the genius Goethe are warped by his power and forget who they are. For Kasparov's trainers, all world-class grandmasters with their own career aspirations, working for Kasparov held the same threat. Consequently, while doing his best work for Garry, it seemed to me that during the course of the match, Gurevich also worked at trying to maintain his own sense of self. In the mornings, he slept late, which was annoying to Klara. During analysis sessions, he argued his points of view against Kasparov more boldly than the others, as if to shield himself from the power of Kasparov's chess vision. In casual conversation, instead of Garry's last game against Karpov, he would talk about his family or the craziness of Rustam Kamsky or the next tournament he would play in or the need to get credit cards.

Garry walked back into the room, smiling, finally ready to go to the park. He had just given a phone interview about game 2 and was feeling pleased. He considered it "a great accomplishment for the art of chess," but he was trying to restrain his happiness, guarding against overconfidence, like his mother. "The match is in the early stage," he said. "One game doesn't mean a thing." It sounded as if he were trying to convince himself. Jacket in hand, he noticed that Josh was sitting over a chessboard in a corner of the room, studying a position in game 2 several moves after the bishop sacrifice. If in the next weeks analysis showed that the position held saving moves for Karpov, then the great win would be tarnished, as Seirawan had predicted. Josh moved the pieces in a variation that Karpov might have tried. Kasparov's neck craned toward the position. Soon they were both sitting at the board, pointing at squares.

"Don't you think it's still winning?" he asked Josh.

"Well, what would you play if he had gone here and here?" Josh asked, pointing. They analyzed for about twenty minutes, mostly without talking or moving the pieces, shrugging, smiling, pointing, nodding. Kasparov was neither patronizing nor overpowering, as he might have been if he had been looking at this same position with a grandmaster.

"Well, the position is completely winning," Garry said.

"Well, it's almost winning," Josh answered.

"Practically winning," Garry offered as a compromise.

Then, as we were about to walk out the door, Klara called from the little kitchen that we must wait a few minutes, she was preparing the snack. Garry was now more than ready to leave, striding in place. There wouldn't be enough time for the walk he had looked forward to. There was a television interview to do after lunch. Then he had to study. But Klara also listened to inner voices and believed that the little perfect moments added up. She knew that the walk wouldn't be entirely successful without the snack. If he didn't eat, she would fret about the afternoon's study, everything would be thrown off. "Ma, Ma!" he called in the direction of the kitchen, impatiently. These two intuitive heavyweights were temporarily out of synch. When she was ready, Klara came into the room with a bag full of cut-up apples and bananas for me to carry. Garry was supposed to eat them while walking around Central Park at his blistering pace.

In game 3, Kasparov again played the King's Indian defense with black. Lately, the King's Indian had been taking a pasting from players current with opening theory, but it was Kasparov who created the cutting edge of theory. With his penchant for complications and his desire to win with black, it was a reasonable choice. Then, on the tenth move, Kasparov sacrificed his rook for Karpov's dark square bishop and a pawn, a speculative sacrifice at the beginning of the game. Karpov was forced to think about it, while trying to shut out the loud rustling and whispering of the audience. Whenever Kasparov played, there was the anticipation of something unusual and the expectation of greatness. Audience excitement after a dramatic move is a tangible advantage for the world champion, a pressure the opposing grandmaster feels on top of the pressure of Kasparov's advancing pieces. Kasparov's expression was brutal: I am coming for your throat, Tolya; I have prepared another new idea for you; remember what I did in the last game? The whispering of fans was so loud that the arbiter had to make repeated calls for silence.

A grandmaster normally fights for hours to gain equality for the black side, but Kasparov had thumbed his nose at the notion and given away material at the beginning for positional considerations. Perhaps more importantly, his exchange sacrifice (the sacrifice of a rook for a minor piece) had layered a clear and much-analyzed position with crags and crannies of complexity, creating a position very difficult to evaluate. Either man could easily lose his way. The player with greater material, Karpov in this case, knew that there might be a crippling response to Kasparov's ploy. If he could find it, during the limited time he had to look (in the first time control, each player had two and a half hours for the first forty moves), then he was likely to win. This was Kasparov's simple but audacious challenge: Can you see as much as I can, Tolya?

At the start of play, minor pieces—bishops and knights—are considered to be worth about three pawns each, and rooks, five pawns. Had there been no positional consideration to Kasparov's sacrifice, he would have come out of the exchange the equivalent of a pawn down, a losing hand. Now, however, Kasparov had a strong hold on the center of the board with his pieces and central pawn. He had both his bishops, which are often more powerful together than a bishop and knight, or two knights. His dark square bishop also had the potential of becoming a super piece, since it could roam the dark squares freely with no Karpov bishop left to oppose it. Were these considerations worth the sacrifice of material?

While the question was being debated by Karpov, and by the chess masters on three floors of the Macklowe complex, Kasparov stunned the house yet again. He offered Karpov a queen sacrifice for Karpov's rook and knight. While Karpov tried to decide whether or not to take her, the arbiter called again and again for silence. A speculative queen sacrifice, unlike most deeply conceived and artistic chess moves, is accessible even to beginners. For even if you cannot calculate the variations, or fully understand the rationale, you cannot miss the queen *en prise*. Karpov considered whether or not to take the queen for the next twenty minutes.

"I am not sure that I could evaluate this position precisely if I had two months," said one grandmaster. "Kasparov doesn't have anything. He is going to lose," said another.

I sat alongside Masha and Klara in the front of the theater. I asked Masha, "What do you think?" and Garry's mother flinched at the sound of my voice. Masha scanned her husband for some telltale sign. Garry sat like a Buddha, focused inward, no movement, except every few minutes he stole a glance at Karpov's nodding face.

"I think it's okay," she said. Klara's face was pained and she never said a word. Each night she sat like this, not speaking, suffering, like the mother in John Millington Synge's *Riders to the Sea* staring out at the black, stormy Atlantic waiting for her sailor son to return. Klara would not smile during the games or say hello or good evening. Part of it was worry, and another part her belief that her own distraction or happiness or anticipation of the win would curse her son's effort. Klara believed that if her focus was pure, Garry would never let down his guard; that his success to some extent hinged upon the purity of her vigil. But this was hard on Masha, who was new to Garry's chess life and was a very different kind of personality. She could not match Klara's intensity, and she sometimes looked a little lost sitting beside her emotional mother-in-law, as if she weren't holding up her end. One could imagine her trying to reconcile her love for Garry with the strain of these games she could not begin to understand, her quick mind wandering illicitly to questions of her own life, what great novel she might be translating in Moscow had she not given herself to traveling around the world with Garry, worrying over the details of his day, wondering how the baby they wanted so much would change the shape of their lives together. Would she still be able to travel with him to tournaments? Would he play better or worse without her? Would Garry find time to spend with the baby? And how wonderful Garry would be later that night if he won. He would tell jokes and laugh through dinner. He would chase her around the big dining room table and gather her up in his arms. She would giggle while he kissed her. He must win. She could not bear to think of how gloomy and tense the night would be if he lost.

She clenched her fists tight and rooted, Garry's best fan, while Klara sat at her elbow radiating her powerful, even censorial suffering. Masha's vulnerability and lack of pretense was a moving statement in its own right. This was her first world championship with Garry, and in her understated way she was making a place for herself on the Kasparov team, bringing aboard optimism and a schoolgirl's smile suggesting the chance that even while Garry faced off against Darth Vader Karpov, there was life besides chess, an idea that Klara might have considered heresy. Josh, who was again with Bruce Pandolfini in the broadcast booth, was very excited about Garry's queen sacrifice. When he walked past us on a break, he gave Masha the thumbs-up sign, and she signaled back and smiled.

The game had become an extended dare: Come fly with me if you are not afraid. "I was inviting him to play in a new territory," said Garry. Taking the queen offered by the world champion was a macho move. You knew that if he offered her, there must be some good reason to decline. But how could a former world champion refuse Kasparov's queen when he had been dared to take her? Karpov nodded as he calculated variations, his sallow face perspiring and taut.

He took the queen.

And now, the situation was nearly impossible to evaluate. When the exchanges were complete, Karpov was up the material equivalent of two pawns, but Black's pieces were more dynamic. The second sacrifice had made a confused situation absolutely chaotic. Pieces were not where grandmasters expected them to be, and therefore their material value seemed liquid and uncertain. "It was like we were playing without the board," said Kasparov. "We were making moves in open space. When you are playing in the air, the normal material values don't work. How should one compare the value of his queen relative to the position I had? I don't know. I was puzzled." Kasparov rested a moment, his nose nuzzling the soft black hair above his wrist and on the back of his hand. It was a self-comforting habit of his, not unlike a child twisting his fingers in a curl. Klara couldn't bear to look at the position, and held her face in her hands.

In addition to imposing complexity, the world champion had introduced the atmosphere of immediate and deadly risk. It was as if his sacrifices had catapulted both of them onto a high wire. A small inaccuracy and one of them would fall. "It takes great energy to play this way," he said. "Because any mistake could be your last mistake."

During the next few moves, while Kasparov's kingside pawns edged forward, Karpov played passively, as though trying to catch his breath. He had a long-term positional idea, a reorganization of forces that would eventually lead to some counterplay, but Black was coming much too quickly. In his lazy plan, Karpov had hemmed in his light square bishop with one of his own pawns, and retreated his knight onto the back rank, where it blocked the path of his remaining rook. "It looks as though Karpov is being driven into the sea," observed Pandolfini on the earphones. Suddenly Kasparov's smaller black army was moving in for the kill. "After the queen sacrifice, I had some quality in return for his greater material," said Kasparov, "but then [his passive moves] gave me some time. I could almost kill him in his camp. He was surrounded, no space, no air."

In this position, Karpov's mighty queen had become withered, virtually without power, with no place to go, and further, she was

stepping on toes, restricting the mobility of Karpov's other pieces.
Nearly all the squares to which she might travel were defended by
Kasparov's active minor pieces. She was suffocating, in danger of
being lost altogether, unless Karpov could find some clever defense.
Karpov's game seemed to be in shambles. In order to salvage something, he sacrificed the queen for a rook and a knight. The resulting
endgame position was hugely in Kasparov's favor. His two bishops
were overpowering and his advancing pawns dominated the kingside, cutting off Karpov's play. Kasparov had all but delivered his
promised blitzkrieg. If he won this second game in a row, the match
might well be over before it began, as he had predicted on Martha's
Vineyard.

But not so fast. Winning from such a highly promising position is
often more difficult than it appears. The player with the advantage
must still guard against a number of tricks, do a great deal of accurate
calculating and have an effective plan. While the losing player fights
for his life with his greatest guile, the one with the advantage may
relax while anticipating his night of glory.

Many in the Hudson Theater commented upon the wreck of
Karpov's position; few noticed that by giving up his queen and
trading into an endgame, even a theoretically losing endgame, Karpov had radically changed the character of the struggle. From the
beginning, he had been lost in Kasparov's home-grown ideas, pum-
meled and perplexed by the assault of Kasparov's minor pieces. The
two champions had played game 3 in the relatively uncharted terrain
of dissonance and paradox. But when Karpov forced the endgame,
bewildering complexities unraveled like a dropped ball of yarn. Karpov was known to be a magician in the endings. His situation was
bad, but by giving up the queen, he had given his pieces a little bit
of mobility, something to work with. And now, the two men were
standing on solid ground. A grandmaster could calculate this position. Karpov's plan was straightforward and pedestrian. He needed
to break down Kasparov's kingside pawn chain to save the game.
That would create weaknesses, and if he opened a file for his rook he
could exploit them. Children learn these strategic principles from
their coaches.

For Black to realize his advantage in this situation called for little

moves, intricate consolidations. It required care and precise technique. Within a few moves it became clear that Kasparov was not
prepared for this. He played impatiently, as if still caught up in the
glamour and boldness of his earlier conceptions. The world champion
made numerous little errors, each depleting his advantage. He pushed
his kingside pawns too hastily before developing his bishop for
support. Then he squandered a pawn for no reason. Karpov waited
for Kasparov to trip over his own feet. This was his best chance. At
just the right instant, he blockaded the world champion's prematurely
advanced pawns. As Kasparov pushed too hard to win, he created
weaknesses in his own structure, which Karpov exploited. When
Kasparov advanced his queenside pawns, Karpov's rook and bishop
were liberated. These pieces began nipping at Kasparov's loose
pawns. Instead of winning, the world champion was suddenly defending: his position was still better, but his advantage was fading.
Karpov had changed the shape of the game, intuiting that it was his
best chance to throw a blanket on Kasparov's fire. He completely
shut Kasparov down in the endgame. After forty-one moves, the
game was adjourned, and the two men and their teams of grandmasters studied the thorny but more or less equal position late into the
night. The following afternoon they resumed play and eventually
agreed to a draw.

Perhaps because there was no day off, game 4 seemed to flow from
game 3, but Kasparov suggested later that the unique challenges of
the previous game drew both players back for more. "Did anyone see
Kasparov's face after bishop f7?" shouted international master Jonathan Tisdall following Karpov's twenty-second move. Tisdall, a respected international player himself, was covering the match for
several magazines, but like virtually all the top minds analyzing in the
pressroom, he was reduced to looking for clues about the position by
gauging the strain on Karpov's face or the flicker of incredulity at the
edge of Kasparov's mouth.

Karpov had brought back his rejuvenated friend, the Zaitsev, for
this game. Early on, employing a different variation than in game 2,
he had attempted to undermine White's center at the risk of weakening his own kingside. His team of grandmasters had worked many
hours honing this variation, but from Kasparov's relaxed manner

Karpov sensed that the world champion and his team had anticipated all of their homework. Karpov began to suspect that he was steering himself into a massacre. "I suddenly discovered a hole in my analysis," he wrote later, ". . . I quickly realized that I was standing with one foot over a pit. I pondered this for about fifty minutes before finding a very sharp and unusual continuation. I had managed to . . . use precisely those nuances of the position which Kasparov's group had failed to find."*

On the twenty-second move, instead of recapturing a piece, Karpov played a highly unusual and brilliant defensive move which both shored his kingside and liberated his queenside pawns. It seemed to give Karpov the advantage, but then Kasparov placed his rook where it could be captured by Karpov's bishop and left it sitting there for the next nine moves. None of the commentators in the Macklowe had predicted this move, which launched an intricate kingside assault. For most of us this game was impossible to follow, but we could feel the power of juggernaut moves, which brought to mind the abiding predicament of these immortal players. During the past decade, each of them had perfected his art largely to distance himself from the other, but instead of distance, together they had created a walled kingdom of two. There was no one else who could compete on their level. Each wanted out of this hateful intimacy, but they seemed destined to battle one another forever. Their intuitions were perfectly tuned and every exotic threat was anticipated and parried with yet another disguised and deadly variation.

"These games are like Hitchcock mysteries," said Mikhail Tal, sitting in the pressroom. "No one knows what will happen next." Tal had won the world championship in 1960 when he was twenty-three, the youngest player to hold the crown before Kasparov. In his prime he had been known as a player able to impose complications that his opponent simply could not figure out in the allotted time, but now Tal made it clear that the depth and abstraction of games 3 and 4 were beyond anything he had ever seen before in championship play. "But for all the complications, at times these games remind me of ice hockey," he said, "fast, hard, brutal."

*Anatoly Karpov, *Karpov on Karpov*, New York, 1991, p. 215.

When Kasparov is feeling confident, as his pieces press ahead he contests the space above the board until he owns it all and his opponent is leaning back in his chair. But in these games, for all of Karpov's supposed physical frailty, he would not yield this space. Garry leaned forward and Karpov didn't budge. The two men were as close as dance partners, Kasparov sneering or talking to himself, his mouth twisted in disgust or concern; Karpov looking cramped and uncomfortable, sometimes calculating with his head nodding sharply.

For hours, game 4 hung in the balance. Kasparov's queenside was threadbare and Karpov's phalanx of pawns was heading for pay dirt. Then Kasparov distracted the march of the pawns by attacking Karpov's weak kingside. If Karpov's defense were not precise, he would be mated, but as the game approached the end, Karpov was getting the better of it. "It was easy for me to play, because I didn't have any pieces on the queenside," said Kasparov, making a joke afterwards. "I had nothing to think about. Positionally, I was completely lost. But still, it was a jungle." Kasparov saved himself by creating intimidating confusion. In the end, although the champion's position was dire, Karpov had used so much of his time in the beginning of the game that he had none left to pick his way through the last dangers of Kasparov's waning attack. On the thirty-ninth move, with virtually no time left, Karpov made a terrible mistake which allowed Kasparov to draw.

The following Saturday afternoon, it was rainy and cold as I hurried through Washington Square Park on my way home from the New York University Bobst Library, where I often worked. In several hours, I was meeting Kasparov for dinner. Each Saturday night during the match, we had dinner together, and I was curious about his mood following these two remarkable games. I wondered if the art of games 3 and 4 would be enough to assuage his disappointment over failing to win either of them. As I approached the chess corner, I noticed a solitary figure seated at one of the marble tables, an old man who was nodding furiously as if he were in a heated argument with someone. He looked up at the trees and spoke to the squirrels, as though attempting to enlist their support. Israel Zilber, the sheriff. All over the world, chess people had heard rumors that he had frozen to death three years before, but here was Zilber, no question. He was wearing a light summer shirt, and behind a mustache and ratty beard his face was deeply creased and weathered like an old seaman's. He was shaking like a leaf from the cold and speaking to the squirrels in Latvian, but I distinctly heard him say the name "Kasparov." Soon his tone became more congenial; he mentioned a few chess moves with an elegant turn of his filthy hand, as though he were offering a reasoned commentary on a game.

"Zilber, Zilber, how are you?" I said in a loud voice, because he had always been hard of hearing, or at least it had always been hard to get his attention. He looked at me and nodded curtly. Then he returned to his discussion of the game, pointing at wet squares on the board in front of him. It was wonderful to see the sheriff again, but also unsettling. I felt the impulse to tell people that he was back.

The sheriff was angry about one of the Karpov-Kasparov games. He pointed at a square and raised his voice. The powerful games forty blocks uptown had called him from wherever he had been. In the old days he had often muttered their names, and I used to think that, sometimes, while he toiled in the park for a dollar a game, in his mind he was struggling against Kasparov for the title. Maybe it struck Zilber as unjust that the two Russians were playing for the championship in his backyard. Zilber talked on and on. I wanted to ask him where he had been playing and if he still recorded his games on little scraps of paper and envelopes, as he had when Josh was a little boy. I wanted to tell him that his old nemesis Mikhail Tal had just arrived from the Soviet Union and was analyzing on the seventh floor of the Macklowe. Zilber was one of the few living players to hold a lifetime edge over Tal. But I couldn't get a word in edgewise. Zilber was talking very quickly, and shivering so hard I feared that he was very sick. He had no socks and his ankles looked raw. I took my coat off and handed it to him, but he paid no attention. He was very annoyed. I think he believed that he could take Kasparov.

By now there were a few of us standing around the table. It was as if drums in the hills had called the guys back to the park on this miserable day. Vinnie appeared, his face swollen, looking sick. Poe was there, another of the men Josh used to play when he was little.

"Fred, this is a miracle," Vinnie said to me. "I feel like I am seeing my father again." Vinnie was feeling very emotional. Perhaps he was recalling the scores of games that he had played against Zilber over the years. Vinnie's genius in chess had been the art of diversion. He could play sharp tactics while singing rap songs, cursing his opponent's mother or quoting Immanuel Kant—whatever it took to win. Against Zilber he had sometimes bellowed in his biggest voice or banged the table, trying to distract the old man, but this was like trying to distract the earth. While Vinnie went through his pyrotechnics, Zilber roared at the trees overhead, forced the exchange of queens, and won with the precision of Karpov in the endgame.

All the park guys gathered around Zilber very quietly. It was a religious moment for them. I quickly walked the half-dozen blocks to my apartment, searched through closets, and pulled out three winter coats, a pair of gloves and some socks. I took a plastic chess set from Josh's room and hurried back to the park, half-expecting him to be gone. Zilber was still there, muttering and shaking. I tried to give him a twenty-dollar bill, but he shook his head no. He had crushed Tal and didn't need my charity. I placed the three coats on the table and urged him to choose one. All the guys pleaded with him to take a coat. After a minute or so, Zilber said very distinctly, "I can do better." I had seen photographs of Zilber in his younger days playing tournaments in Europe and Israel, and in each he had looked like a man-about-town, perfectly groomed in a tailored suit. Perhaps this other life still seemed accessible to him. Vinnie shook his head, admiring Zilber's sense of style and pride. In truth, all three coats I had brought were a little shabby. This was the happiest I had seen Vinnie in years. The rumor was that Vinnie was dying of AIDS, and a few months later, he was gone.

Before I headed home, I remembered to offer Zilber the chess pieces, which he accepted with a "Thank you." When I left it was almost dark and getting colder. All but one or two of the guys had quit the park, leaving Zilber to argue in Latvian. That was the last time I ever saw him. The pieces were set up and the sheriff was waiting for someone to come by and play a game.

*   *   *

Two hours later, in the Regency Hotel, a waiter wheeled in a neat
room service table with places set on white linen and a warming
cabinet below filled with soup and hot rolls. He uncovered steaming
dishes of chicken, potatoes and vegetables. Garry had also ordered
a jumbo shrimp cocktail in case one of us felt like nibbling, and he
had remembered to order me a beer, which was thoughtful. His mood
was subdued. The television was playing subliminally in the background, Indians rushing past on horseback while a cowboy took aim
from behind a rock. Garry glanced at them. It was an odd experience
watching him play Karpov and then coming here for supper or for
a walk in the park. The Macklowe Kasparov was thrilling the chess
world with his courage and refined positional understanding, but the
more absorbed I was by the games, the more I forgot about Garry.
Indeed, Garry seemed irrelevant in light of the world champion who
moved the pieces on the big screen. Kasparov was a forbidding
presence, a piece of history. Playing for the world championship for
month after month must have been a schizophrenic experience for
him.

Garry ate his soup, and I noticed that he had developed a rash at
the corner of his mouth. It made him seem vulnerable, beatable. He
looked tired. He got up from the table, went to a chessboard and
played through a variation.

"It's very bad," he said, referring to the strain. "Even if I rest or
take a time-out, it's always on my mind. It feels as though I am living
years of my life in a few months." He watched the Indians and tried
to relax. "I think it's dangerous to live this way," he said. "You can't
rest when you're worried that you might lose the spirit of fighting
chess."

He ate his chocolate cake, watched the Indians for a few minutes
and returned to the chessboard. He moved the pieces for both sides,
clicking them ahead in the rhythm of a canter. The sound of his
clicking pieces made him feel better. We kept chatting about this or
that, but every ten minutes or so he played through a variation. I
mentioned that Josh had played the King's Indian the past weekend
for the first time, and that throughout the game he had tried to use

the ideas of quality, time and material. Garry was pleased. He cantered the pieces ahead. He picked up the paper and said something about his friend Viacheslav Fetisov of the New Jersey Devils. I mentioned the appearance of Zilber in the park, but he didn't respond. He was allowing himself a little bit of Garry this weekend, a few minutes here and there, but not so much that he would lose touch with Kasparov.

I told him that Tal had called the last two games Hitchcock mysteries and wondered if the match would continue at this level of abstraction and intensity. Garry's expression became a little tight. "How could it?" he said. "We are human. For how many games can you do it?" And then a few minutes later, he said, "The third game could have been a masterpiece, but it takes energy. I didn't have it."

Masha came into the room wearing jeans and her hair in a pony tail. Garry gave her an affectionate pinch and she smiled in a way that said he was her entire life. She climbed into his lap. Garry had decided to take a sick day on Friday because he had felt tired and disappointed. The blitzkrieg had not worked. He had trained for the early knockout, and now he sensed that he might have to go the distance. While she cuddled with him, he looked over her shoulder at the chessboard.

In game 5, cautious opening play led to a lifeless middlegame. As Kasparov had all but predicted two days before, this was a working day off for the two grandmasters. For the first time in the match, Kasparov did not push to make a fight. It was interesting to notice that, without tension on the board, there was no excitement in the theater. Karpov and Kasparov appeared relaxed onstage. Upstairs in the pressroom, chess journalists played blitz, only occasionally glancing up at a monitor. Klara even smiled once or twice before the players agreed to a draw.

In game 6, with the black pieces, Karpov outplayed Kasparov in the opening. Garry played quietly, no sacks, no fire. Karpov played the early middlegame in his inimitable fashion, absorbing Kasparov's threat before it could gain momentum, skirting complications, setting up for later. Jonathan Tisdall pointed out that Garry wasn't tapping his foot on the floor, and wondered if he was tired. Soon Karpov held the advantage, and his well-coordinated pieces were poised for an attack. But then he began making mistakes, four or five bad moves within a short period, which threw the initiative back to Kasparov. In the pressroom, grandmasters were asking one another, how could this happen, so many bad moves? Whenever Karpov or Kasparov made errors, grandmasters on the sidelines were perplexed, as though the natural order had been violated. Kasparov explains that making mistakes and even grievous blunders is "normal" when playing for the world championship, where the tension becomes blinding, particularly as the match goes on. During a pressured, five-hour game, unwanted thoughts intrude upon clever variations. Players cannot help worrying about losing, or how their next move, a crucial one, will be rated by a world of experts and fans. At stake is a lifetime of glory and power, to be cheered by thousands back in Moscow, to be wealthy, to have heads of state ringing up, to be judged kindly by history. It is easy to overlook a weak square or an open diagonal eight moves ahead when a man is worrying whether or not he will be king.

Now Kasparov smelled blood and found his rhythm. After playing badly, he had a chance to score a point against Karpov. The world champion found little ways to increase his advantage. He took possession of key squares and diagonals. This was not a game in Kasparov's surrealist style, with startling sacrifices leading to refracted advantages. The way was clear, and Kasparov was playing like a machine, perhaps more like Bobby Fischer than quintessential Kasparov. A modest player could follow the punishing and relentless advance of his pieces. Karpov was getting squeezed, as players like to say, and he was in bad time trouble. All match he had been getting into time trouble. Earlier in his career, Karpov had been known for his fast play at the board, but in the last few years he had needed more time to think and had often been in a rush to make his last moves before the time control. When a player has to make eight or nine moves in a minute, it is terrifying for him, but also thrilling. Some players become time-trouble junkies. They crave the rush of fear, the thrill that only comes when big decisions have to be made very rapidly. Some players use time trouble for inspiration, even grow to rely upon it, but that is a form of Russian roulette. Often, with just a beat or two to go on the clock, God does not tap a grandmaster on the shoulder with the right move, and his instantaneous move is a humiliating blunder.

With game 6 all but lost, Karpov had pratically no time to come up with a last-ditch plan. His jaw was tight and his sallow face squeezed bloodless from grim pressure. His hands grasped his forearms, while his legs twined around one another beneath the table. Wrapped up this way, his whole body jerked, a spasm of indecision; maybe he had glimpsed disaster six moves ahead, needed another variation quick. His head bobbed up and down as he calculated. As the seconds ticked off, the muscles in his face swam this way and that, and he took on a greenish cast, as though he were about to become sick.

Karpov is such a compelling villain when he is down and out. Time pressure washes aside the cool inscrutable Karpov. He wins over fans with extraterrestrial suffering. The shadings of his diaphanous skin suggest weakness, mutability, a frantically beating heart. With seconds left, he found time to wipe his sweaty stringy hair away from his eyes. Forget his decade of dirty tricks, his supposed bribes and blackmail. It's hard not to feel for him when he opens his mouth straining for a deep breath, his teeth so little, like baby teeth. How can you not pull for him, with an avenging Kasparov dug in and poised to flatten the little guy like a linebacker?

Karpov shot his hand out finally, and moved his queen to e7. An ugly move, blocking in his bishop, but it was a defense no one else had thought of. Maybe it would hold. There was not enough time left for anyone in the theater to calculate. Karpov played his next four or five moves without pausing more than a second or two. Once again, he had rolled his fear and strain into an intriguing defense. His king was attempting to walk away from Kasparov's mating net. But it didn't quite work. Karpov had made things tough, but Kasparov still held a winning position.

Then, on the forty-first move, after both players had made time control, those familiar with the world champion's habits expected Kasparov to walk away from the board, relax for a minute or two, and then take his time to find the winning plan. They expected that, after thinking for ten or fifteen minutes, he would seal the killer move, and after analyzing through the night, he would finish off Karpov the following afternoon. It is often an advantage to be the one to seal the move before the adjournment, because then your opponent must guess what you have chosen, and has to divide his time studying a number of possibilities.

But Garry couldn't restrain himself and moved immediately. Maybe he had become caught up in the pace and desperation of Karpov's time trouble. Maybe he was strutting for his fans. Whatever the reason, Kasparov's move was a blunder. He blocked the very square that his queen needed to pursue the mating attack, which gave Karpov time to organize his defense. It was an error that would cost him more than this game. Throughout his career, in such situations, he had taken his time and then sealed the move. Why hadn't he done it this time? he thought after offering Karpov a draw. He was disgusted with himself. He had thrown away the win.

Game 7 began in the fashion of the prior two. Kasparov's opening play was passive, and he gave Karpov an advantage without a fight. But Karpov seemed to be uncomfortable with the early initiative and his middlegame play was diffuse. It was as if each of them had been asked to play the other's role, but neither could do it very well. The two players were in something of a muddle, when Kasparov seemed to rouse himself and lashed out with his queen. Fans came to attention—Kasparov was on the attack. But no sooner had he taken his hand off the piece than Kasparov clutched his head as if something were wrong. Then he walked quickly off the stage. The news spread like fire, Kasparov had blundered horribly. Karpov considered the position for half an hour before responding.

It was the kind of mistake that beginners make. One move, and the world champion's position was dead lost. "That's incredible, a blunder of this magnitude," said grandmaster Larry Christiansen. On stage, Garry squinted at the position, looking at it from different angles with bombastic profundity, as though he were considering great winning plans. I have often watched children do this when they have losing positions and are desperately trying to pretend that they are winning. Garry moved and blundered again, giving away a pawn for nothing. He had gone chess-blind and shook his head incredulously.

"I can't recall Kasparov being in such a position." said Bruce Pandolfini, shortly before the end. "He doesn't have a useful move."

When Garry resigned, Klara shook her head, no, no, and then hid her face in her hands. On the big screen, there was a close-up of her suffering. She twisted in her chair to avoid the camera. Masha tried to help her stand, but Klara was weak-kneed. One might have thought the mother had just lost her son. "This is terrible. This is unfair," said Masha, and gestured angrily to the cameraman to stop taking their picture. But this inspired him to zoom in closer.

Karpov didn't want to leave the stage. He looked out at the audience, drinking deeply of the moment. They were cheering for him. Karpov was winning them over with his grit. It must have reminded him of Moscow in 1984, when he had been the reigning world champion crushing Kasparov while fans standing outside the majestic Hall of Columns chanted, "Tolya, Tolya."

The loss of game 7 was a defining moment for other grandmasters in the theater. Kasparov had suddenly become beatable—three large blunders in two games. For young grandmasters, the world championship seemed a little more accessible than before.

"Garry played yesterday's game as if he wanted to lose," said Andrew Page, when he called me from London the following morning. Though he was upset, his voice was ringed with dry amusement, and I could imagine a little ironical smile. I think of Andrew as a gentle anarchist. He often speaks without monitoring himself and enjoys toppling the status quo. He had been worried about this match from the beginning and had said so, while Garry was telling all of their friends that he would crush Karpov. Page had believed that Garry would pay a price for not training properly and that his bragging belied a lack of confidence. "If he keeps throwing away wins, at least one good thing might come out of it," he said. "Maybe I can get away from chess and get serious about my life."

For years, Page had been coming to matches and tournaments,

fretting over games that he did not understand, but that were central
to his life and livelihood. Were Kasparov to lose the match, Page
would be devastated financially, and he would grieve for Garry,
whom he loves like a brother. But at the same time Garry's loss of
the world championship was an intriguing possibility for this eclectic
forty-five-year-old who by disposition craved new horizons, and at
different points in his life had been a student of political science at
Oxford, a race car driver, an actor, an inventor of games, a writer, and
a businessman. As Andrew traveled from London halfway around
the world to meet Garry at a chess tournament or a business meeting,
he sometimes mused that his side of their complicated relationship—
friend, manager, business partner—ultimately typecast him in the
role of super-valet. For all the glamour and financial potential of
living the Kasparov life, Andrew was still not sure what he wanted
to do with himself. He wondered if he should be a novelist or
screenwriter. He wasn't at all sure that making millions would make
him happy. Andrew had spent many of his most creative hours
chasing Garry's dreams, and like the champion's world-class grand-
master-trainers, he wondered if his association with Garry prevented
him from coming into his own.

   "The problem with being on Garry's team is that there is little time
for anything else in life," he said. "I should be spending more time
on the business and less time chasing around the globe packing his
bags and getting his chess stuff for him. But when I leave him on his
own, look what happens. Garry has been getting bad publicity lately.
At least in part, I think it is because a couple of years ago I was
traveling with him everywhere. Back then, I would arrive before a
tournament, and the publicity was terrific because I would talk to the
press and smooth over things if he had been misunderstood. I would
force Garry to be nice to a few players. The chess world quite liked
him at the time. Now, with no one there to do these things, he is
getting enemies."

Page and Kasparov began their complex association in 1983, when
Page was in charge of the European operation for a chess computer
company and approached the young grandmaster for an endorse-

ment. Andrew says that, six months later, he felt guilty about the financial arrangement his company had offered Garry, and visited a Kasparov exhibition on the continent to renegotiate. "Garry's face fell," recalls Page. "He thought I was going to take away his money, and I said, 'No, I'm going to give you more money.' And that was a start of a long friendship."

To date, their business deals have been numerous, extremely ambitious and frequently without profit. In 1984, they started a management company, which initially focused upon tapping the financial potential of Kasparov's chess life. But soon they were both thinking about a variety of far-ranging ideas. In 1987, Andrew traveled with Garry to Azerbaijan and met many people. They laid plans for the export of apples and pomegranates. They negotiated to build fruit juice concentrate plants and a brick factory. They looked into the secondary extraction of oil. "I was flying around the country in helicopters, meeting with high-level politicians. We did a great deal of work there. The potential was in the billions. Just when we had everything ready to roll, the Sumgait massacres took place, and we had to get out," he said, putting an ironical spin on the Armenian tragedy.

Then, Page, Kasparov and some friends began a joint venture in Moscow, and in August, 1990, Garry instituted the first private shareholding company since the Russian Revolution, which included a number of high-profile Moscow anticommunists, such as the eminent historian Yuri Afanasev. To greater and often lesser degrees of success, Page, Kasparov and his friends worked on a variety of projects: a motor car distributorship, the export of Russian sculptures, renting hotel rooms at reduced rates to airlines for their flight crews, the purchase of Moscow's GUM, which is the largest department store in the world, the financial management of Soviet athletes who wanted to make a living in the West, the purchase of a radio station with which Garry intended to spread the gospel of anticommunism and Andrew imagined to be a commercial radio station.

Andrew Page pointed out that, perhaps more than the idea of making money, Garry enjoyed the sport of bending and breaking communist rules and being a business pioneer, one of Moscow's first capitalists. In the first months after the fall of communism, with

Moscow reeling from unemployment, Kasparov was planning to
open factories to manufacture arrestingly attractive chess sets for
young children. While Kasparov explained to American businessmen
the urgent need to find work for Moscow's unemployed, it was not
at all clear that there was any market in the United States for these
chess sets. Andrew said that Garry always looked to incorporate
politics and business. "And it never bloody worked. Garry has proposed many big ideas, but the political angle always obscured the
commercial one. Frankly speaking, doing business is not his forte. He
enjoys it as an intellectual exercise. He goes off in wild enthusiasm
for one of his projects and then he thinks that because he has been
interested for a few minutes, something will happen. He leaves it to
the others to follow up and do the nitty-gritty. But in Russia, everyone is as inexperienced as Garry. By the time he is on the seventeenth
idea, they've dropped the first fifteen, so nothing happens and our
cash flow is terrible. And then Garry doesn't like to get his hands
dirty, so he has an important meeting and won't go and say, listen,
chum, you owe me a favor, so do this. He'll go and have a nice
political conversation. In the most impressive way, he'll describe the
current situation in Russia and forget to say at the end, listen, we
want to put on a rock concert."

Andrew Page arrived in New York City a couple of days after
game 7. Since the beginning of the match, he had been commuting
back and forth to London. He had a lot to discuss with Garry, but
he knew that their business discussions might not happen. Sometimes
he would arrive in New York and Garry would not be in the mood
to talk about problems in the Muscovy Company. This was particularly the case when Garry was playing badly. Recently, Page had
discovered that some of Garry's Russian partners were less than
reliable, and he had been getting a cold shoulder from airlines that
he and Garry had counted on to fill their subleased rooms in Moscow's Cosmos Hotel. Now, difficulties in the match made the business problems seem worse. Their financial setup was shaky, and it
depended upon Garry's retaining the world championship. Top political figures in Moscow and CEOs in the States were always pleased
to have a working lunch with the world champion—even a world
champion who was sometimes reluctant to talk about business deals.

It also struck Page that, if Garry lost this match, he would have little to show for being world champion for most of the past decade. In the past four encounters with Karpov, Garry had been forced to pay most of his winner's purse to the Soviet Sports Committee. This time, Garry was refusing to pay and it would be the first of the matches from which he would see any substantial money. By nature, both Garry and Andrew were attracted to new ideas and lacked patience for detail work. But if the Englishman didn't make sure the contracts were drawn properly, spread sheets were scrutinized and the like, they would both lose their shirts. Perhaps it was because of this compromise to his nature that Andrew felt impatient when Garry refused to talk about business deals, regardless of the tragedy of their cash flow. Sometimes it seemed absurd to Andrew that so much in their lives hinged upon Garry's winning a chess game, or in this case, losing. He knew that he might have to fly back to Europe and do some stalling, until Garry won a game or two and his spirits improved. Better than anyone, Andrew knew the futility of trying to buck Garry's state of mind.

I was nervous about going to see Garry after the loss of game 7. I had heard from Masha and members of the coaching team that it was better not to be around him while Kasparov was digesting defeat. I had called to suggest visiting another night, but he asked me to come. Garry was so pleased to be visited; he walked quickly across the room to shake my hand. He looked at me with the guilty smirk of a little boy: What can I do? I was bad. Do you still think things will turn out okay? I rubbed the back of his head, as though he were Josh. "Yesterday was a bad time for me. It was the worst blunder of my career." He shook his head slowly. "Fred, I was in a black hole. A black hole." He was still in a black hole. Things had gone wrong and he didn't have the answers. Garry seemed physically diminished. His shoulders were stooped. His body felt soft. He was like a puppy. You could tell him to sit or stand, suggest turning on the television or taking a walk, and he would do it without question. He had broken trust with his sense of timing. "I feel shattered," he said. Chess masters know that life tips on edge after a crucial loss. The game itself—the sixty-four squares, the little men, years spent memorizing variations, planning elaborate tricks—feels idiotic, absurd, useless. Particularly when a player has been feeling immortal, as if he cannot lose, defeat can throw him into a state of chaos and blackness.

I must admit that there was something wonderful about seeing Kasparov cut back this way. He was entirely without pomp or pretense and not at all embarrassed about his condition; this was part of him, as well, like a gimpy leg. In his body English and bedraggled expression, Garry said, I am shit. Kasparov hated losing more than anyone I had ever known, but when he lost he wanted to feel it all through him, to embrace it—perhaps this was the only way he had learned to get defeat out of his system. But also, it seemed to me fair for the champ to take his turn on the mat. He had crushed so many egos over the board, and I found myself thinking of instances when I had seen him wither men with a remark or a disgusted expression. When I suggested that there was something just about his having a taste of this side of life, Garry seemed to glimpse it for a moment, but then he sighed and said, "I hate losing."

"Fred, I couldn't sleep for four days before this game," said Klara. Garry's mother always feared the worst. Danger was everywhere. "There were little things in his earlier games," she said. "I could see it building. After enough little things go wrong, something big will go wrong." Klara was always looking to read the future. She examined all clues: the color of the fruit on the table, the expression on her son's face an hour before the game. And then when he was playing, she engaged in war alongside him. "When Garry plays, I repeat the whole time, danger, danger, bad, bad, bad, danger. I try to warn him. It is like we are soldiers together in the ditches. When the enemy attacks, you cannot raise your head for even a minute. If you raise the head, you are killed. You must not relax. I must never relax and then he will not relax. Even when we are at a great distance, Garry and I can feel each other's mood. One time in a game, I relaxed and said, 'It is good,' and Garry lost."

For Klara, Garry's losing felt like a constriction of her chest, pain and weakness in her limbs. But more, her universe had suddenly become terribly bleak and although this had happened before, the horizon of doom appeared endless. All familiar references were askew; happiness and even the small pleasures of a day were impossible for her. Bright future plans seemed like nonsense. Camaraderie was alien. Friendly smiles made her feel hysterical or humiliated, and she could not quite hold the idea of Garry in her mind—it fragmented into defeat and malaise. After he lost, tomorrow was ominous. Tomorrow there was another game, and he could lose again. The only thing that would cheer Klara was for Garry to win. That would be salvation, even ecstasy, but then she would restrain her celebration, for fear that it might curse her son's next effort.

As the night went on, Garry looked at his poor play from many angles. He tried to be analytic, but his reason was shaded by self-reproach. He was trying to spit out a part of himself. "From the start of the match, I didn't have enough energy, and then every game has been a big fight, with me pushing the attack, Karpov trying to hold. The sixth game was very bad for me. A bad sign. Since 1984, I've had this rule to seal on the forty-first move. Seal the move, Garry. Think about it for five or ten minutes, and seal. I'm sure I would have found the winning move. It wasn't so difficult. . . . Yesterday, the instant I took my hand off the queen, I wanted to resign, but then I went back to my room off-stage and said to myself, okay, let's see what he plays. There were three ways to win and Karpov didn't find any of them. With the move Karpov played, he gave me a great chance to save the game. He was still better, much better, but maybe I could draw. But then I made a second blunder. Two blunders in one game. Unbelievable. I had already resigned in my soul. A mental block. Unbelievable. . . .

"Five years ago I had this impression: To beat Karpov was like lifting a world record weight." Garry grunted with the effort of hefting six hundred pounds. "In this match I'm still thinking this way, but it doesn't make any sense. At this point in our careers, I am a much better player than Karpov. I think this is obvious. He is no longer a world record weight for me. Just do it easy. Relax, Garry. Don't be so tense. But I can't do it. Why can't I do it? For me this is so unpleasant, this contradiction. You see, Karpov didn't deserve to win. I did it to myself. Anyone with two eyes can see that. All these mistakes. I've given him a chance . . . It's a good lesson. I deserved to lose. The anger is only against myself. I lost it. I made the mistakes."

We turned on the television and watched a horror movie, and afterwards we talked about Gorbachev and the likely possibility of war in the Middle East, but the conversation looped back to losing. The way he saw it, the central problem in the match wasn't Karpov, but himself. He had to understand Kasparov better to beat Karpov. "I believe that before you can judge the value of a policy, you have to understand the objectives," he said. "What is the American administration trying to accomplish in the Middle East? What is the goal? Have two hundred thousand American boys been shipped to Saudi Arabia to protect American interests? To create a free oil market? Or to remove Saddam Hussein and destroy Iraqi forces? Now it seems to me that nobody knows what the goal is, including Mr. Bush. In the newspaper, I read that Senator Dole says, 'We're fighting for oil.' Then it's Mr. Bush, 'No, we're fighting for democracy.' Nobody in the world knows exactly what America is trying to achieve. Maybe the same thing is wrong in this fifth match against Karpov. Coming into this, it was important for me to demonstrate the art of chess, but somehow in doing that I have lost my way, I've neglected to win games where I've had an advantage. In game three, for example, when I sacrificed the queen with a great position, I was feeling the greatness of the game, and said to myself, 'I've got it.' But I didn't have it yet. The same thing happened again in game six. Okay, I've played a great game, but not yet. Seal the move, Garry.

"In the beginning of the match, I was so pleased with the high quality of the games that I forgot that the art should serve the match. At the heart of this, I suppose, is the conflict between the artist and the sportsman. But for sure, art is not the sufficient goal in a world championship. In the history books, brilliant wins and lucky wins look the same. The second game was a masterpiece and the seventh game was a game of blunders, but in the history books they are scored one win for Kasparov and one win for Karpov. From this point, I have to remember that my goal is to win the match. I have to win the match."

* * *

But Garry's resolution and lengthy soul-searching that weekend was less than effective. Game 8 reproduced the frustrations of game 6. Kasparov built up a massive attack and then allowed it to slip away. He seemed to lose his mettle at the critical moment. When he needed a few bold moves to put Karpov away, he lost heart and played safely. But even while his attack was formidable, he appeared restrained in front of his pieces, his body heavy and plodding. There was no intimidating glare, no contesting of the space above the board. As usual, Karpov was in time trouble. As he sweated and quivered from strain, he found the best moves, and it was Kasparov who lost his cool and blundered a pawn.

"The young Kasparov would have won this game easily," he said to me afterwards. "Any Kasparov would have won." Garry had become an insecure player, second-guessing himself at the critical moments. He was playing without flow. He should have lost this game. During the adjournment session, Kasparov was unshaven and his clothes were rumpled. He looked beaten. In his heart, he felt beaten. Somehow he managed a staunch defense and drew after eighty-four moves.

We continued to meet regularly. Garry would often refer to the young Kasparov, as though he were a missing person. There were few smiles, no banter. One evening, Masha said to me that the hair of her twenty-seven-year-old husband was becoming gray before her eyes. There was a predictable arc to our meetings. For an hour or so, Garry would talk about his bad play and wonder what was wrong. He complained of having no energy. Garry had been in the best physical condition of his life eight weeks before on Martha's Vineyard, but now his body had gone flaccid. He rarely left the hotel, except to play Karpov. I suggested that he needed physical exercise, at the least to begin walking. But he cringed at the thought. The city seemed a fearful place under these circumstances. On one or two occasions, I coaxed him to take a late-night walk and his gait was slow and stiff. He smirked, as if to say, look how I am walking.

I would try to reassure him. Once I said to him, "Try not to worry so much about winning. Worry has become your enemy. Just play the games. Try to enjoy the games a little. The winning will come if you can loosen up." I had said similar words to Josh at times when his game had gone sour. "I'm sure things will turn around," I said to Garry.

"I hope so," he answered in his littlest voice.

As the New York half of the match drew near the end, it became clear to me that Kasparov's depression had more to it than his poor play. At the end of each visit, he wanted to talk about events in the Soviet Union. He was thinking more about Soviet politics than he had during the first weeks of the match. He spoke with sadness about the miners' strike in his country, and with anger about Gorbachev's recent demands for increased power and the decision to send Yergeny Primakov to the Middle East as a special envoy to head off a U.S. war against Iraq. Kasparov considered the "special envoy" a publicity stunt to demonstrate to the Soviet people that Gorbachev was still a formidable world leader more or less in step with George Bush. "I wonder if George Bush knows where Mr. Primakov was last January," said Garry. "He was in Baku for ten days during the genocide of Armenians. He is responsible for mass killings. He had Soviet troops standing by, but he did absolutely nothing to stop the killing. Then he conducted the invasion of the city with these troops on January twelfth, when the city was absolutely empty. Primakov has great experience for the Middle East; he knows how to send Muslims to kill Christians."

After the games Armenian-Americans would pass pieces of paper and books on stage for Garry's autograph. One of the books was a lengthy and gruesome account of the massacre of Armenians in Sumgait. Kasparov read this litany of murder and rape and often talked about it. He asked all of his friends to read the book. Garry's chess variations had become reinfected with memories of the loss of his home, and with worry about missing friends and members of his family. At the time, he had still not told me the details of his last weeks in Baku, but he remarked that he would never be able to return to see the grave of his father. Increasingly, Garry felt leaden. He complained frequently about having no energy, and on stage he appeared listless. He also complained that the ceilings in the hotel were too low and that the air was foul and that the city was too noisy. He felt trapped, and yearned for clean air and space. We talked about depression, and putting a name on how he felt was somewhat reassuring. It suggested an end to it somewhere ahead. I described the aftermath of a boating accident several years before, when Josh and I had nearly been killed. For more than a year afterwards, I told him, everything seemed gloomy, life had no purpose and I often felt fearful. "It passes," I said, and he nodded.

On the day before the eighth game, Kasparov had received a phone call from an Armenian advocate, a lawyer. The man said that an old Armenian lady, a distant relative of Garry's who lived in New York, wanted to come to the Regency Hotel to visit. "I was willing to break my training routine to meet her," he said, "because as a child I had heard wonderful stories of her rich and prosperous life in the States." While he told me the story of this woman and her family, he became very emotional.

"When she was a girl, she lived in Azerbaijan in an area which was decimated by the revolution. In 1918 and 1920, there had been horrible slaughters of Armenians, a million people had died, and the surviving Armenian population lived in terror. In 1921, the Nagorno-Karabakh region, with a predominantly Armenian population, was forcibly made a part of the Azerbaijani Soviet Socialist Republic. This was another big wound to the Armenians living there. Like everyone else, this woman, then in her twenties, had lost members of her family and was desperate to leave, to find a place to begin a normal life. Somehow she managed to save a little money and emigrated to the United States in 1922.

"The rest of her family stayed behind and their lives were difficult, at best. She had two brothers. In 1937, her oldest brother, who was the father of four children, was branded an enemy of the people and sent to a labor camp. He committed suicide there. The younger brother came to live with his dead brother's children, three boys and a girl. The youngest of the boys eventually married my mother's sister, and I've heard about the trials of this family mainly from him and from my aunt. Anyhow, the surviving brother struggled to support them as a builder. His niece, the oldest of the children, had been born in 1922, the same year her aunt left for the States. She also worked hard to help the family. In Baku, this girl became one of the best teachers of English. She made her money preparing students and doing some translating. I took some lessons from her when I was a boy.

"It is a typical story for this time in Azerbaijan. Survival was a struggle. The family had little money. The uncle and his brother's eldest daughter worked to help the three younger children get an education. During Khrushchev's time, the dead brother's reputation was cleared—he was 'rehabilitated,' that was the term they used. There were government decrees, with lists of people who were no longer considered enemies of the people. Little good it did.

"This family had more than its share of problems. The surviving brother had a daughter, and when she was grown and married, she gave birth to an abnormal child, Down's syndrome. Soon after, this woman died of cancer and her husband abandoned the family. The support and care for this Down's baby passed to her father, an old man now, and the rest of the family. Meanwhile, the daughter of the dead brother lost her husband. She was also getting old now. Okay, what I am describing here is not a tragedy. In all families, people get sick and grow old. But this family wasn't very successful. None of them. They grew old with less than their measure of happiness.

"But during these troubled years, this family often thought of the lady, a member of their family, after all, who had escaped this misery to live in the United States. Several times she had visited and brought presents, and because she lived in America, they concluded that she was very wealthy, that she must live in a wonderful mansion and drive a large shiny car. In their minds, over the decades, their missing aunt became the American dream. The splendor of her life grew to fairy-tale proportions. Thinking about her made them happy. One of us has done well. As a boy I heard about the good fortune of this woman, but in truth I didn't think much about it.

"In 1988, in response to the Armenian demand that the Nagorno-Karabakh be reunited with the Armenian Soviet Socialist Republic, things became bad for Armenians living in Sumgait. For this poor family, and for other Armenians, history was repeating itself. There was a big campaign to move all Armenian people out of Baku, too. All Armenian people lost their jobs. My mother's sister, a dentist, lost her job at the end of 1989. It didn't matter that she was my aunt.

"The Armenian population of Baku lived in terror. People could feel that horrors were coming. Everyone understood that you should leave as soon as possible, but it is difficult to pack up and leave your home.

"In 1990, the central government orchestrated the pogroms against Armenians living in Baku. My people, Armenians, were raped, tortured and killed.

"Those of the old lady's family who survived were very badly off. Her brother and his niece were very old now and they had no money. They were jobless, homeless. They had to emigrate to Yerevan, Armenia. They were lost there in an ocean of refugees, two hundred thousand Armenian refugees. It was just after the earthquake and the entire population was suffering. They were old people, ripped out of their lives.

"Not knowing what else to do, these people wrote their wealthy relative in America: Can you help us?

"When my mother and I heard that this old rich lady was coming to visit, it made us very happy. Probably she would bring money to send back to her poor relatives in Armenia.

"She arrived at the Regency Hotel with the lawyer who takes care of her family. I interrupted my preparations to meet her. When I came into the room, I was very surprised. This very frail old woman wore the clothing of a poor person. She cried and cried. She said that she had heard that her family was miserable. She wept for her brother with no place to live, who tried to care for this abnormal child. She said that this tragedy was the fault of the communist system, an evil which had forced her to emigrate nearly seventy years before.

"Finally, her lawyer explained that the woman had brought money to be distributed among members of the family. I said that I would make sure that the people received it. I was handed a thick envelope. Inside was seven thousand dollars. 'This is her life savings,' said the lawyer. For a moment, I was speechless. "Her life savings?" For all of these years, I had heard about this wealthy relative living in America. The bills in the envelope were tens and twenties, old bills. She had been collecting them for decades, maybe hiding them in a box under her mattress. Seven thousand dollars in seventy years.

" 'We cannot take this,' " I said, intending to send money to her relatives myself.

" 'I have to give it to them,' " the woman insisted.

"I asked the lawyer to leave the room with me for a few minutes. I asked if the woman had any other means of support and he answered that she had a pension. 'She believes that her life savings must be distributed to her relatives suffering in the Soviet Union,' he said, describing a sacred duty. I had a quick word with my mother, who said, 'You know, it's holy money. You cannot reject it. It is a last will. It must be heeded.'

"The woman wanted the money divided among her surviving relatives, but the major share would go to her homeless brother so that he might be able to buy a little house. A place to live quietly and die quietly. I said to her, "Then send all the money to him, and let me look after the others." But no, it was important to her to send a little to each of them.

"This is a story that for me demonstrates the wheel of history. The Armenian lady emigrated to save herself from communism. And now she had to use her life savings to help her relatives after the tragedy organized by the communists once again. It is a tragedy of the Armenian nation and a tragedy of the human mind warped by communism. These poor people from my homeland have lost their sense of the world. I don't think this old lady tried to mislead her relatives in Azerbaijan by pretending to be wealthy. Her relatives had this impression because of the poverty of their own lives and their distorted image of the West. They don't know what it means to be rich, what it means to be poor. Today they are homeless, jobless and must accept aid from a poor lady in New York. But a last irony in the story is that the four thousand dollars she sent to her brother in Armenia will be enough to make a big impact. It will be enough to buy a house. A final resting place."

In early November, 1990, Mikhail Gorbachev's popularity was at a low ebb in the Soviet Union. There were serious meat and bread shortages in Moscow. Gorbachev had been jeered by the military as well as the liberal press, and Moscow intellectuals were calling for his resignation. All over the Soviet Union, regions were asking for more autonomy, and from his home in Vermont, Alexander Solzhenitsyn belittled Gorbachev's reforms and called for the dismantling of the Union. But in Washington, George Bush continued to offer the Soviet leader unflinching support and his highest praise. He applauded Gorbachev's winning of the Nobel Peace Prize.

"In the Soviet Union, the response to Gorbachev's winning the Nobel prize is very bad," said Kasparov one evening over dinner. "He is hated in my country. People demonstrate against the inhumanity of his policies. For example, a large protest was held recently by the Committee of the Soldiers' Mothers to protest the death of boys in Afghanistan and of many thousands who died because of the feudal structure of the Red Army. The mothers of tens of thousands of dead soldiers consider it a mockery that Gorbachev won the Nobel prize."

Garry was reading all the political news from home that he could get his hands on. He was placing daily calls to Moscow. "You cannot isolate yourself from current events," he said. "How can I not be affected by events in the Soviet Union? I have relatives. I receive phone calls and I know how bad it is." He and I were talking much more about Soviet affairs than about the match. The political turmoil and crumbling economy at home provided something of an escape from the grim chess life in New York, but it did little to help his game. Kasparov again played badly in game 9, and would have lost if not for a huge blunder by Karpov. Game 9 was a draw. In the tenth game, playing with the white pieces, Garry had no stomach for the fight. He offered a draw on the eighteenth move, which was highly unusual for him, and Karpov accepted. Andrew Page, who had dashed back to England for the day, said over the phone, "Garry's playing these games like he doesn't want to win." Andrew decided that Garry just wanted to be finished with the match, to get on with the next phase of his life. I took this to mean a career in politics.

"If Gorbachev has been doing such a good job, why is his country completely in shambles?" Garry asked me one night, gesturing towards an editorial in the *Times* which praised the Soviet leader. Kasparov considered the Gorbachev regime a corpse, and it seemed preposterous and immoral to him that the Bush government and the American media were trying so hard to revive it. "Gorbachev is the last Russian dictator and soon he will be out. But did you read

Hedrick Smith's cover article about the Soviet Union in *The New York Times Magazine*?" he asked, referring to a piece that had run on October 28, which was generally sympathetic to the Secretary General.

"Yes. His thesis seems to be that Gorbachev's reform movement has been effectively stalemated by the character of the Russian people," I answered.

"It is a lie. If a writer said the same about blacks in America, that their problems stem from a lack of ambition, laziness, and a tendency toward alcoholism, he would be branded a racist. My country was raped by communism. You should feel sorry about it. This nation saved Europe from fascism, and now it's saving Europe from communism because the Soviet people are paying all dues. Eastern Europe is free now, almost free, and whatever happens, Russian people will fight for independence. Hedrick Smith's article is an insult to the Russian people."

One afternoon, during Kasparov's last week in New York, Andrew Page received a phone call from grandmaster Ron Henley, who was one of Karpov's trainers. According to Page, Henley said that he was calling from the office of the man who produced the Teenage Mutant Ninja Turtles, and that they had come up with an idea for a promotion that would involve Garry and Anatoly going down to Atlantic City, or possibly to Las Vegas, for a month. The two grandmasters would set up shop at one of the casinos and play all comers at speed chess for a thousand dollars a game. Presumably, they would win most if not all of the games, and the money would go into a big glass cage. At the end of the month, they would play a match for the money. "This idea was totally out of context. Completely frivolous," recalls Page. After all, Garry was depressed and playing terribly, in danger of returning the world championship to Karpov. While Henley talked, Page was thinking, "This is a trap. Someone is taping this conversation. They are trying to sucker Garry into something preposterous while he is down." It seemed to Page like a trick, an elaborate distraction. Karpov would have known that Garry would never agree to this stunt.

"I asked Henley, 'Does Anatoly know about this?' and he put

Karpov on the line. He may actually have been on another extension the whole time. Karpov said that this was a great way to see America and make a lot of money, that he and Garry could go on tour together from casino to casino. It was mind-boggling that while Kasparov and Karpov were engaged in this grim struggle, with so much at stake, Karpov was proposing this . . . fluff. I said to him that I would give the idea consideration and hung up. I didn't know what to think." Maybe the former world champion truly believed that there was money to be made with this Ninja Turtle producer, Page calculated. For if it were some kind of trick, Karpov wouldn't have gotten on the phone, he wouldn't have wanted to get his fingers dirty.

"But how could Karpov bring himself to suggest such a thing?" I asked, recalling the years of bribes and dirty tricks and the bombing of Zurab Azmaiparashvili's home. My incredulity amused Andrew. He explained that the rules of the game were different in the Soviet Union, where there was a Wild West mentality, and where chess had long been a tool of communism, tainted by the chicanery of the KGB. In his cheerful tone, Andrew suggested that perhaps Karpov was adapting to a new time and place—perhaps the enmity of these perennial warriors could be forgotten if the profits were high enough. I couldn't tell whether or not he was putting me on. "When Karpov comes to America, he is looking to make money," explained Andrew, as though the profit motive forgave all else. But, after one more phone call from Henley, the idea was never alluded to again.

In game 11, Kasparov once again played the black side of the King's Indian defense. Early on, he sacrificed a rook for a bishop to weaken White's center and to get an attack on the dark squares. He used less than eleven minutes for his first eighteen moves. The rapidity of his play suggested that the line had been carefully plotted in advance by him and his team. Although some analysts, among them Yasser Seirawan, spoke of the courage and deep vision of Kasparov's sacrifice, others suggested that Kasparov's plan from the beginning was to draw the game, because only six moves later, the world champion forced a draw by perpetual check.

Many masters expected Kasparov to go all-out for a win with the

white pieces in the last game of the New York half of the match. It
was reasoned that with game 12 taking place on November 7th, the
anniversary of the Bolshevik October Revolution of 1917, Kasparov
would have little difficulty finding his fire and resolve. So much for
prognostications. Game 12 was the very embodiment of Kasparov's
frustration throughout the New York half of the match. Once again,
sharp opening play on the white side of a Ruy Lopez earned him a
powerful middlegame position. On the twenty-seventh move of the
game, Kasparov jimmied his queen deep into the heart of Karpov's
kingside. It appeared to be the start of a kingside onslaught. On the
following move, Karpov attacked Kasparov's queen with his knight,
a predictable response, but then instead of repositioning his queen to
the rook file to continue the attack, the champion reversed engines
and retreated her, which made little sense. Kasparov was seeing
phantoms. With this retreat, his promising game had fizzled into a
more or less equal position, and ten moves later he offered Karpov
a draw. Karpov did not accept immediately. Objectively, Karpov was
no better than even, but he took his time. It was as though he sensed
that Kasparov's knees were wobbling, and the challenger was deciding if this was the moment to put him down.

    After they agreed to the draw, Garry admitted that ghosts were
playing havoc with his game. "It was only game twelve, but with the
break coming, it felt like the last game," he said, trying to make sense
of his indecisiveness. "And you tend to think, c'mon, it's the last
game. Don't take too much risk. But it's not the last game. Game
twelve is not game twenty-four. You want to forget this voice of
caution, but you cannot. That's what happened. I was pressing him.
My plan was to bring my queen to the kingside. Karpov's pieces
were on the queenside, but the king was on the kingside. The plan
was so obvious. Kasparov in any kind of form would play the moves
without hesitation. After I played Qf5, Karpov thought for eight or
nine minutes, and during this time I began to second-guess myself.
Then when he attacked my queen [with his knight], I retreated her for
no good reason. I started thinking *too* much. So I retreated my queen
when Qh5 was the obvious decision. There was no need even to
calculate—just make the move. There are some moves that should
be played by instinct. A chess player must trust himself, in the same
way that a pianist believes in his fingers."

* * *

When I next visited Garry at the Regency, there were half-packed cartons, piles of books and magazines, and miscellaneous knickknacks strewn around the floor of the sitting room. Garry was slumped on a sofa. "I feel awful," he said. He kicked at some junk near his feet. The room was oppressive with failure and the chaos of leaving. Masha and Klara were noisily packing things in boxes in a room across the hall, and none of the other members of the team were around. Soon they would all be flying to Lyon. "It's a pity, a pity," he said. "So many mistakes. It's incredible, really, so many mistakes in a world championship match, and most of them by me." Earlier that day, the match organizers had held a press conference, which Kasparov had not attended. He had not wanted Karpov to see him in this beaten condition. "I do not want to help Karpov. You understand?" Garry had trouble all through him. He was confused. He felt as though he had let his friends down. When I asked him a question about the match, he put up his hand to say, let's not speak about it, but then he couldn't help himself. "That blunder was like a wound," he said referring to game 7. "It was bleeding, working somewhere inside for the rest of the games. When you are psychologically unstable, it [a blunder like this] kills you. For me, every game since the end of game six was painful."

After ten minutes or so, Garry walked across the hall to a room where he often played practice games against his trainers. After a few minutes, I looked in. He was sitting in a straight-backed wooden chair and his shoulders were stooped. Klara was looming over him, chiding or counseling, I couldn't tell. He looked up at her and then turned away. His face was flushed.

The last two or three times I had visited, I had brought with me an autographed copy of grandmaster Pal Benko's endgame book, a volume that Benko had published himself and which he had asked me to give Kasparov. I believe there were a hundred copies or so in this new edition. Each time I came, I forgot to give it to Garry, or his mood was so bad that I thought that he wouldn't notice it. And then when I returned home, I felt guilty. Benko had been one of the top eight players in the world in the fifties. He had played many great wars against Bobby Fischer, had beaten Fischer three times, and often showed me other games where he had had Bobby on the ropes but then allowed him to escape.

Now, as a sixty-year-old, Benko was still thin and fit, and though he was a most congenial man, he often wore a fierce preoccupied expression, to go along with his jet-black hair and bushy eyebrows. If you didn't know him, you might think Benko was a little danger-ous. In his small Jersey City house, Benko slept for much of the day, and each night he analyzed games and composed beautiful but nearly unsolvable endgame problems in which the pieces did magical things: Knights had the power of rooks and two pawns might well be more powerful than five. But at sixty, Benko felt bad that he no longer received invitations to attend regal tournaments in Europe and that he rarely had inquiries from new students. It seemed stupid to Pal that once a man gets a little old, people assume he is no longer any good. He smoldered at the thought that recent Russian emigrés were getting all the top students. Why was it that if you were Russian, he wondered, people automatically assumed you were a great player or had deep wisdom for teaching? Perhaps with a sense for the passing of time, Pal drove himself to compose problems ever more elegant and deeply plotted, and occasionally he showed one of them to a hot-shot Russian trainer, and Pal would stand by impatiently, his face tight with annoyance and barely-concealed scorn, while the guy couldn't begin to solve it. Benko spent six months a year in Hungary working with the three Polgar sisters, and when he was in the New York area, he sometimes taught my son Josh, but often he remained in the little house in New Jersey that he had inherited from his father.

When Garry came back in the room to sit among the boxes, I handed him Benko's self-published book, half-expecting him to drop it at his feet. But instead, he started reading. "This is very important," he said, as he slowly turned a page. Garry's face softened. He moved his lips and smiled as he calculated a witty move. For the next hour or so, he lost himself in Benko's book, which contained interesting and instructive endings culled from numerous games, along with Benko's sharp analysis. Garry was enjoying chess for the first time since the start of the match. But there was one troubled moment when he looked up from the book and said, "I wonder if there are any of my endgames here." He turned quickly through the pages and then double-checked. "I've played some good endings." There were none, and he was disappointed. This was something of a sore point, because many grandmasters considered Karpov stronger than Garry in the endgame; maybe Garry even thought so himself, but he never told me this. After a minute, Garry had settled back into the book and was calculating a variation and biting his nails a little. "This is very important," he repeated.

Sometimes I think that Garry's earnestness and moral tone inspire the dark side of Andrew Page. Before leaving New York, with Garry bereft over his poor play, with the entire team in gloomy spirits, Andrew placated himself and brought cheer to the camp by playing a little dirty trick. Throughout the history of Karpov and Kasparov's championship matches, there have been numerous examples of one team or the other accusing the organizer of favoring the opposition. For example, in the past Karpov has claimed that Kasparov received better living accommodations, and Kasparov has made similar complaints. Andrew's trick played upon Karpov's ongoing suspicion that Garry received preferential treatment. According to Page, the French organizer provided first-class tickets to Lyon for Karpov and Kasparov, and in addition each team received economy-class tickets for the trainers. But before leaving New York, Page arranged with Air France for Masha also to sit in first class, and paid the extra fare himself for Garry's grandmaster trainers to sit in business class. Andrew knew that, to Karpov and his group, it would appear as though the organizer had given Kasparov preferential treatment, and that later, when the organizer denied it, Karpov still wouldn't know for certain. "When we walked on the plane, Karpov's group filed to the back, muttering," said Andrew, relishing the memory. "It was a nice dirty trick. It made our guys feel good."

8

LYON

When *New York Newsday* reporter Manny Topol arrived in Lyon to cover the second half of the match, he was eager to get started. It was unusual for the paper to send a reporter abroad on a lengthy sports assignment. Before unpacking his bags, Manny went to the playing site, the Palais des Congrès, to set up in the pressroom. Topol, at fifty-five, was short and slightly overweight, with a bad leg that dragged a little when he walked. His dress, "disheveled fifties," fit well with his sympathetic but slightly needy expression.

Manny went directly up the broad, winding staircase to the pressroom to arrange to have a private phone line installed at his desk, so that he could contact his office in New York. He took a look around and set up his computer. The room was big enough for two hundred reporters, but there weren't more than fifteen or eighteen in the room. He walked around to say hello, but hardly anyone spoke English. There were only a couple of familiar faces from the Macklowe pressroom, and no one was here covering the games for *The New York Times* or, to the best that he could tell, from any of the wire services. Manny concluded that he was the only journalist from the United States covering the match on a daily basis. He scratched his head. This was a surprise. In New York, there had been seven hundred reporters, including a slew from metropolitan papers. Manny had told his editor that Lyon would be a media circus. "This is really big," he had said, explaining that Kasparov was in danger of losing the title, which might put the world champion in danger back home. Manny's editor and some of the guys in the sports department and on the crime beat with whom he had worked for years may have wondered why he was pressing so hard to go to Lyon to write about chess, but Manny was a top reporter, and there was no doubt that he would deliver good stories.

Sitting beside a drafty window, Manny could feel the frigid wind gusting across the snow-covered Parc de la Tête d'Or which bordered the Palais des Congrès. While Karpov and Kasparov shook hands on a television monitor, Manny looked around the cold and nearly empty pressroom, feeling uneasy. Working the crime beat, Topol had learned that there was power in numbers; if you stuck with the other reporters, you would never miss something crucial to the story. When he had been a rookie covering front-page homicide cases, this had been an essential fact of life, but, over time, Manny had learned homicide like the back of his hand and didn't need anyone's help. He had written many prize-winning stories and had covered all the big ones. Manny particularly favored stories in which murder was driven by lust. He knew how to build these stories.

A few veteran chess writers, bundled in overcoats and scarves, watched the opening moves, while in a corner of the room, unlikely though it seemed, a man with a professional salon chair was giving free haircuts to the scant group. Many of the world's top masters, who would normally camp out in the press room providing reporters with analysis, anecdotes and a player's feel, were away representing their countries at the chess Olympiad in Novi Sad, Yugoslavia. Manny loved the locker-room camaraderie of reporters at a large event, such as the New York half of this match or the Super Bowl. He never missed going to the Super Bowl and the *grande affaire* the league threw each year for its football writers. But there was no big party of journalists in Lyon. Manny was the party. He dialed his editor on the phone. "It's terrific here," he said. "The place is jammed with reporters. You could cut the tension with a knife."

The reason there weren't more international journalists in Lyon was not a deep mystery. In addition to the normal attrition that takes place during your average three- or four-month sports event, with the Persian Gulf War about to explode, newspapers were sending correspondents to the Middle East and trying to save money in other areas. Wire services and major newspapers assumed they could pick up the story about the world championship from one another. Circumstances had conspired to make Manny the primary, if not the exclusive, pipeline to the United States. In addition to his million-plus readers at *Newsday*, the *Los Angeles Times* news service would pick up his stories and pass them on to another 100 or 150 newspapers around the country, an opportunity that any journalist would relish.

But Manny wasn't happy. There was a problem. Manny knew next to nothing about high-level chess. He did not have a clue about opening theory, critical squares, weak bishops, or rook and pawn endings. When he imagined himself sitting alone, trying to analyze tonight's game for his twenty-five million readers, he broke out in a cold sweat. In New York, with a veritable army of masters on hand, he could casually eavesdrop for technical information, and his articles had been inspired by the waves of passion that had swept across the pressroom. He had sometimes traded anecdotes about brutal murders and sports corruption, or the latest inside word about whether the Jets rookie had enough smarts to start at quarterback next year, for insights about the King's Indian and the Ruy Lopez. But Manny contemplated the large empty Palais des Congrès pressroom and wondered who was going to explain to him the meaning of Kasparov's latest opening novelty, or why it would excite chess players for generations to come that Karpov had moved his king to g2 rather than h1.

After a two-and-a-half-week break to rethink his strategy, Kasparov, with the black pieces in game 13, opted for a sound line in the Grunfeld defense rather than one of the sharp variations he favored in the King's Indian. This signaled a departure from the attack-at-all-cost style with which he had opened the match in New York. "In some of those games, I committed suicide," he reflected. In Lyon, living in a spacious house with a view across the Parc de la Tête d'Or, Garry was more lighthearted, and seemed resolved to play in a more flexible and self-protective style. The onus to win the match was still on Karpov. The players were tied 6–6—each win counting for a point, each draw a half-point—and if they continued to draw, Kasparov would retain the championship.

In game 13, Karpov deftly forced the world champion to trade queens and play out an ending in which Kasparov was considerably worse. Karpov's two bishops were poised to nurse home a passed pawn in the center of the board. He had made a career of squeezing wins from such positional advantages. The players traded off their light-square bishops, and then Garry violated time-honored principles of endgame play by placing his pawns on the dark squares, where they might be vulnerable to Karpov's dark-square bishop. In *Five Crowns*, Yasser Seirawan suggests that the ugliness of this plan belies its courage and resourcefulness. But with this highly unorthodox pawn placement, Garry had liberated his own king to slip ahead to a key square. The king and pawns together formed a shield against Karpov's dark-square bishop and, utilizing an active rook as well, Garry was able to equalize and draw. He had managed to keep Karpov from taking the lead in the match by using deep and unexpected ideas in the endgame. Pal Benko might have wanted to put this one in his book.

Game 14 was exciting from start to finish, with sacrifices launching attacks and counterattacks. Karpov and Kasparov wrestled the initiative back and forth, and as both players grew short on time, they were still attacking. When it seemed for a moment that Karpov, up the exchange, was getting the better of it, Garry quickly found the key defensive idea and drew the game. It was a tense fighting draw, the seventh draw in a row.

When newspapers report successive draws in long championship matches, the public assumes that the games are lifeless and monotonous. More often, the opposite is true. When the players fight hard for wins, consecutive draws might be thought of as violent skirmishes within one huge battle or mega-game, which builds in tension through hundreds of moves, and which may indeed prove to be decisive in the match. The big one, encompassing many games, becomes increasingly more tense for the players and fans, as it continues to expand with more skirmishes. Everyone knows that the end of this standoff must come. The suspense increases with each drawn game. The players know only too well that, for all the days of buildup and irresolution, once the blood begins to flow it is likely to be a torrent. Fans and players look for clues to when the break may take place by scrutinizing telltale signs in prior games. After someone finally wins a game, the player who is down a point can no longer afford to safeguard his position. He must take greater risks to win, which in turn will alter his opponent's style. The contestants will play the next stage of the match on a tilted board where draws may be the exception.

"In New York and Lyon, when we began drawing many games, it wasn't because of our lack of will to win," said Kasparov. "It was the result of a terrible fight . . . We didn't score because of the tension. The tension kept building. We made mistakes. Who will make the decisive mistake? It is like Russian roulette—you feel this tension in your fingers. You are very nervous. Every move is a big responsibility. The importance of every home preparation is huge. In each game the importance of a mistake grows larger. I hadn't played a world championship for three years, and I had completely forgotten what this kind of tension feels like . . . Draw, draw, draw, draw. It is like a kettle boiling. The tension is getting too strong for the players. One day the mistake will be crucial. You make a mistake and you are dead. One mistake could cost me the title. It feels like you are playing for your life."

Before the start of game 15, chess enthusiasts in Lyon were betting that the first one to break the cycle of draws would take the match. Sitting at the board, Kasparov continued to look drained, but despite being on the receiving end of heavy blows, he appeared to be more in control of his game than in New York. In this one, Karpov played a fantastic opening novelty and came within a breath of winning. Again, Kasparov bailed himself out by trading into an inferior endgame. Then he created a stiff defense around his king to hold off Karpov's menacing pieces, and save the draw. Playing in the fashion of his opponent, Kasparov had neutralized the former world champion's aggressive early play by employing uncanny endgame technique.

*   *   *

When Manny Topol stared at a double-edged endgame position on the television monitor, his forehead furrowed and he took his chin in his hand. He knew that he was in trouble. During the many weeks of the match, Manny had become rather good at identifying the strength of direct attacks in the middlegame. He had learned that if Kasparov sacrificed his rook for a bishop, but in turn opened diagonals and files for his remaining rook, queen and bishop, the sacrifice was probably worth it. He had learned, in the language of Kasparov, that the quality of pieces can be decisive: fewer pieces dynamically placed on the board can overwhelm a material advantage. This was not so hard to grasp. After all, teamwork, feints and displacements proved decisive in many sports. But in the endgame, the principles were both many and frequently paradoxical, and you had to know them to have any idea who was better. To begin with, the playing field of the endgame is nearly barren, with only a handful of survivors on the sixty-four squares. In the first weeks of the match, Manny had been inclined to think that with just a few chessmen to keep track of, the action ought to be easy to follow. But he had soon discovered that he was wrong.

The great endgame player can be defined by his ability to read the meaning of disengagement and empty space. He judges the importance of unoccupied squares, of the critical number of spaces separating the two kings, of the number of steps a king must traverse along empty pathways to achieve a goal that would be a complete mystery to an amateur. In this sparse terrain, pieces yield space to edge around one another. But the implications of these austere and seemingly indirect moves are often more grave than in the middlegame, where the loss of a tempo—when a player is stalled from his plan for a move—frequently means no more than the loss of initiative in a hectic battle. A player can struggle back from middlegame errors. But the loss of a tempo or an inaccurate move in the endgame is likely the end of the game; you lose.

The stupefying principles of endgame play, explained to him by the pressroom grandmasters, left Manny befuddled. To play beautiful endgames, for example, you have to know, as Kasparov did in game 15, that one can be significantly behind in piece activity or even in material and still manage to survive by constructing a clever defensive formation or fortress. But to do this a player must know the engineering principles involved. In some fortresslike positions, the knight and bishop protect critical squares so that neither the king nor queen can invade, and the game is a draw. Creating a fortress or attacking a shaky defensive setup, and especially promoting a pawn, often depends upon the manipulation of tempo. In arriving at a critical position, at the end of a long variation, it may be essential for it to be your opponent's move rather than yours, or vice versa. To gain winning and saving tempos, one must understand the principles of opposition, *zugzwang* and triangulation—interactive techniques so delicate and complex that they sometimes confuse the greatest endgame players. Over the decades, there have been countless articles, many books, thick encyclopedias, exploring the intricacies of rook and pawn endings, knight and bishop endings, king and pawn endings. Today, computer research has changed evaluations of critical endings previously thought of as incontrovertible and fully explored. The jungle of endgame theory continues to thicken, and the active tournament player must keep up with this proliferation of data.

But learning all the endgame principles is still a long way from being able to feel the ending, as Kasparov might say. When the queens come off the board, the character of the game shifts, and the master must change his demeanor as well as his technique. The Marines are no longer storming the hill. The endgame is chilly and minimalist, and to play effectively in this new terrain, the heedless attacker must quiet himself and be patient, precise and perhaps a little detached.

In the pressroom, Manny intimated neediness and naiveté, not unlike the television character Columbo, which he used to his advantage while slyly rummaging for material for his stories. Chess masters began to look out for him, and crucial analysis fell into Manny's lap in time to meet his deadline. During the beginnings of games, when neither of us could follow the opening theory and we had time on our hands, Manny, in his understated style, would hold me captive with tales of murder and lust. One evening, he spoke of the insatiable sex life of the child murderess Alice Crimmins, and recalled her love-making with Pasquale Picassio, the barber, in the back seat of his automobile parked behind the barber shop in Queens, New York. During a King's Indian defense, Manny reminisced about Lynnor Gershenson and concluded that her case was, in the end, a story of enduring love. The pretty junior high teacher and her principal had plotted to have the man's wife chloroformed to death while he lay asleep beside her, as though some third party had committed the murder. Ten years later, when they came out of jail, they married with the ardor and commitment of young love, and moved into the same house where the crime had taken place. Manny told me many stories during the openings, and in turn, I would find myself recalling something that Kasparov had told me the night before, and occasionally it found its way into one of Manny's articles.

Despite the depleted pressroom in Lyon, Manny, old pro that he was, developed key sources. In the thick of difficult endgames, he was often to be found analyzing with grandmasters Spassky, Speelman and Seirawan, and the tactically gifted American senior master, Maurice Ashley. Of course Manny took notes from these sage chess thinkers, but he also worked at the games himself, which was the reason his articles were lively and accessible to so many. As the months passed, Manny watched and learned, and chess began to open up for him. More and more, he related these battles on the board to other dramas that had engaged him—war movies, pro football, boxing, murder stories—and he began to feel the exhilaration, fear and despair that pushed Karpov and Kasparov to find great moves. By the end of the match, Manny knew that he wanted to write more about chess, but his deepest connection to the game remained something entirely personal. More than all else, the great games of Karpov and Kasparov brought back memories of his father.

Manny's father, Isaac Topol, had been born in a small town on the border of Poland and Russia in the region called White Russia. Isaac was a chess master, and as a young man he valued the game beyond all else, except his family and religion. He was a scholar of Judaism, and sometimes he would ponder connections between the mysteries of the Talmud and the game that dominated his fantasies.

In the late twenties and early thirties, there were pogroms against

Jews throughout the area. Synagogues were closed and desecrated and Jewish homes were broken into. People were beaten by fascists and anti-Semites. Isaac's father was beaten and murdered. The Jewish community was terrified and many wanted to leave, but it was very difficult. Isaac somehow managed to get a ticket to Palestine, but then he gave it to a married friend and it was impossible to get another. He was afraid that he would be killed. He wanted to travel to the United States, but at the time there were harsh restrictions on Jewish emigration. Isaac had no money. What was he to do?

Isaac conceived of a plan to walk out of Poland. He laid out his route carefully. To survive, he would stop in places where there were little chess tournaments, or cafés and outdoor parks where chess players gathered and he could hustle games for food or money. That's what Isaac did. He moved from town to town, playing games, walking, occasionally riding on the back of a truck, sleeping in the homes of chess players or in a barn or beneath a tree. He chess-hustled his way south through Poland to Czechoslovakia, hiked through Austria and Switzerland, skirting Germany, and into France. After more than half a year, he arrived in Cherbourg with barely enough money to pay his passage to Argentina. Many of his friends and family who had remained at home were murdered, but in this unlikely way, Isaac survived. He stayed in Argentina for a few years, subsisting as a chess player and peddler, then met and married an Eastern European immigrant and eventually they gained entry to the United States.

When Manny was a teenager in Brooklyn, his father would talk to him about chess. "It's more than a game, Manny," his father said in Yiddish. Chess had given Isaac pleasure while growing up in a grim land, and then the game had saved his life. Naturally, he wanted to pass this gift on to his son. Isaac taught Manny the basics and they played many games. "I never won one," said Manny. "He played an old-fashioned game. Now, from watching Kasparov, I know it's the Ruy Lopez." But at the time, Manny had never thought to ask. Isaac tried to tell the boy how chess could sharpen his thinking and help in many areas of life. "Mainly he was trying to get through to me. This was the best way that he could be my father," said Manny, trying to hold back his tears. But while Isaac was explaining the magic of Capablanca's endgames to his son, Manny was thinking about Jackie Robinson. He wanted to go outside and play baseball with his friends. Probably because his father wanted him to play so badly, Manny resisted learning chess. He loved his father, but Isaac's European customs and thick Yiddish accent were an embarrassment to Manny. For the youngster, chess was also from the old country.

"I should have listened, I should have listened," he said, more than forty years after Jackie Robinson had prevailed over the Ruy Lopez. "There was a life philosophy beneath those chess lessons, but I couldn't hear him . . . Oh, what I would give today to have one more chess game with my father."

Karpov played the opening horribly in game 16. After fifteen moves, his pieces were misplaced, and Kasparov's pair of bishops and queen-side rook dominated the board. After a half-dozen more moves, Karpov was down a pawn and his position was technically lost. And then he staged a remarkable marathon defense. For many moves, he dodged and weaved, avoided Kasparov's mating threats, sacrificed an exchange in order to survive, and when the two players neared the fortieth move, both in time trouble, it was Kasparov who once again played inaccurately and squandered most of his advantage. The preeminent Russian chess coach, Mark Dvoretsky, will remind a gifted student that if he has a poor position but remains alert, sooner or later he will have an opportunity to pull himself back into the game. The fifth world championship match between Kasparov and Karpov was proving this again and again.

But when play resumed on the second day of game 16, Kasparov still retained an edge. The world champion was up the exchange for a pawn, Karpov's black pawns were disconnected, which made them vulnerable, but on the other hand, the players had bishops of opposite color, which often made winning in the ending difficult. Within a few moves, Karpov's defensive idea became clear. Using his bishop, knight and two central pawns, he created a fortress in the center of the board for his king. The pieces controlled many squares, making it hard for Kasparov to break through. At this point, grandmasters in Lyon gave Karpov excellent drawing chances. But Kasparov kept coming ahead. He squeezed Karpov with his rook, bishop and king, edging in, eventually loosening Karpov's pawns, the main pillars of the fortress. The structure began to change in shape, then apparently fell away in different directions, but suddenly erected itself again, this time more formidably. It was all part of Karpov's plan and was nimbly shadowed by Kasparov. "For thirteen games, I couldn't beat Karpov," said Garry. "Unbelievable, thirteen games. And then I had a chance to win. A chance. But Karpov showed a great defense." By move sixty-five, most grandmasters in Lyon, including former world champion Boris Spassky, considered the position drawn and Karpov's defensive conception absolutely dazzling.

The assessments and predictions of even top grandmasters often have a static quality, however. Their conclusions are reasonable enough based upon a current position, a snapshot in time, but they often miss the living and slithering progression of the game, which can only be truly felt by the players themselves. "Karpov created a castle for his king," said Kasparov. "But . . ." The world champion shook his head slowly, and sniffed the air, as though recalling a rotten smell from within the fortress.

At the very point where most analysts were predicting a draw, Kasparov realized that somewhere very far ahead, perhaps forty or fifty moves ahead, if he could combine mating threats with invasionary probes of his king and bishop, then he could once again shake the house apart and this time win. He continued to maneuver patiently, slowly dominating squares near and within Karpov's defensive setup. His little probes caused Karpov to weaken himself, and cracks appeared in the walls of the fort. Soon, Kasparov controlled Karpov's knight with his bishop, taking away all its moves. Towards the end, Karpov was a fighter with one arm, and worse, he had been maneuvered into a situation called *zugzwang*, which meant that *any* move he made had to be self-weakening. When Karpov resigned on the 102nd move, Kasparov's king had invaded the fortress and he was about to deliver mate.

"The psychology of the match had changed," said Kasparov afterwards. "It's something you can't explain if you're not playing these games. In games thirteen, fouteen, and fifteen, there were hints of a change, of a different direction. The results of games are important, but it is also important to notice the shift of direction in the match. You can feel it. In game fifteen, Karpov had a big advantage and could win, but in the end he was worse and I offered a draw in a very good position. Somehow this was linked to my win in game sixteen. Why? I don't know why. Except that as a player, you can sense when you are ready to press an advantage and sometimes it relates to the games that came before."

The progression of draws had ended. One can imagine how devastating the loss of this marathon was for Karpov. He had been so close to winning a half-dozen games in New York and Lyon, and now this. One might have imagined him reeling with the unenviable task ahead of having to make up two wins in the final eight games— and this psychological deficit alone made his performance in game 17 all the more remarkable. In this one, he simply destroyed Kasparov, who appeared weary following the long sixteenth game. Karpov tricked Kasparov into small positional mistakes and then slowly took control of key squares all over the board. After he had cut the knees out of Kasparov's feeble counterplay, his win was simple.

Karpov's fans might have predicted such a comeback. In the past, he had been remarkably resilient following Kasparov wins, often gaining back the point in the following game. But it was hard to understand how either of them could come back from such heart-breaking losses. Kasparov was probably the more vulnerable at such times. After every defeat, he struggled with self-doubt, and his sense of failure often overwhelmed attempts to be lighthearted and opti-mistic. Immediately following the loss of game 17, Kasparov was inconsolable and slipped into a long simmering rage. In the imposing mansion where he lived on the Boulevard des Bêlges, across the park from the Palais des Congrès, his trainers and his wife maneuvered to stay a room or two apart from him. "Things are very, very bad here," his mother told me, when I visited the following morning. Garry was upstairs in a funk. "He has no emotional energy to fight any more," she said, as though describing the end of the championship. Defeat hung on Klara like a shawl. A few minutes later, I spoke with Garry's friend from Azerbaijan, Kadzhar Petrosean, and he said almost the same thing. "Very bad. Very bad." He shook his head sadly. Masha gave me a sorrowful smile. All of this despair and rage. She had never imagined that defending the world championship would be like this. The walls of the mansion were bleak with losing. The park outside the big picture windows in the living room was gray with winter gloom. The entire house—wife, mother, cook, trainers, driver—was in mourning. How do you gather yourself to win from such a condition of misery?

Karpov was beginning to resemble the Karpov of 1984, who had pulverized Kasparov in the Hall of Columns in Moscow at the beginning of their first match. Confidence swelled through his body. His haughtiness was damning. While he played his first moves in game 18, he hardly glanced at Kasparov's responses, and played very swiftly, building up a big advantage on the clock. Several times, he looked out at the crowd, as if they were his legion. In the opening, he offered a pawn sacrifice in exchange for play in the center of the board, and the advantage of two bishops as opposed to Kasparov's two knights. It was a carefully prepared line, and on the twenty-first move, as Kasparov scratched his head, Karpov strode off the stage as a kind of exclamation point.

When Garry sees a new variation, his first response is often surprisingly casual. What is Karpov up to here? Garry raises an eyebrow. Rocks his head from side to side. He looks with the curiosity of a tourist in a new land.

Three of Kasparov's coaches, Dolmatov, Gurevich and Azmaiparashvili, were sitting behind Klara, Masha and myself. They were discussing Karpov's novelty and how Garry should answer it. In risky situations, Mikhail Gurevich sometimes counseled Garry to seek practical solutions that held a measure of safety, but Garry tended to go for broke. The coaches were still annoyed with Garry after game 17. He had played badly, and then afterwards had become angry at them. And now here was this novelty, which no one on the team had anticipated. If Garry lost this game, there would be hell to pay tonight. "What can you do?" one of them remarked. The trainers reminded me of coaches in the National Basketball Association who got together for beers after the game and commiserated that no matter how well you mapped out the play, if your guys didn't make the jumpers, you lost. During the past two and a half months, Kasparov had missed a lot of open jumpers.

Klara sat with her head leaning to the side. She could not bear to look at Garry. She turned around and asked a question of Sergey Dolmatov, a candidate for the 1993 world championship. He answered her politely. This, too, was part of his job.

Now Garry was digging into the position, layer by layer. What does Karpov want? What is my enemy here? Are these two bishops so powerful? What about the pawn sacrifice? Is it any good? Should I give it back? What does he expect me to do? How can I surprise him? After a period of looking and sensing, he began to calculate concrete variations. The tendons in his face were working. His jaw was grinding. After a time, he smirked, seeming to say, this sacrifice will win Karpov nothing. The audience was reading all of this by watching Kasparov on the big screen. He was a fan's delight. His face told every secret.

Klara looked off to the side. Occasionally, she turned her head a little to glance at the image of her son, but never at Garry himself, though we were sitting no more than a dozen yards away. Most of the time she stared off into space with eyes that were tiny slits.

Garry wiped his mouth with his thumb and forefinger. It was a gesture which said, let's clear the slate and look at this one more time with a fresh perspective. Let's try to see the position more clearly.

In the pressroom, I noticed that the fourteen-year-old Rumanian prodigy, Gabriel Schwartzman, was having a conversation with Michel Noir, the mayor of Lyon. Gabriel was a remarkable child. At the time, he was very short; with his baby face and bangs he could have passed for eleven. But Gabriel spoke five languages fluently and was one of the three or four best chess players in the world for his age. I had known him for several years, from international youth tournaments, and whenever we spoke I had the uncomfortable sensation that he fully grasped my meaning while I was still struggling to bring it into focus. Gabriel sought out adults for conversation; he had

little interest in palling around with other teenagers, but was pleasantly curious about them. When he was with me, he would inquire
about Josh or relate an observation of his own about my son, as if
we were two caring parents engaged in shop talk. I had never seen
Gabriel run or play, except with chess pieces or a computer data base.
To get to chess tournaments around the world from Rumania, he had
learned how to wheel and deal with organizers, airlines and sponsors.
Like Kasparov, young Gabriel knew that his chess life had forced big
trade-offs. His arresting smile played against gestures that were
road-weary, and hinted of an awareness of the transitory nature of
things.

Gabriel spelled out to Michel Noir the terms of a match he desired
between himself and Eloi Relange, the youth champion of France.
From his confidence and tone, it sounded like he was tidying up a
done deal, though this was the first that the mayor or anyone else
had heard of it. Gabriel spoke of appearance fees, the prize fund, even
suggested a playing site in Paris, unless Noir preferred to have it here
in Lyon. Noir, one of the smoothest politicians on earth, was taken
aback by the composed quality of this short boy with his Buster
Brown face and weary eyes. The mayor was at a loss for words, and
while he vacillated, Gabriel noticed me standing by and immediately
improvised boldly. Since he was planning to go to the United States
soon to play the champion Joshua Waitzkin, he said, with a pregnant
glance in my direction (which I took to mean, Mr. Waitzkin, why not
a match between me and Joshua?), the U.S. match would provide
momentum and advance publicity for the French match, which would
make it attractive for a commercial sponsor. Perhaps Air France
would be interested? What do you think, Mr. Noir? Noir did not
know what to think. Young Gabriel was a show-stopper. He and his
father had arrived here from Rumania like gypsies, with little money
in their pockets and nowhere to stay. In the pressroom, Gabriel
traded his bewitching smile for peanut butter and jelly sandwiches,
which he shared with his father. While I watched him, I was again
reminded of the privations of this sport. If Gabriel had been born
with comparable talent in tennis, he would already be a millionaire.
There is no other sport in the world like chess, where the world
champion can make millions and the third or fourth in line is fortu-

nate to make a few thousand, and after the first twenty, you're out of luck, buddy.

"They have both lost their confidence, but the question is, who is more afraid?" Former world champion Boris Spassky was commenting on game 18 for several journalists who were taking notes. Since losing the world championship to Bobby Fischer, Spassky, an engaging showman, had spent much of the past twenty years traveling the world doing analysis at important tournanments, and giving simultaneous exhibitions and speeches in which he described his match with Fischer and enticingly alluded to recent conversations on the phone with Bobby. Occasionally he played in serious tournaments. But now, in his early fifties, Spassky seemed to lack heart and stamina. In such events, he often sought quick draws, much to the dismay of tournament organizers who had paid his appearance fee. Before the reporters in the pressroom, he was pompous, theatrical, funny. He imitated the high nasal speaking voice of Karpov. Mimicking Kasparov, he lumbered around like a gorilla on speed. He grabbed his nose with his hand to signal that there was something rotten about how Karpov and Kasparov were playing, but teasingly refused to elaborate. Then he crossed his fingers to signal that the game would be a draw. "They do not want to fight." His melodic voice dripped with disgust.

Nearby, grandmaster Iosif Dorfman was speaking to another Russian grandmaster. "They both play very strange," he said, in response to Karpov's pawn sacrifice. Dorfman is one of the several great chess trainers in the world. From 1984 through the last match, he had been a respected member of the Kasparov team, but this time he had not been asked back. "When you are on the inside, you have a feeling for the order of the openings," he said, meaning that the players cunningly set one another up for later games with opening choices in earlier ones. "But now." He shook his head. He didn't know if Kasparov had lost all direction, or if being on the outside, he had lost all perspective. After serving on Kasparov's team, to be a spectator was strange and humiliating. Dorfman was confused about why he had not been invited back.

Later, Garry explained to me that it had been nothing personal. "We needed a little change," he said. "A breath of fresh air. Each time

I like to change one member of the team. Bring in some new ideas."
It made sense, but it was also cold-blooded. Dorfman's dismissal did
not leave him in the same position as, say, a professional football or
hockey coach who has lost his job but knows that he is likely to be
picked up by another team in the league. In the chess world, the
descent from the world championship team is precipitous. In the
pressroom, Dorfman looked forlorn, a man who had been cast out of
paradise. Maybe in the next match, Mikhail Gurevich would be on
the outside looking in.

Kasparov has said that, in the struggle to outdistance one another,
he and Karpov have been able to push the outer limits of the game.
At the same time, each has learned to play in the style of the other.
In game 18, while Kasparov pondered his response to Karpov's pawn
sacrifice, he found himself having to defend a relatively passive
position while up a pawn. He was the guinea pig, as it were, for
Karpov's carefully-devised gambit, a classic role reversal. "There is
no question that the novelty is a good one," offered senior master
Maurice Ashley, who was known for his own creative sacrifices and
tactical melées. "It creates a lot of problems for Kasparov."

"Karpov decided to use this innovation because he knows that
sometimes after I've lost a game, I'm vulnerable in the next one,"
explained Kasparov. "He wanted to catch the initiative." But in this
match so far, novelties had often failed. The one who had had to play
against the deeply-researched innovation, with his back against the
wall, so to speak, had often found inspiration to create a winning idea
over the board. "Game 14 showed something about the psychology
of innovations," observed Kasparov. "I made an innovation. It was
a long, exciting plan. But in my home preparation, I had made an
error. In the game, I spent twenty-eight minutes on my first eighteen
moves, and Karpov spent one hour and forty-two minutes. Later on,
when the complications started, Karpov was better prepared for it.
[He understood the position better.] He made better moves and got
to a winning position. I had to concentrate very hard to save the
game . . . Of course, sometimes the innovation is very good and
wins," he added.

The pressroom was far more populated than usual for game 18, because Bessel Kok, chairman of the Grandmasters Association, had scheduled a GMA meeting for that evening. In the past few months, the chess world had slipped into a state of organizational chaos. In the June agreement between the GMA and FIDE, the two warring organizations had agreed to split a share of revenue from world championship matches and to divide a number of organizational responsibilities pertaining to chess worldwide. But in the months since it had become less clear who was in charge of doing what. The grandmasters tried to address this muddy question. Then they squabbled for an hour over several technical rule changes.

There was an air of unreality about the meeting. In the theater and on the monitors in the pressroom, Kasparov offered a pawn sacrifice to win back the initiative. None of the grandmasters seemed to notice or care. This was arguably the pivotal game of the match, but Bessel and the grandmasters were locked into their own agenda. It was as if the commissioner of professional football were holding a league meeting to debate the merits of instant replay, while Joe Montana was in the midst of a thrilling fourth-quarter drive in the Super Bowl.

Making things even more bizarre, many, if not most, of the propositions discussed directly or indirectly impacted upon the world champion. Should the current practice of adjournments during tournaments and the world championship be continued? The ensuing debate was grave and acrimonious, as though the outcome would be written in chess history for centuries to come. But if Kasparov retained the championship, he would certainly refuse to allow this board to legislate any change in the playing rules for his defense in 1993. What about the grandmasters' ambitious plans for GMA tournaments in the future? Little more than wishful thinking. No one at this meeting knew if Kasparov would even agree to play in GMA tournaments, and without his name and charisma, it was difficult to believe that organizers would put up big sums to hold these events.

The grandmasters seemed oblivious to the futility of their decision making. Running through this lengthy meeting was a general distaste for Kasparov, and a reckless optimism that professional chess could do without him. Garry's withdrawal from the GMA before the match had angered a number of his colleagues, who grumbled about his need to get his own way. One of the grandmasters called Garry "a demagogue impersonating a democrat," and another branded him "a typical communist." A large majority of the players favored Karpov in the match, and several days before, when he had won game 17, a group of them stood and cheered. In 1984, Karpov had been much hated in the chess world, but grandmasters in Lyon were calling the new Karpov "a regular guy" and "a gentleman," claiming that when you got to know him, "he was very kind."

Bessel seemed to be the only one who truly understood that without Kasparov the GMA was an empty shell. He wanted Garry to take back his position as president of the organization. Privately, he spoke of his break with Garry sadly. "It was a good synergy between us," he said. "A very forceful, driving top chess player and someone who could structure and think strategically how to build up an organization. Garry and I both wanted to have a totally independent organization [from FIDE], but I like to make tangible progress, to sign a contract and then get on to the next goal. Garry is the man who says no way, we have to go full bore, no compromise. He thinks I'm too slow. I think he is too rough. He says we should take over the interzonals.* I say, who is going to organize it? Who's going to find the sponsors? Garry is always one year ahead. He doesn't look backwards. He always looks forwards. I admire him, but he doesn't [think in terms of infrastructure]. We have to create a strong base. Sometimes Garry makes jumps in logic. We must build step by step, and he doesn't think this way."

As the grandmasters debated into the second hour, Nigel Short, who was considered a possible challenger for the championship in 1993, introduced a new topic—the necessity to focus more or less exclusively on improving the careers of only the very strongest of the world's grandmasters. The organization was in no position to assist weaker grandmasters as well, he said. While Nigel was explaining his position, which made a few of his lower-rated colleagues

*The regional tournaments to choose the qualifiers to compete in the candidates matches. The winner of the candidates matches is the challenger for the world championship.

uneasy, fourteen-year-old Gabriel Schwartzman raised his hand from the back of the room. "Gentleman," he began in his Rumanian-accented English. "Vat about the children? Vat about the children?" Gabriel pleaded that the GMA must find some means of financial assistance for talented but impoverished teenagers around the world who wanted to develop into strong players. If not, he said, professional chess was ultimately doomed. While Gabriel spoke, I recalled the army of children in the streets of Timisoara, Rumania, where I had first met him at the international youth world championship two years before. Rumanian players with unsmiling faces and threadbare clothes had seemed physically hungry for wins when they squared off against rosy-cheeked Western opponents wearing high-performance Nikes. The grandmasters in Lyon had no answer for Gabriel. "Vat about the children?" Gabriel's unexpected plaint silenced the drone of chess politics for a minute or two, and soon after the GMA meeting sputtered to an end.

I returned to my seat in the theater beside Masha. "What do you think of the position?" I asked her. "Maybe it's a draw," she said, fearing that it might be worse and hoping that I would contradict her.

Klara's countenance was unchanged from two and a half hours before. She looked off to the side through eyes that were glazed and distant. While Garry played, his mother experienced their doom. The loss of the game. The loss of the world championship. Her eyes were unfocused, like someone in a trance.

I felt compelled to break through the black cloud. "Everyone in the pressroom thinks that Garry is winning," I whispered to Masha.

"Really," she answered, terrifically surprised but at the same time trying not to betray any emotion to Klara. It was not suitable to appear happy next to a mother who was holding a tragic vigil. But from being a chess parent myself, I suspected that Klara was also playing a tricky high-stakes game. If she suffered the loss powerfully enough, maybe the gods would take pity. She had already endured so much pain of losing. Garry had no more energy to go on. They were both so needy. If she could convey this convincingly . . .

On some level, Klara's pain played a role in the game that was going on a dozen yards away. Garry has said that he is aware of his mother's suffering while he plays and that her involvement is necessary. "We are connected," he says. "One unit." She concurs. "Every move he makes is a piece of my life." They both feel that her suffering will enhance his power to win. But in the fifth hour of game 18, her anguish was starkly in counterpoint to what was happening on the chessboard. After thinking for an hour, Karpov had made a mistake declining Kasparov's pawn sacrifice. He had hoped to maintain something of an attack, but his evaluation of the position was faulty. After Garry had deftly blocked all of Karpov's play, he was up a pawn and going after another. Kasparov held a big advantage. He kept improving the placement of his pieces. He chased Karpov's queen off a key central square and was preparing to push his passed pawn. He was playing wonderful chess. Garry looked toward our section in the audience and seemed to be sending a message. "Ma, Ma, will you look, I am winning."

It was a message that Klara did not want to hear. Garry turned our way three or four times, but she refused to meet his glance. Her face was averted to the side, as though to say, he has been winning many times in this match, and then he didn't win.

Garry was sobered. There were still obstacles. He needed to keep pushing Karpov's pieces back, to restrict their movement. He planned to trade into an endgame, but first he wanted to increase his advantage. Advantages have a way of disappearing in the endgame against Karpov. Perhaps Garry reminded himself, I am winning but I have not yet won. I had winning positions in games 3 and 6, but I didn't win.

The big screen above the players showed a close-up of Masha. In the soft focus she looked like a tragic heroine. The moment the camera switched to Karpov, she giggled. Masha's youthfulness and delight bubbled all around the edges of Klara.

On the thirty-sixth move, Garry brought his rook to the seventh rank. Bruce Pandolfini calls a rook on the seventh "a pig." The rook is a beast there, living in the enemy camp where it can feed on the opposing pawns. On the following move, Garry's knight jumped to a strong central square, and every amateur in the theater could see that he was completely dominating Karpov.

Karpov was pushing himself to the limit to defend. His lips quivered while he calculated variations, all losing. Every ten or fifteen seconds, he took little glances at Kasparov. The glances were like a nervous tic and Kasparov never looked up. He was riveted on the position. The silence in the theater was intense. Coughs sounded like little explosions. Karpov couldn't find a way to squirm out of this one. He had started this game looking like a king and now the reality of losing was seeping into him. Karpov touched his forehead with a trembling forefinger. Losing game 18, probably losing the match. He was nearly forty years old now. Maybe he would never fully recover after losing this match that he had had every opportunity to win. His cheeks looked bloated. His glances at Garry were pathetic. What will you do to me next? Like a fish squirming on the deck. What will you do to me next? Kasparov wore his cold killer face. He loomed over Karpov, calculating the most efficient method to finish him. On the forty-first move, after taking his time to think, Kasparov walked briskly off the stage as though he had an appointment. He went to seal his move, without having to worry that the camera might record what he had written. Then he came back on stage to calculate one more time, to double-check.

The following afternoon, when play resumed, Kasparov played swiftly and without error. He simplified into a rook and pawn endgame, which he won with economy and perfect technique.

The next evening, when I arrived at 17 Boulevard des Bêlges the snow was falling hard with four or five inches already on the ground. Before I had taken off my overcoat in the hall, Garry and Masha came through the heavy front door behind me, covered with white flakes, stomping their new fleece-lined boots. They had been walking and were fresh and happy from the new snow, deciding which movie they would go to see tomorrow afternoon. They hugged and kissed in the hallway. There were ski resorts nearby, and Masha said how wonderful it would be to go on vacation. Garry was always so busy. They had never been on a vacation together. They made an unspoken pledge to do it. Arm in arm, they walked to the living room, where Garry glanced for several minutes at CNN. They were still

holding hands, but she knew that she was losing him. He had been
away from chess for the entire afternoon. The muscles in Garry's face
began to tighten. Karpov is always dangerous after he loses. He
called sharply for Gurevich and Dolmatov, who were upstairs, and
within a few minutes the three of them were in a foyer off the
enormous living room, analyzing a variation in the King's Indian
defense.

Garry had to decide what he would play on Wednesday with
the black pieces against Karpov. The last three games had been
wins. Karpov and Kasparov were passing the pressure back and
forth with each game, and the pattern of wins now seemed as
imposing as had been the long streak of draws. It was crucial to
break the pattern. If Karpov won this next one, they would be
even once more and it would be Kasparov's turn to sweat it out.
For the next game, Garry was inclined toward a variation which
sacrificed an exchange for some initiative. He had played this in
game 11. Both trainers thought it was too risky. Gurevich argued
his point of view strongly in his deep, dramatic voice, moving his
knight ahead, tapping it onto the square with the end of his forefinger to emphasize the problem with Kasparov's setup. Kasparov,
who was sitting on an edge of his chair, smirked at the move and
threatened the knight, banging his pawn down as if it were a nail.
They continued this way through the lengthy variation, with Gurevich tapping his pieces into place and Kasparov answering almost
immediately with a move, followed by a resounding bang that
echoed through the mansion.

Masha and I were in the living room, glancing at CNN while we
talked. "I never dreamed that I would fall in love with a chess player,"
she said. "Because they are very reserved people, very diplomatic,
but Garry wasn't like that. From the beginning I was struck by how
open he was to all fields. We never discussed chess. We talked about
literature and the feeling of life or politics. When he read a novel, his
appreciation of the characters and of the author's theme was always
unusual, something I didn't understand or hadn't looked for.

"But then it seemed very scary to be in love with the world
champion. Because there is so much hysteria about chess in the
Soviet Union. He was hugely popular. So many girls wanted to be

in love with him. I wondered, how will I cope with it? And then, when we were first married, there were difficulties. Now I know that chess is his obsession and I know when to be in the background. There are times when I should go away, but at first I didn't know these things. I was newly married and in love and I thought that I should be in first place. It should be me and nothing else. At first, I felt hurt that there is chess and chess, and then Garry is a very social person; it was not only me. Garry belongs to the whole world and this was very hard to accept."

Play solid, was the message of Garry's two trainers. If you draw the rest of your games you win the match. But each time they tried to exploit their material advantage against his more speculative variation, he improved his position. Inch by inch, his guys came ahead. "The difference between us is that Gurevich thinks that there is a good practical way to play," said Garry. "He sometimes says to me, 'Come on, Garry, you're playing against human beings.' But I want to find the best, best, best. I'm looking for the best move. I'm not playing against Karpov, I'm playing against God." On each move Gurevich tapped his piece with his forefinger, a pleasing grace note, and Garry secured his own with a resounding rap. There seemed to be a tacit understanding that the trainers would not hammer their pieces into place as loudly as Kasparov.

"For the first months of our marriage, Garry's moodiness was difficult for me," continued Masha. "He can be very nice, attentive, affectionate, and then suddenly he is engrossed in his thoughts, or for some reason that I don't know he becomes gloomy. I've learned that it does no good to say, 'Garry, please don't let it happen.' You have to cope with it, wait. It is best to let him live through it. Then soon he will talk about what has been bothering him, share his feelings. At first it was distressing to see how absolutely changed he would become. Often it was a concrete problem, but sometimes not, and I began to realize it is his nature. Of course the worst time of all for him is if he loses a game. He is almost destroyed. It is a tragedy for him. You have to understand that for a person like Garry, to win is indispensable. If he loses, it is as if he loses part of himself. For this reason, I cannot even bear to consider his loss of the championship.

"Everyone thinks, world champion's wife, wealth, pink colors. There is another side to this. Now, when he is defending the title there is so much more pressure than in his normal life, and that life is many times more concentrated and tense than the normal life of most people. Many working couples come home every day and share domestic problems. But Garry is on the road a lot and often I cannot travel with him. Sometimes when I am with him, I have problems to discuss, but I feel that I cannot because I don't want to upset him, he needs to be in good form for a tournament or some public event. I try to protect Garry, but, you know, our lives are always on the surface. Everybody talks about us and all facets of our lives are written about. Journalists want more and more. I am a reserved person and I don't like it."

Garry's bang was lordly. You could hear it distinctly in the kitchen where Klara supervised Kadzhar's cooking. It pleased her. Klara was smiling, tasting the potato soup. The phone rang. It was Garry's friend Viacheslav Fetisov, defenseman for the New Jersey Devils, calling from New York to congratulate Garry on game 18. Klara was gracious on the phone, but she didn't want to disturb Garry's study, and Slava's jubilation also made her uneasy. "Not another word about congratulations," she chided. Klara felt as though she finally had things in order. Garry was leading the match, but was not overinflated with confidence. At this point, congratulations was not the right message, and besides, it was bad luck. During the match, Garry for the most part seemed oblivious to his mother's magical thinking. As he had grown older, he professed to believe less in superstitions than he had as a teenager, when lucky numbers and the use of parapsychologists were factors in his chess life. Now his attitude seemed to be: Who knows about these things? There is probably nothing to it, but what's the harm in covering all the bases?

After a few minutes, Klara came into the little room where the men were analyzing. Klara was not someone who blended into the woodwork. Her face suggested the direction of a powerful mind. She sat at the table and, resting her chin in her hands, began to analyze. This was one of the rare times during the match that I saw her enjoy the chess. She had wrung all the dread and suffering out of herself the night before. I was struck by how well she understood the game. She commented on Garry's weak pawn structure. She pointed at squares, made quiet suggestions. The two trainers were cordial. She was the boss.

In a nearby room, Alexander Shakarov scrolled through game after game on a computer screen. He was checking for King's Indian variations similar to the one that Garry had been looking at with Gurevich and Dolmatov. During the period of time that I had been a regular in Garry's homes on Martha's Vineyard, in New York, and now at the mansion in Lyon, Shakarov was almost always to be found sitting in front of the computer, like the radar man on a warship scouring the screen for bogeys. If he missed a little trick that someone had played in Bulgaria in 1976, it could cost Garry a game, it could cost him the championship. Garry and Shakarov had met in 1972, when Shakarov had been coach of the Azerbaijan junior team. They had worked together regularly since 1977, and I think that for Shakarov, life apart from Garry held little meaning. Love and loyalty were written on his gray, stern face. In January, 1990, after Azeri thugs had broken into Shakarov's apartment in Baku, Kasparov had managed to save his friend's family by using his local connections with the KGB. Sometimes Shakarov traveled abroad with Garry to tournaments, doing double duty as trainer and bodyguard. He guarded Garry so fervently that his manner was offputting. I believed he would not hesitate to step in front of a bullet for Garry.

As the men analyzed, Klara grew bolder in her assessments. The trainers responded seriously to each of her observations. She began to push Garry to play a move, looked to the two trainers for support, and finally Garry said with exasperation, "Ma, Ma," and turned his palms over, what are you doing? You are the mother, we are the grandmasters. She smiled and left the table with a girlish pout.

Again and again, Garry demonstrated that his understanding of the key positions was deeper than that of his trainers. His analysis was wicked, teasing. They could see to a distant point, but he would show them what lurked around the corner. "When I started working with Garry in 1985, for the first week, I couldn't sleep nights," said Mikhail Gurevich. "Every day he demonstrated feats of mind that were absolutely incredible." But this type of work was not the most comforting for a world-class grandmaster with championship dreams of his own. Garry's sneers must have made wounds. Great as they were, for months Gurevich and Dolmatov had been repeatedly forced to see that they were not in Kasparov's league.

"Thank God, Garry is not the president of the United States," Gurevich needled during dinner. "He thinks the United States should just drop a nuclear bomb on Iraq." Indeed, this was a somewhat simplified version of Garry's position. He had serious doubts that George Bush would push hard enough in a conventional war to finish off Saddam Hussein, and worried that the dictator was likely to remain a threat to peace for years. On other nights there were spirited arguments about the morality of using the big bomb, but during this dinner, Garry chewed his food and didn't comment. He wasn't in the mood for talking politics.

Kadzhar cooked his massive meat meals in the most unpredictable fashion. When I came here for dinner, there were always eight or ten at the table and he had prepared liver for one, beef for another, fish for me, chicken for Klara, rice for Garry, potatoes for Gurevich, and on and on. I asked Masha, "How does he know what to give to whom?" "It is part of Kadzhar's magic," she answered. We all ate Kadzhar's meals as though fortunate to have good food during bad times. Heavy and overcooked, they had little in common with the dainty sculptured delights Kasparov was served at Paul Bocuse in Lyon or at the Four Seasons in New York, but he seemed to appreciate these meals more. He ate with a peasant's relish, spearing more meat from the platter in front of him, reaching for a tomato or pickle and taking a big bite, not talking, chewing with ardor, his lower lip glazed with Kadzhar's sauce of sour cream and dill.

"Fred, did you see the championship crown?" he asked me after dinner, referring to the Korloff trophy, forged of bronze and gold and studded with more than a thousand diamonds. According to the organizer, it was worth a million dollars and would go to the winner, in addition to his share of the prize fund. "Don't you think it's ugly?"

"You could sell it," I said.

"But wouldn't that be immoral?" I went to answer but he didn't care to talk more about it. On most evenings I found Garry to be less accessible here in Lyon than in New York. He no longer seemed wounded and was much less inclined toward introspection. In New York, he had been beleaguered by a running commentary within himself about the nature of his problems, he had been thinking himself into paralysis. In Lyon, something had given and he was insatiable for the game.

After Kadzhar's high-cholesterol dinner and a piece of chocolate cake, Garry challenged grandmaster Zurab Azmaiparashvili to play blitz. Garry asked me to sit beside him, so that I might experience the heat and danger of the fray, but in truth, my sense was not of a man engaged in mortal combat; rather, Kasparov effortlessly directed great stores of energy and power towards poor Zurab. White or black, Kasparov was always the aggressor. He played each of the opening fifteen or twenty moves instantly. He built up a strong center with his pawns and pieces, as though laying the cinderblock foundation of a house. His center crawled ahead. Inexorably, he took more space, infiltrated Zurab's defense. He played without emotion, delicate fingers not so much making moves as releasing force. Zurab looked as though his neck were in a noose. Once or twice each game Garry paused for ten or fifteen seconds to calculate, and the energy of his attack spilled ahead as he pointed in rapid-fire fashion from square to square, there, there, there, there, until he freed his men to finish the rout. In each game, Zurab pulled back, trying to figure out how to save himself. His army on the run, Azmaiparashvili was a gun-shy general, sweat running down his face, running out of time, blundering soldiers, getting mated. "Come on," Garry said impatiently, giving him a move back. He didn't want blunders ruining the game. Then he grew bored. Not enough resistance.

Following the blitz games with Azmaiparashvili, Garry and all the trainers, besides Shakarov, sat at the dinner table playing poker before bed. Shakarov remained in front of the computer screen, searching for problems on the horizon. Klara sat a few feet away from her son, knitting and nodding to some secret tune. After an hour or so, when Masha guessed that her husband was nearly finished, she came down the stairs and watched the men with an earnest expression. The snow was still falling and the mansion beside the park felt warm and sleepy.

On many off-days, Garry played blitz games with his trainers or with visiting grandmasters. He was reveling in chess. One night, when all the trainers were off to a movie, he began to analyze a position with two elderly friends from Moscow. The white side appeared to be winning, but the advantage was elusive. The game was a remarkable puzzle. The two men, lifelong students of chess, were caught in its enigma, but not as absolutely as Kasparov. As the hours passed, the men moved off from the table and came back, but Kasparov never moved from the board. He murmured over moves, smiled lovingly at times. Watching this, I felt the game of chess as a powerful river with no beginning, no end. A lover of the game might travel on it for a lifetime. A great one, like Kasparov, would change its direction a little, but the river remained essentially the same. Around midnight, when the two old men finally left the mansion, Garry hardly noticed. The world champion was alone, his lips moving through the variations, as though consorting with a companion.

Although Manny Topol was hooked on chess, his editors back in New York were more reserved. "Manny, we hope you're not calling in with another tension-packed draw," was a greeting he received more than once when he dialed the office. Always a tad insecure about his chess analysis, hoping for page one but suspecting that his story would be relegated to the bottom of a page in the middle of the book, Manny would respond, "This is really big," before beginning to dictate. But Manny knew all too well that Kasparov's subtle control of the dark squares was not page one material. He was always on the prowl for something explosive, or at the least, something tasty with which to hook the average *Newsday* reader. Alas, during a long sports season, fans of the nineties had come to expect sex and corruption to go along with bunts and home runs. But game 19 offered little promise for sex and corruption. The opening was a lullaby. Kasparov had decided against the aggressive variation in the King's Indian, in the end heeding his trainers and choosing a more solid and slow developing line. After seventeen moves, there were no exchanges of pieces, and the tight picket lines of pawns indicated that there were no fireworks on the near horizon. The two grandmasters appeared to be settling into a game of subtle and intricate probes and maneuvers. Manny knew that his editor would not be enthusiastic about this opening.

Grandmaster Anatoly Lein sat at a nearby table, analyzing the opening with another eminent grandmaster, Yefim Geller, one of the few players in history to hold a winning record against Bobby Fischer. Though Lein was almost sixty, he was still a formidable opponent at international events. Most evenings, Lein and Geller sat alone, poring over the moves, making it scathingly clear that they didn't want strangers peering over their shoulders. Occasionally, when Lein would rise from the table, Manny, or myself or some other journalist, would approach the grandmaster, who had lived in America since 1976, to ask his opinion about the position. Lein was rarely forthcoming, and sometimes answered with a withering stare.

When Manny asked Lein his opinion about the opening of game 19, the grandmaster's response was even more offputting than usual. "I have no idea," he said, with a smug expression. Manny, the old sleuth, decided that Lein was keeping secrets.

In truth, Lein had perfected the art of the secret. I had known him for years, but on some days the grandmaster would look at me and walk past as though we were complete strangers. On other days, he would rush over as though we were special friends. He would drape a muscular arm across my shoulder and guide me to a secluded corner of the room. After looking around to make sure that no one was listening, he would begin to whisper urgently in his Russian accent, and soon I would be making furtive glances at anyone who might come within earshot, though the subject matter might be the difficult life of an American grandmaster, or even the gloomy weather outside.

If Anatoly Lein had a suspicious side, which might be said of a number of expatriate Soviet grandmasters, there was good reason. He had made his mark in the Russian chess world in the sixties and early seventies, at a time when the Party controlled the chess lives of its stars, and when a player, particularly if he was outspoken, had to concern himself with the KGB as well as the variations of his opponents. In the summer of 1992, the world was appalled to learn that East Germans had fed steroids to their adolescent swimmers to reap gold medals in past Olympics. For decades in the USSR, the Party had done much the same to its brightest chess players, trying to prove to the world that communist minds were the best. According to Lev Alburt, who was a top Soviet grandmaster in the seventies, the Soviet chess life was a reflection of the decadence and injustice of the society at large. Grandmasters were expected to do whatever was good for the state, and tactics were employed that were both bizarre and criminal. Alburt recalls that players were sometimes fed stimulants and encouraged to employ hypnotists. Top grandmasters were asked to draw or to lose key games in international events, when it would improve the chances of a countryman to win the event. As mentioned before, many Soviet grandmasters have related stories of KGB officials or chess bureaucrats blackmailing talented players into offering their brightest ideas to Karpov when he was the world champion. Alburt says that, to a lesser extent, grandmasters were coerced to work for Botvinnik and Petrosian, as well, when they were world champions, and that it was very risky for a player to refuse to help when he was asked.

Scores of top Soviet masters emigrated to the United States in the seventies and eighties, Lein among them, desiring political freedom, and concomitantly to free themselves from the intrigues and corruption of the Soviet chess life. They hoped that in the West free enterprise had operative significance in their profession. But arriving here, they soon discovered that the United States was a chess wasteland. Over the years, Lein has become embittered by his inability to make a decent living playing in U.S. chess tournaments. Despite his reputation in the Soviet Union as a prominent coach, it has been nearly impossible for him to find students here. But more, the U.S. chess world, in its spiritual and material misery, has spawned its own sad compromises. It is so difficult for strong masters here to make a living from the game today that, frequently, in the final round of a tournament, the two players vying for first place will agree in advance to draw the game in order to share the first and second place prize monies, and occasionally a down-and-out player will agree to "dump" the critical game and then split the first prize with the winner. Agreeing in advance to draw key games is so widespread in U.S. chess that strong players, as well as organizers, take it for granted, and in off-the-record conversations point out that chess professionals must somehow make a living. Recently I argued with several strong masters, who derided a third master for refusing to enter into such arrangements. "What's wrong with sharing the top prizes?" said one of them, outraged by the suggestion that prearranging games ripped the sporting heart out of tournament chess.

In Lyon, Anatoly Lein was perhaps more circumspect than usual about his ideas. A half year before, he had developed what he considered to be a very promising novelty. At this point in his life, Lein was more interested in achieving recognition for his ideas than in winning tournaments. He had worked on this idea for a number of weeks, written copious notes. Then he made the mistake of showing it to another top U.S. grandmaster. This man was soon to play in an important international competition abroad, and Lein decided that this tournament would be a perfect showcase for his novelty. "I said to him you can use it, but don't show it to anybody, don't analyze with anybody, and give me credit for this." Weeks later, Lein's novelty began appearing in various newspapers and magazines, played by a third grandmaster and credited as the brilliant conception of the grandmaster to whom Lein had loaned it. "There was nothing to be done about it," said Lein with resignation. He had written letters to various publications, but it was already too late, chess people already thought of the variation as the brainchild of the other man.

In the telling of this story, Lein seemed to be saying, this is the life of an American chess player today, there are too many of us, too little money, too little recognition to go around. In Lyon, with journalists hungry for quotes, it must have been tempting for Lein to give interviews and fill the morning newspapers with his analysis. But he was a proud man, and it seemed to me that while he desired recognition, he could not bear to take the risk of being embarrassed. He knew well that pressroom analysis rarely held up to scrutiny.

Sometimes it took weeks or more for a grandmaster to thoroughly understand a deep position of Karpov's and Kasparov's. He would let others take the glory or play the fool.

For several hours, game 19 was an exercise in fine tuning. Pieces maneuvered for tiny advantages behind their staunch lines of pawns. On move eighteen, Kasparov slid his bishop to the f4 square, a mildly provocative move. Karpov chased the bishop back with his knight pawn. That was what Kasparov had hoped for. By pushing the knight pawn, Karpov had weakened his kingside a little. But there were no big threats here, nothing that Karpov couldn't easily defend. Once again, spectators commented that Kasparov looked drained, and afterwards he said that he had felt weary before moving the first piece. His strategy was to try to draw this game, and then to go all-out to win with the white pieces in game 20. What he did not want was for game 19 to drag into an adjournment, so that he would have to play out a demanding position on the rest day. "Psychologically, I wanted to survive game nineteen," said Garry. "I wanted to survive and play game twenty. And this worked against me."

"They are like two fighters feeling each other out," commented Boris Spassky. "They are doing nothing. It is even." He crossed his forefingers to signal draw, draw, his face registering contempt. For the past few games, Spassky had been telling the press that Karpov and Kasparov were afraid of one another and that their play was feeble.

By the twenty-ninth move of the game, the position had reached a condition of stasis. Neither player was doing much and either might have offered a draw. But on the following move, Kasparov sacrificed a pawn in order to gain a strong queenside square for his knight. "This is a typical Kasparov decision," commented Maurice Ashley. "He sacked material for dynamic play. Maybe at this point in the game Kasparov knew that the right match strategy was to draw, but he is not the kind of player that can easily do this. He was wavering between planning to draw and craving to win."

This pawn sacrifice caused havoc in the pressroom. International master Jonathan Tisdall called it a blunder and predicted that Kasparov would lose. But after a few more moves, Tisdall and virtually everyone else had changed their minds. With Kasparov's rook deep into Karpov's queenside, and his queen controlling a key file, the world champion now appeared to be winning. "Kasparov's sacrifices are often more difficult to assess than the sacrifices of other grandmasters," observed Ashley. "He sees more deeply through the jungle of ideas, and therefore the compensation he gets is not as obvious, because it comes further down the road. When he sacrifices material, it appears that his opponent has many viable responses, but then when you analyze closely, you see that most of those are complete losers. In the pressroom, we watch his games and are inclined to say, look, Kasparov sacrificed a pawn, and he has nothing tangible in return, he has no attack, and there are weaknesses in his position, he must be losing. Then four or five moves later, with Kasparov's rook penetrating Karpov's position and another rook poised to deliver the death blow, we can finally see the value of the sacrifice."

Chess lovers in Lyon were just beginning to understand Kasparov's unexpected sacrifice and attack, when something odd happened. They observed the world champion and Karpov shaking hands. Many in the theater assumed that Karpov had resigned, but that hardly made sense, the position was bursting with fight. Now the two men began to analyze on stage. This was very strange to watch. They were both smiling, moving the pieces, chatting. They hardly seemed like enemies. I had never seen Kasparov listen so attentively to another player. Suddenly the crowd was rustling and murmuring. Word had spread that Kasparov had offered Karpov a draw. How was this possible? Wasn't Kasparov's final position completely winning? The two players continued to analyze together. Neither could bring himself to break off the exchange. This meeting seemed to cut through mountains of enmity, which further heightened the confusion of the audience. Toward the end of it, one could see that Kasparov's smile was more forced.

In the pressroom, there was bedlam. No one could figure out what Kasparov had done. Manny asked Lein for his comments, and the grandmaster said portentously, "Ask Spassky." Spassky was standing nearby, talking in Russian to several grandmasters. The former world champion's face was red and he was gesturing dramatically.

"I am more than disgusted," said Spassky to Topol. "This is unbelievable. I am shocked." Spassky was so upset that he lapsed back into Russian for a few sentences, then back into English. "Kasparov had the advantage and he [offered a draw]. I have never seen anything like this in my whole life. . . . I am sick over this. He is a beggar. My only thinking is that there was an agreement before the game."

Manny couldn't believe his ears. An agreement before the game! That means fix. The world champion fixing games! Manny couldn't wait to call his office with the news. His mind was racing. This is like point-shaving. Now I'm in my world. He recalled point-shaving cases he had covered. The last one had been the Boston College scandal in 1981, when the player Rick Kuhn had been sent to jail. Manny was searching for analogies for his *Newsday* readers. He would never forget the response of Sherman White's father, after his son had been indicted during the 1951 scandal involving Long Island University and City College players. White's father had said, "I sent my son to college to become a crook."

"They must have decided beforehand," repeated Spassky, who was surrounded by a large group of players and journalists. He was calmer now, with the aspect of a man who had been personally vindicated. He had been telling us for days that there was something strange about how they were playing, and here was the proof. "Why else would such a thing happen? In the end, Kasparov's position was completely winning," he reasoned.

But even while Manny listened to Spassky make the case for corruption at the world championship, he began to see the story disappearing in front of him. "I knew almost immediately that it didn't add up," he said, with a hint of sadness. "Almost always in point-shaving stories, organized crime is in on it. There is a lot of money to be made. Millions are down on the games, and they use a complicated network of betting. It can't be too obvious. I've written stories on this. But the mob isn't here in Lyon, booking action on King's Indians. What would be the gain for Kasparov and Karpov to agree to draw this game in advance? Why do it?"

As Spassky continued to claim fix, Jonathan Tisdall, unshaven, a little portly, and with the I've-seen-it-all-before-and-worse manner of a veteran war correspondent, was nearby, bringing some perspective to the scandal. "Boy, is Spassky going to feel badly about this in the morning," he remarked. "In every world championship I've covered, after two or three months the grandmasters on the scene become bored and homesick, and one or another of them begins to talk about a conspiracy or fix. It's bullshit. Just because a player gets nervous and makes a mistake does not make it a conspiracy." He explained that it was not unusual for a world-class player in the heat of battle to misjudge a position, to get nervous and offer a draw when he had winning possibilities. "I've done it many times," he added.

Late that night, I was rushing to finish an article on game 19 when Anatoly Lein knocked on the door of my hotel room. He wanted me to know that he and Geller had been analyzing for hours and had concluded that the final position of the game, promising though it had appeared for Kasparov, was unwinnable. He said that Kasparov's offer of a draw had been entirely proper and that other grandmasters in Lyon were beginning to come around to their view. It was unusual for Lein to approach a journalist with his opinions and he was very excited. I asked him if I might include his comments in my article and, after a hesitation, he agreed. This was no small decision for Lein, but this time he had decided to take the proper credit for his timely analysis.

The following afternoon, when I visited 17 Boulevard des Bêlges, Masha whispered that Garry had been brooding about game 19 all day. He had not yet heard about Spassky's remarks, and when I read them to him he appeared shocked. Later in the afternoon, I pressed him for a response. "I remember when I was a boy in the seventies and the Spassky-Fischer match was an issue in the Soviet Union," he began. "Botvinnik [the ex–world champion who was Kasparov's mentor] often made comments about the match. During his lectures he said that Spassky sold the match to Fischer, that Spassky lost the world championship because he was bribed by Fischer. I thought that what he was saying was very bad, and I said to him once, 'It is impossible, Mikhail Moiseyevich.' But he remained convinced. He is still convinced today.

"I think that he said this thing because of a disease that infects some ex–world champions. Botvinnik was feeling pushed aside. He was suffering from feeling unimportant, from feeling outside of the spotlight. And also he was jealous about the money that Fischer and

Spassky earned. When Botvinnik was world champion, the money was peanuts. And now I think that Spassky feels the same thing. People don't care about him anymore, so he tries to build his ego by attacking my character or my playing style, or Karpov's. Probably he's jealous that we are earning three million dollars in this match. I think he feels left behind by the world changing around him. He says these crazy things to be noticed for a moment or two."

I said to Garry that from watching him and Karpov on the stage, it appeared that they were becoming more friendly. "No, I haven't changed my mind about Karpov," he replied. "But you have to realize that he is the only serious opponent for me. I am talking chess with the number two in the world. I wouldn't go to a restaurant with him, but who else can I really talk with about these games? Spassky? Who else can Karpov talk with? Karpov is the man who understands chess at the same level as I do."

We were already seated at the table for dinner when Andrew Page arrived at the Kasparov mansion. Page quickly asked Garry what had happened last night, and Kasparov became red in the face while trying to push out the words. "I offered him a draw in a winning position, so what?" The game was eating him up. No one would be able to enjoy this meal. But I was the bearer of good news. I told Garry that I had spoken with Lein, and that he and Geller had determined that the final position was probably unwinnable and that his draw offer to Karpov was perfectly appropriate. Garry grimaced a little. "But unfortunately their analysis is incorrect," he said. "While I looked at it with Karpov, it became clear to me that I was much better at the end, maybe winning."

Although Kasparov concentrated much more effectively on chess in Lyon than in New York, his Soviet political life still percolated. After several weeks, the wives of Kasparov's trainers came from Moscow. At the Kasparov mansion, big meals were accompanied by stories of food shortages at home and of friends collecting paper, books and wood to burn in order to survive the long winter in case Moscow ran out of fuel oil. The wives spoke nervously to their husbands about economic collapse and political repressions that were surely coming. During the middle of December, political and business friends and associates of Garry's visited Lyon on a charter arranged by Andrew Page. They watched games, hoped for a word with Kasparov and spent long nights in their hotel talking about deteriorating conditions at home.

One visitor, Zhelnin Vadim, was a member of Kasparov's political party, Democratic Russia, which had about 25,000 members. "There are two main movements in the party," he explained. "In one, the approach is to have a party that will have the broadest possible appeal. In the second approach, mine and Kasparov's, the party must conform strictly to the principles of liberalism and anticommunism." Vadim conceded that this schism might ultimately hamper the effectiveness of the party, but argued that it would be wrong for the anticommunist faction to compromise. "It is clear that Kasparov's growing involvement in politics is a concern to Gorbachev, because Kasparov is so popular in his country, but mainly because he is so visible in the West." At the time, intellectuals in the Soviet Union understood that Gorbachev's main pillar of strength was his outside popularity. Sakharov and Kasparov were the two Soviets who had most consistently and visibly attacked the regime in the Western media, and after Sakharov's death Kasparov's opposition was even more conspicuous. In the first months of 1991, friends of Kasparov, such as his political mentor, Vladimir Bukovsky, warned Garry that his relentless criticizing of Gorbachev was not without risk.

"Right now, we all fear that there will be repressions coming soon, and no one knows what form they will take," Vadim continued. "Will there be the elimination of undesirable forces, Stalin's type of repression, killing people indiscriminately, or something more hidden? Some members of our party believe they will use hooligans to attack all real and perceived enemies. Soon it may be illegal for political parties such as ours to meet."

During the last weeks of the match, Kasparov looked forward to Vladimir Bukovsky's visit. A biologist by profession, Bukovsky had written chillingly about his years spent in Soviet concentration camps because of his political views, in the book *To Build a Castle: My Life as a Dissenter*. After gaining his release in 1976, Bukovsky had settled in Great Britain and had given up his profession to organize anticommunist movements. In the early eighties, he had founded Resistance International, an umbrella organization of anticommunist resistance movements worldwide, and later he had established an organization of freedom fighters, with branches within each of the Soviet Republics. In July, Bukovsky, along with Vaclav Havel, had organized a conference in Prague to address the problems of achieving a transition from communism to democracy in the Soviet Union. Kasparov had interrupted his training in Spain to attend for four or five days, and had been elected to the executive board, with some objections. Several members of the conference had complained that Kasparov had been a member of the Communist Party for years. Bukovsky had responded that Garry had broken with the regime in 1989, long before it became fashionable and even safe, before Yeltsin and the prominent historian Yuri Afanasyev had done the same, and had become one of the world's most effective critics of Soviet Communism. Bukovsky had said to friends that after spending years in the gulag with his life hanging by a thread, he had gained a sixth sense about who can be trusted. He trusted Garry.

During each of Bukovsky's several days in Lyon, he visited Kasparov in the late afternoon. The two of them would walk slowly off from the imposing mansion into the deep shadows of the Parc de la Tête d'Or. They spoke of the likelihood of civil war and what might be done about the present disarray of the anticommunist movement at home. During these walks, Kasparov looked solemn and much older than his years, his head inclined towards the graying Bukovsky, his hands clasped behind his back, like a president taking in the point of view of a trusted advisor. Bukovsky urged Kasparov not to return to Moscow after the match. He considered it dangerous, although only moderately so. He gauged that it would be politically imprudent for Gorbachev to kill the world chess champion, but Bukovsky predicted that after George Bush attacked Hussein in the Gulf, Gorbachev would take advantage of this "news cover" to rain harsh repressions upon all Soviet dissidents. Besides, he argued, Kasparov could do more for the cause speaking out in the West. "We can do more sitting here, trying to break through the barrier of the Western press," he told Kasparov. But Garry was determined to go back to Moscow after defeating Karpov. When they returned to the mansion, Kasparov would immediately begin preparing for the next game.

"Gorbachev is a good tactician and a lousy strategist," Bukovsky said one night, employing chess parlance to convey the idea that Gorbachev had bought himself time in power by clever maneuvers, but that he did not foresee the long-term consequences of his actions. "Mind you, he has been very cruel. He has used one nation to stir up another. Many people have died as the result of his tactics." Bukovsky argued that it was Gorbachev's repeated ploy to instigate ethnic conflict in the republics and then to rush in with troops to save the day. "In practice, Gorbachev has said that these stupid people are children who can't live without central power.

"Garry is very quick. I was amazed how fast he learned," said Bukovsky. "And because he is a chess player, you don't have to tell him much. You tell him two moves and he tells you the rest. He sees the whole field. But in truth, though he was a member of the Party when we started exchanging views, he had already arrived at similar conclusions about the system.

"Two years ago, we would meet and Garry would say, yes, yes, we have to do something. But our discussions were theoretical. I didn't feel that he was someone who would pull off his jacket and start working. But after the massacre in Baku, he was completely changed. It shocked him. It traumatized him. This spring he was speaking a new language. "The main enemy is Gorbachev," he told me. 'We have to finish off Gorbachev.' He was obsessed.

Asked about the likelihood of Kasparov's becoming a political leader, Bukovsky was uncertain. He characterized the world champion as an original thinker, with a strong grasp of Soviet and world affairs. "He has enormous potential, but Garry is overcommitted," said Bukovsky. "Now he seems to want a career in politics, but who knows in five or ten years? He might burn out before then. He wants the changes to come fast and they don't come fast. You have to be patient. Otherwise, you are easily traumatized. Also, if politics in the Soviet Union becomes direct and simple like in the West, Garry will become bored with it. I would never enter politics in the United States. I would rather collect garbage."

On December 20, several hours before Kasparov played a tense

adjourned position one afternoon, news shows carried stories about
the abrupt resignation of Soviet Foreign Minister Eduard Shevardnadze. In the foreign minister's parting remarks, he warned that the
Soviet Union was heading toward dictatorship. By and large, the
Western media interpreted Shevardnadze to mean that forces from
the right might soon topple the Gorbachev regime. Kasparov and
Bukovsky dismissed that view. "It is perfectly clear to anyone who
knows Soviet politics from the inside that Shevardnadze did not
mean that there was danger from the right wing," Kasparov said, a
couple of hours after drawing the game. "He meant that the danger
was Gorbachev. It was Gorbachev who was the potential dictator.
Shevardnadze has a good name in the West and he doesn't want to
lose his reputation. He has given this warning that Gorbachev's
government is preparing for war against its own nations."

"He was smart enough not to point to Gorbachev and say, you
are the bloody dictator, because then it would be his last day," added
Bukovsky. "Oh, a plane crash, a car crash, but he spelled out his
message for everyone in the Soviet Union."

I asked Garry if he had mulled over the meaning of Shevardnadze's
remarks while playing out the tough endgame against Karpov. "No,"
he answered.

"It never came to mind?"

"No."

In New York, such important news from home would have
nagged at Kasparov's moves and made the match itself seem trivial.
He would have been impatient to make calls to political allies in
Moscow to discuss the new crisis. "In New York, I would begin to
study chess, and I would say to myself, 'Mistake, mistake, you will
be punished for it. Politics is everybody'." But in New York, Garry
had frightened himself with his blunders and distracted chess, with
his depression and inner chaos. He had tasted defeat. During the
practice sessions and games in Lyon, he was focused purely on chess.

Early on in Kasparov's career and in his earlier matches against
Karpov, he had been a big favorite among both players and fans. But
now there was a decided drift. Karpov had many fans in the Lyon

audience. After years of enduring crucial defeats against Kasparov, the old world champion had taken on a noble cast. He had become like George Foreman, old and with a potbelly, but still throwing leather, someone with whom a middle-aged patzer might identify. A few years before, grandmasters had been thrilled by Kasparov's attacking style and intimidating energy, but players had become turned off by his aloofness, his unwillingness to compromise, by his appetite for the spotlight and his ability to win despite innumerable distractions—perhaps this was the biggest offense of all. It was belittling and even confusing for a grandmaster who had devoted his life to the game to watch Kasparov duel effectively against the number two in the world while maintaining his war of words against Gorbachev in interviews and articles in the Western press. Toward the end of the match, grandmasters were yawning over Kasparov's most brilliant attacks. One strong GM spent his evenings sitting in the snack area sipping espresso. His cultivated look of boredom expressed the complaint of most titled players in Lyon—we are fed up with this champion who is likely to hold the crown for the next twenty years. I asked this grandmaster about a particularly inventive Kasparov combination, and he answered curtly, "So what?"

Following game 19, the grandmasters in Lyon were giddy with the talk of scandal. Even grandmaster Bachar Kouatly, the organizer of the Lyon half of the match, could not resist engaging in gossip. "If it is true it is terrible," he said within earshot of Boris Spassky, who, before the start of game 20, was once again surrounded by journalists and players, holding his nose. "It stinks," he said. "It's terrible for chess when the players leave such a suspicion."

In the Kasparov house it was Masha who was most hurt by the surge of distaste for her husband. "Everyone roots against us," she said, referring to Kouatly and a group of GMs from the GMA who sat beside him during the games. "When we come into the theater you can see hate in their eyes."

By the morning of game 20, the talk of scandal, the glee and gossiping of other players had become fuel for Kasparov's rage. Garry was unapproachable. His trainers didn't want to be near him. Andrew Page and a friend came for breakfast, and left after ten minutes. But Klara and her son were conspiratorial in their silence.

Klara moved through the house moody and sullen. She was pleased by her son's fury, protective of it. She was certain that Garry would win.

It was hardly a game. Garry attacked like a hurricane. By move twenty it was clear that Karpov was getting blown off the board. No one watching was sure exactly where he had gone wrong. There must have been some terrible move. But Karpov hardly seemed a factor at all. The game had barely started and Kasparov's bishops, knights, rooks and queen were bearing down upon Karpov's king. Before playing the decisive combination, Kasparov rushed back on stage with his tie loosened, looking like a street fighter. When Garry unleashed his queen sacrifice, Karpov's face went to jelly—he never saw it coming. But by then his position was so riddled that if Kasparov hadn't won with this combination, he would have won with another. From the opening moves, the result of this game had seemed inevitable. With game 20, the match was essentially over. Karpov would have to win three of the remaining four to take back the title.

In the pressroom, while answering questions, Spassky's face was covered with sweat. A reporter asked, "What sense would it make to prearrange the draw in game nineteen and then win this one with a blitzkrieg?"

"Now I don't know what to think," Spassky managed. Two days later, when the former world champion was again questioned about game 19, he admitted that he must have been wrong.

Kasparov elected to take a time-out following game 20. Typically, the loser of a game in a world championship decides to take the time off, but after his powerful win, Kasparov was elated and felt that he needed to regain his equilibrium.

After a three-day break, the twenty-first game was played on December 19. It was a titanic struggle, with the initiative seized and then lost again and again. Late in the middle game, Kasparov was losing ground. With his king under attack, and his pieces in disarray, many thought that he would lose. Kasparov defended tenaciously, trading queens to stop the mating threat, but giving himself an inferior endgame. He was able to negate Karpov's advantage in the ending by maximizing the potential of his few pieces and finding unusual ways to attack. In the later games of the match, Garry was confident of his ability to save difficult endgame positions. It pleased him to outplay Karpov at his own specialty. After the drawn twenty-first game, Karpov called for a time-out.

On Saturday, December 22, I came to Kasparov's house, looking forward to the usual late lunch, but everyone had already finished eating. Marsha offered to make me something, but I told her not to bother. Garry had spent the day reading *Master and Margarita* by Mikhail Bulgakov. It was his favorite novel and he had read it five or six times. He read passages of it aloud to Masha, while Beethoven played from the stereo. Garry was happy to have some time away from chess. He and Masha snuggled on the sofa, and after a time he stood and waved his arms in a silly imitation of a symphony conductor. All of Garry's trainers but Shakarov were off with their wives, and the big house felt hollow and chilly. In the bleak afternoon light, the living-room furniture seemed particularly unappealing: a frail seventeenth-century chair slid beneath a modern writing desk, a shiny new Scandinavian leather sofa beside an ornate eighteenth-century clock, paintings of different periods and moods clashing. The high-ceilinged room was a mismatch of pricey things put together at the last minute by the organizer, hoping to impress a difficult world champion.

"So maybe I'll win it next Wednesday," Garry said, and then at my surprise explained that the organizer had called that morning to ask if he would accept a technical time-out on Christmas, so that the staff could have the holiday off. It would mean nearly a week off between games. I was not thrilled by the news. Of late, there had been more time-outs than games. I had already explored Lyon and had eaten too many Salade Lyonnaise lunches with Manny Topol. I envisioned more winter mornings sitting in my little hotel room, staring at the green curtains, pining for Christmas in New York with my family. I was feeling homesick. It was difficult to say this to Garry, but I did, and then he didn't know how to respond. For some reason, I chose to prolong the awkwardness of the moment. I said something more about missing my kids. The vein in Garry's forehead swelled. I was changing the rules. Fred's melancholia was not on the agenda. After a minute, Garry replied that Bob Burkett (who had organized the New York half of the match for Ted Field) had flown into Lyon that morning from Los Angeles, only to discover that the game had been canceled. After dropping in to say hello, he had immediately flown back to Los Angeles, a twelve-thousand-mile error. Garry laughed at this and I could feel my jaw tightening. What was the point exactly? If Bob Burkett could take it without complaining, I should be able to? We all have to be warriors?

Again, he read from the book. Then he spoke to Masha in Russian. I looked at him, and shrugged: What are you guys talking about? Garry took a deep breath. He was tired of translating for me, but he did. According to Garry, Bulgakov was the greatest of all Russian writers: Had I read *Master and Margarita?* I hadn't. It was Garry's opinion that this was the most important novel in the Russian language. Could I think of a similar example in American literature, a book that had influenced generations of writers? I mentioned *Moby Dick*, not quite able to recall from my college days exactly how Melville had changed the shape of American literature. Garry shook his head, no, he doubted that *Moby Dick* had been as influential as the Bulgakov novel. "Moby Dick was huge," I quipped, stealing a line from my friend Steve Salinger's novel, but wishing that I had been able to come up with a more crushing literary retort. Garry and I were peeved with one another. The match was too long. I was too much in his house. The unexpected days off would be a torture. Hoping for concordance, I mentioned that Tolstoy and Dostoyevsky were among my favorite writers, and Garry said that he had read them as a teenager and hadn't liked them. He urged me to read *Master and Margarita*. How could he not like Tolstoy? I resolved not to read *Master and Margarita*.

"Perhaps if you read Tolstoy and Dostoyevsky when you are older, you will feel differently."

"Maybe," he said.

Some friends of Garry's from Moscow dropped by, and he went with them into another room to talk. I began to think about leaving before the end of the match. For all practical purposes, the match was over. Garry would have to lose all three to lose the championship and I already had more than enough material for my book. I told Masha that I was thinking about going home early. There was a direct flight from Lyon that left at noon the following day. In order to go, I needed to talk to Garry for fifteen or twenty minutes about the past few games, for an article that he and I were coauthoring for the international weekly, *The European*. This change of plans made Masha uneasy, but I didn't think too much of it. I had decided to go home for Christmas.

Garry's friends left after an hour, and he immediately went into the computer room and replaced Shakarov, who was pained to break off his search for dangerous variations, at the terminal. Garry called up a video game and began to play. After a few minutes, I walked over to him, and without looking up from the screen, he proposed that we should get together tomorrow, he was in a bad mood. I answered that I needed to speak with him for a few minutes this evening. "Go ahead, I'm listening," he said, while punching the keys. Josh and I had played out this same scene many times in the past. "Go ahead, Dad, I'm listening." I wanted to rip Garry's hands off the keyboard. While he pushed the buttons and bobbed and weaved with his head, I explained that I wanted to return to New York tomorrow, but that we needed to talk tonight about the past few games for our article. "Can't we speak about this tomorrow, Fred?" he said. Trying to remain calm, I explained that tomorrow was the only direct flight of the week from Lyon to New York and it left at twelve noon. If we didn't work for twenty minutes tonight, I would have to take the train to Paris to get back to New York.

"I'm not in a good mood now," he repeated, while sneaking a look at his burgeoning score.

"How about tomorrow morning at nine?" I asked, trying to calculate if I could still catch the plane.

"You know that I don't like to talk in the mornings. Why don't you come about twelve and we'll take a long walk and work afterwards." Twelve! What was this about? Garry's self-indulgence was maddening. He banged the keys, smiling like a video junkie. Was he paying me back for Tolstoy and Dostoyevsky?

I walked back to my hotel, kicking the pavement. I wasn't going home for Christmas. On the phone from New York, my wife Bonnie reminded me that Garry was in the middle of playing for the world championship. Funny, but I had forgotten. I was stuck on the idea that he disliked Tolstoy and Dostoyevsky and wouldn't look up from the video game. Being friends with Kasparov, particularly when he was engaged in combat, was not an association involving two equals. During a world championship match or strong tournament, Garry catered to himself more or less exclusively, brought himself into form for each game with a regimen of chess study, stimulated by politics, literature, video games, friends, in just the dosages that felt correct. But even during more peaceful times, friends of Garry's came to realize that in almost every interaction, choosing the moment to talk, walk or eat, Garry's sense of timing prevailed. It was an unspoken covenant in all his relationships, except perhaps with Klara.

During the past year, I had come to recognize that Garry was different things to different people, and that it stimulated him to try on different personae much as he renewed himself as a player by trying new variations in the opening. Despite Andrew Page's criticisms of Garry's fledgling business adventures, he remained hopeful about the potential of Garry as an entrepreneur. Andrew had staked his future on Garry's success as a business mogul, and sometimes he must have bit his lip when Garry's eye was elsewhere and he was not in the mood to discuss the latest deal. For Vladimir Bukovsky, the match was background noise while he and Kasparov conspired to overthrow the evil empire.

For me, Garry revealed himself as the chess world champion who might have been a poet or novelist. Garry knew that I was most intrigued with his vulnerable side, and at times he risked showing me that part of himself. Perhaps it was my limitation, but I never entirely believed the public Kasparov, the haughty, disdainful, implacable warrior. Even while he mounted an attack against Karpov, his face hardened with resolve, I felt his vulnerability, how easily he could slip up and lose. As the father of a player, I have learned that while a fierce fighting face is reassuring to the player and to his father, and perhaps intimidating to his opponent, one false move and the best show of machismo goes to shame. While Garry played, I sometimes recalled him watching cartoons, searching for the little boy inside. I heard him wrestling with self-doubts. "Fred, I feel devastated . . . I feel empty."

But, while Garry fought Karpov, the little boy inside was perhaps an enemy. Their nine-hour games were a kind of death march, and to endure them was inconsistent with admitting to friends that he would feel better if they would remain in Lyon to the end, instead of going home for the holidays. I had forgotten too easily that there was hardly an hour during these past three months when the match did not nag and pull at him.

By the next morning I was on a more even keel. Garry was upstairs when I arrived. I chatted with Mikhail Gurevich for twenty minutes. "The other day, in the twentieth game, Garry saw the final combination early in the middlegame," he said. "He saw twenty moves ahead calculating deep and complicated variations. It was absolutely incredible." During the last two weeks, as Garry had come into top form in his practice sessions, Gurevich had yielded ground. Instead of sharply debating the nuances of a position, Gurevich had nodded his head, yes, yes. It also seemed to me that he had argued less with Garry about politics over dinner.

Gurevich spoke of the match reverentially, as he might describe it in thirty years to his grandchildren, the miracles that he had watched the great Kasparov perform. We talked a little about the Linares invitational in March, which would be the strongest group of grandmasters ever assembled in one tournament. Mikhail had been invited, and he was curious about the prodigy Gata Kamsky, who would also be playing. He wondered to what extent Gata's incendiary father would be a factor in the games. For Gurevich and the rest of the Kasparov team, this match was already history, although there were three games to go. Like me, they were making their plans to go here and there, a vacation, a tournament. Within this atmosphere of people getting ready to leave, thinking about their own lives, Garry still had to play the last three games.

Garry came down the stairs. He looked rested, happy. "How are you doing?" I asked.

"Much better than yesterday," he answered, an acknowledgment that something less than wonderful had taken place the previous evening. After chatting and looking around, sizing up the morning, he mentioned that his mother would be walking with us in the park. Soon they were both wearing new French walking boots trimmed in leather, fashionable here this winter, and Garry put on his brown English racing cap.

As we clumped through the hard snow, Garry and his mother discussed the building feud between the GMA and FIDE over which of them would organize the candidates matches. They spoke in Russian, with Garry pausing after five or six sentences to translate for me. His manner was subdued and, I thought, hinted at contrition.

Garry still wasn't sure what he would do regarding the GMA. He maintained that chess professionals had become dependent on the personal largesse of Bessel Kok, instead of establishing viable working relationships with commercial sponsors. For professional chess to work in the long run, he said, it had to be a business, with the potential of turning profits, rather than the plaything of a rich man. Kasparov disagreed on key elements of international chess management with Kok, but perhaps more to the point, Garry had crossed a line with Bessel. Their own power struggle had eclipsed discrete issues. Garry no longer trusted Kok and didn't see how they could continue to work together. Each time that Garry penned an article in a chess magazine explaining his position relative to the GMA and Kok, a dozen new articles came out attacking him, a deluge of criticism. For years he had been the popular boy on the block, and now it had become chic for grandmasters to call him a bully. Even Garry's old friends were speaking out against him, mostly relative to his decision to leave the GMA. His childhood friend grandmaster Lev Psakhis said that Garry's character had changed for the worst, that he had lost his way trying to live too many lives at once. Boris Gulko wished that Kasparov would devote himself more exclusively to chess.

This criticism was upsetting but it also cut both ways. Garry's horizons were different than they had been a few years before. More and more, Garry found that keeping company with other GMs was boring, limiting. But what to do about the GMA? Some of Garry's advisors were suggesting that he should enter into an arrangement with Ted Field to create a new independent organization for professional chess management, which would effectively take the world championship away from both FIDE and the GMA. Field had apparently indicated a willingness to support his plan, though it would split the chess world into warring factions overnight, and would probably result in each of several organizations claiming its own world champion. For the time being, Garry was inclined to do nothing, to stay on the sidelines and watch. The weariness on his face said that he had no heart for this particular war.

After forty-five minutes, we came to a lovely little zoo buried in snow. "Do you see the big lion?" Garry asked, his face suddenly spread into a smile. I had to look for a time before I saw the animal sitting on a snowy rock. Klara was ecstatic. She grabbed Garry's arm, said something in Russian, giggled. They had often come here together, and their happiness was so large and private that it felt odd to be with them. Klara gave pieces of apple to Garry to eat and then some to me, and when I tried to refuse, she said, "No, no, no." There was no choice. On the walk we must eat apples. Garry called Klara "Ma, Ma," so lovingly, and she chided him, "Garry, eat, eat."

We came to an empty pen, and Garry banged on the bars. He banged and banged. "Don't worry, he will come." Garry would have banged for an hour. This was important. After five minutes, a huge beast came lumbering out of a shed, a water buffalo with enormous thick horns. "I come to see him every day," said Garry, grabbing one of the horns and holding it firmly. Apparently, the beast was used to rough treatment from the world champion. When he let go, the huge animal licked Garry's hand and wrist with its thick tongue, and Garry fed him banana peels and apple cores. Then Garry wanted me to see the ducks. He knew each of them individually. "You must see this one," Garry said, pulling me along the lake. "Look at the intricate colors, as though it were made of porcelain. Look at the one over there. It is the creation of an impressionist artist, not a real duck." Garry laughed and laughed. "Look at its eyes. They're not real."

In half an hour we were back at the house, and Garry was on his way upstairs for his nap. "Will you stay for lunch?" he asked quietly. When I said that I would, he looked pleased. He is a most complicated man, and one must know the rules to be his friend. Garry would sleep, and I would read a magazine and watch CNN. In time, he would come back down the stairs and we would enjoy a big meal. For the past few weeks, he had been promising to tell me a story about his father. Perhaps it would be this afternoon.

Five days later, Kasparov began game 22 knowing that a draw would secure the world championship. But on move eleven, Karpov presented Kasparov with a choice, a variation leading either to a sure draw or to a murky game in which both sides had winning chances. Kasparov chose the latter. Later, it came out that Karpov's preparation had taken into account the likelihood that the world champion would almost certainly choose not to embarrass himself by clinching the title with a cheap draw.

In the ensuing middlegame position, Kasparov was once again forced to play the role of counterpuncher, adopting Karpov's style, while it was Karpov who tried to demonstrate that less was sometimes better than more: Garry was up a pawn, but he was forced to weight his material advantage against Karpov's dangerous piece activity. Toward the end, when Kasparov's position began to deteriorate, he once again relied upon his superb technique, forced a number of trades, simplified the position in textbook style, and finally clinched the draw by perpetual check.

And he clinched the title as well. Ironically, it was a stellar Karpovian effort by the champ which ensured his reign for at least three more years. The score stood at 12–10. Now even if Karpov managed to win the last two to tie the match at 12–12, Kasparov would still retain the title. The victory was his. But not completely. The last thing Kasparov wanted was to back into the world championship with a tie. Karpov would proclaim to the world that he was as good a player, and that Kasparov had retained his title only because of a technicality. This would be a nightmare for him.

In game 23, however, Garry collapsed. He had a bad position out of the opening and never played with conviction or a coherent plan. In the middlegame, when he was under attack and needed to make a solid defense, Kasparov threw away material for no reason. He did not seem to want to play on. "Kasparov unconsciously dumped this one," said Bruce Pandolfini. "He didn't even play like a good grand-master. He just didn't show up. Various commentators have specu-lated that since Kasparov had already won the world championship, he didn't have sufficient motivation for this game, but I don't think that's the whole story. Kasparov lives to make great art in chess, but he needs creative energy to raise the game to another dimension. He manufactures pressure, obstacles, crises, even distractions from chess, whatever it takes to get up for it. By losing game twenty-three, Kasparov put himself in a must-win situation in game twenty-four."

As the match approached the end, Manny Topol was understanding the game much better and had developed a hunger for it. Some veteran chess reporters in Lyon were impatient to leave, but Manny wished there were more games. Before falling asleep, he would think about sparkling piece sacrifices and tricky endings. Jonathan Tisdall and other reporters were discussing the category 17* tournament, the strongest round robin of all time, coming up in March in Linares, Spain. In serious tournament play, Kasparov had not finished below first place in the last ten years, an unbelievable record, but there had never been such a formidable field taking aim at him before. In Linares, Karpov would be seeking revenge, and the young stars Gata Kamsky, Viswanathan Anand and Vassily Ivanchuk would try to make their reputations by shooting down the champion. Manny was already figuring how to break it to *Newsday* that he should spend three working weeks in a village in the foothills of Spain. He needed to convince them that chess was a sleeping tiger in America. He would point out that there were persistent rumors that Bobby Fischer wanted to make a comeback. Fischer would put the game back on the front page. Linares might be a hard sell to *Newsday*, but Manny had an appetite for chess and its surrounding intrigues, and it was hard to say no to him when he wanted something.

While Kasparov and Karpov took time-outs near the end of the

*FIDE categorizes international round robins according to the average rating of players. The average rating of the fourteen players in Linares, 1991, was 2658, at the time the highest tournament average in the history of chess.

match, Manny wandered the streets of Lyon, trying to understand the tragedy that had struck the Jews in World War Two. Since he had been a boy, Manny had read Holocaust literature and questioned survivors. Both of Manny's parents had lost close members of their families in pogroms and concentration camps. The Jewish community of Lyon had been decimated. More than 4,000 had been murdered here, and twice that many had been deported to die by Klaus Barbie, known as "the Butcher of Lyon." One night, Manny attended services at a synagogue built during Napoleon's reign, and discovered that Garry Kasparov was a hero to the elderly congregation, though no one seemed to know the least thing about chess. Among Lyon's Jews, communism was synonymous with anti-Semitism; Kasparov was a friend of Israel, an enemy of communism.

One afternoon, Topol visited an elderly Jewish dentist who lived directly across the street from Kasparov's mansion on Boulevard des Bêlges. The man told him something of what it had been like back then.

"My father-in-law was killed by Barbie," said the dentist. "When my wife was a girl, she lived in this same apartment. She was walking in the street when her father was taken. When she came back home, he wasn't there. She waited for him and he never returned." The dentist turned towards a window which looked across the street to Kasparov's residence. Although he, too, knew nothing about chess, he was rooting for his famous neighbor, because he understood that Kasparov was sympathetic to Jewish issues. "Let me tell you something," he said, pointing to the house alongside Kasparov's. "Barbie arrested eighty Jews there." The dentist slapped his leg sharply three times. "They were shot right there."

Manny was determined to interview Klaus Barbie, who, old and sick, was being held prisoner in a jail in the center of the city. One day, Manny walked three miles from his hotel to the imposing stone prison, which resembled a medieval fortress. After walking around its entire circumference, Manny pounded on the tall, thick wooden doors. The guard who opened the peephole saw no one at first, because Topol is very short. Manny demanded an interview with Barbie, but they didn't allow him inside. Klaus Barbie died of cancer some weeks later.

A few days before the end of the match, Manny Topol, grandmaster Max Dlugy and his wife Marina visited a medieval village thirty kilometers north of Lyon. Dlugy, twenty-four, had been world junior champion at nineteen, and was now one of the strongest grandmasters in America. All afternoon, Manny struggled with his shyness. Odd, Manny thought, when he was with mob bosses or all-pro linebackers, he was perfectly at ease, but with great chess players he was nervous and a little bumbling. Nevertheless, he loved to hear about their intricate winning plans, their psych jobs, and their dreams of glory. Max Dlugy had spent the previous evening with Kasparov, and confided to Manny that he had beaten the champion in blitz, three games in a row. Manny reflected on this as the rented car sped through the Rhône countryside. Three games in a row against the world champion! He wondered if Kasparov had dropped three in a row before, but was too shy to ask Max. Maybe Max could be world champion someday, Manny thought.

Then on the drive back to Lyon, Dlugy surprised Manny with the news that he was retiring from professional chess. After graduating from high school, Max had given himself six years to become one of the top twenty in the world, and he had fallen a little short of that. Now, at twenty-four, with a wife and baby girl, he was resolved to try another career. There was no money to be made playing chess tournaments in America, and commuting from Englewood, New Jersey, to tournaments in Seville, Hastings or Haifa was not very sensible for a married man. Manny, who called his wife in Long Island each evening, could see the point. Max would begin a job as a foreign exchange trader as soon as he returned to New York. Lyon was his farewell to professional chess.

Manny took this in: a currency trader. Max sensed his disappointment and explained further. He had chosen chess over Yale and it just hadn't worked out. A young player couldn't get a first-class chess education in America. If he managed to become a grandmaster, he still couldn't support himself. Chess and America didn't make a good fit. America's most talented young players were making the same decision. Grandmasters Michael Wilder, Nick DeFirmian and Michael Rohde had also determined to give up professional chess so that they could earn a reliable living. It was the sensible thing to do, Max said, and Manny nodded.

Back in Lyon, Manny took his usual evening walk beneath the

grimy elevated subway on Stalingrad Avenue. He scratched his head. All very reasonable and also a little tragic. A currency trader. Giving up childhood dreams went against Manny's nature. In that moment, Linares in March seemed farfetched. Just when I'm easing my way into chess, all the great young American players are dropping out, he thought.

On New Year's Eve, Karpov and Kasparov played the highest-stakes chess game of all time. If Kasparov won or even drew game 24, he would get the Korloff trophy, worth about one million dollars, as well as $1.8 million of the prize fund. If he lost, they would divide the Korloff trophy and each player would get $1.5 million of the prize fund. One chess game for eight hundred thousand dollars. But Kasparov had further raised the ante for himself. Before the game, he had decided that, if he won the bejeweled trophy, he would sell it and create a fund for Armenians who were destitute and homeless after the slaughter in Baku. It was a classic Kasparov gambit, spilling chess off the board, matching his best moves against Gorbachev's genocide, revving himself up this way to destroy Karpov with his best chess. For Garry, 1990 had begun tragically in Baku, and if he thrashed Karpov in the last game, he would end the year as neatly as a sonnet.

With the white pieces, Kasparov played the English opening for the first time in the match. After relatively few moves, the players deviated from known theoretical lines, and for a time the battle was tense and unpredictable, with both players falling into time trouble. After a couple of positional mistakes, Karpov's queenside attack began to fall apart, and Kasparov rapidly achieved an overwhelming position. And then he offered Karpov a draw.

Many people were surprised. Garry seemed to be developing a habit of offering a draw when Tolya was losing. A few in the audience thought that Kasparov was being excessively cautious, that he didn't want to risk losing with so much at stake. But most commentators regarded the draw offer as an act of *noblesse oblige.* Wearing his best Boy Scout face, Garry later told me that he had decided in advance to offer Karpov a draw from a winning position. "It showed strength and fair play. I didn't need the win."

However, Bruce Pandolfini suggested that Garry's motivation had been more knotty. "Garry has never blown away Karpov," commented Pandolfini. "At the beginning of each match, he has said that he wants to crush Karpov, run up a big score, kill him off once and for all. But I wonder if it's true. In game twenty-four, he had a chance to put some distance between himself and Karpov, but he chose not to. I think that, on some level, it worries Garry to get too far ahead. Professionally, Karpov and Kasparov are almost a single entity. It was the same with Bobby and Boris. After their match, each was incomplete without the other, and although Bobby cut himself off from most of the world, he stayed in touch with Boris. It is risky for Kasparov to annihilate Karpov. What would be left? Who else could motivate him to study and play his best? Most likely, his next opponent will be little more than a weak sparring partner and there will be little worldwide interest in the match. Kasparov will be out there by himself."

It was true that when Garry assessed his art, he frequently spoke of Karpov as an aesthetic counterpoint, or even more intimately, as a function of his own chess identity, much as God assumes clarity and holiness relative to the devil. "I play creative chess. Karpov normally plays destroying chess," Garry said to me, a couple of weeks after the match. "You need his chess to appreciate mine, and of course sometimes he plays brilliant moves, too. It's as if the two of us are racing in a velodrome. You have the leader who splits the wind, and someone who follows."

"But don't you think that he has made an art form out of following?" I asked. "Preying upon you with finesse? Remember, you said Karpov sucked the energy out of you like a spider."

"Yes, that's true. But the good thing about this match was that he couldn't take this energy from me. There was nothing to take."

9

THE TRAVELING CHESS
SALESMAN

Following the championship, there was no skiing vacation, as Masha had hoped. Kasparov flew to Moscow to address business problems and to meet with political allies, and then left for a lengthy business trip.

Before the riots in Baku, when Garry had visited Moscow, he and Masha had lived with her parents in a small flat south of the center of the city, on Donskya Street. Now this flat was their only "home." The building was virtually indistinguishable from scores of other dreary walkups in the neighborhood. Downstairs was a club that had been closed and boarded up for some time. Broken pipes dangled above the street entrance, which was effaced by ripped-off advertisements, scratched paint and the dents and pry marks of multiple break-ins. Inside, the dark hall was damp and foul-smelling. Apparently no one ever cleaned here.

The apartment was cramped for four adults. It consisted of a sunny kitchen just big enough for a little table, a bedroom down the hall and a small living room with walls of flimsy wood paneling, knickknacks in every cranny, classical records and books jamming the shelves, and, on the floor, boxes filled with clothing and the sundry stowage of two families. There was no place to put anything away. To get a big fancy flat like Karpov's, Garry would have to make a deal with the Soviet Sports Committee, and he wouldn't do that. But there was a nice feeling to this tight place. Perhaps it was the spirit of Masha, optimistic and sunny, the refrigerator brimming with tasty morsels purchased with hard currency, comfortable corners to sit, an inviting home to visit and have good talks.

In the morning, the sleepy world champion sat at the kitchen table in a sleeveless undershirt, eating toast with butter. Then he moved slowly to the bathroom to shave. He lathered his face in a small mirror which reflected laundry hanging about. He nicked himself repeatedly as he scraped his heavy beard again and again, going for the executive close shave.

While he dressed, I noticed a handgun tangled in the straps of Masha's purse on the bedtable. "You must have it during these times in Moscow," he said quietly. Downstairs, a half-dozen burly men stood beneath a cluster of barren trees, looking like a gang of toughs. They kept an eye on the door, chatted and kicked at the dusty ground. When Kasparov, dressed in jeans and a sports shirt, trotted down the steps and slid into his navy blue Mercedes, he was flanked by two of them, while four more followed in another car to intercept attacks. "He is like John Lennon here," explained Arkady Murashov, a People's Deputy who would become Moscow's Commissioner of Police a year later. "When he walks on the streets, everyone wants to touch him. It only takes one crazy. It's smart for him to have bodyguards."

"Maybe I would be safe without them," Kasparov mused. "But who knows? In the West this would not be good for my image but here it is fine."

By the time Kasparov arrived at his sprawling offices in the center of town, he was in high gear. Above the beeping and printing of the fax machine, he called out instructions to a leggy secretary who wore a practiced, condescending smile. In his office, he sat at the head of a long conference table and immediately began making phone calls, fine-tuning his itinerary for a whirlwind trip to Europe and the States the following week. Kasparov had managed to get a special line, which permitted overseas calls without the innumerable false starts and disconnections that plagued Moscow's phone system.

Several times on the phone, I heard him use the term "joint venture." That year, all of Moscow's pioneer businessmen were doing joint ventures, and the term itself seemed to connote adventure, to go along with big profit. Throughout the morning, business associates came in and out of the office to see him; they spoke of a negotiation with Alitalia about the airline's renting Kasparov's leased rooms in the Cosmos Hotel for their crews, and about a pending telecommunications deal. There was a tense, closed-door meeting with several partners, to discuss another partner who was perhaps skimming profits. Even while communism was still making its last furious fight, Kasparov was getting an education in the dirty tactics of the new game.

One day, when Andrew Page was in Moscow, he peered into Garry's office and then shook his head. How fast this young bumpkin from Baku had picked up the capitalist affect and lingo, if not, alas, the deep fiscal moves and savvy of Kasparov's billionaire friend, Warren Buffett. But the possibility that Kasparov's chess brilliance would translate to business acumen kept Page hoping. After an hour, the historian and activist Yuri Afanasyev came to talk with Garry about politics, and then they discussed a business idea. In his office, the businessmen were all freedom fighters. According to Page, this explained in part why many of the deals conceived here were losers; priorities were invariably mixed up. Afterwards, Kasparov raced off in the Mercedes to discuss a deal with a man who had just opened Moscow's largest computer distributorship. Then it was lunchtime.

Garry normally ate lunch at his mother's, which was a short drive from the office, and the lunch break often took much of the afternoon. While Garry was inside, the bodyguards settled across from one another at a chessboard in the lobby. They were trying to blend quietly into the landscape of a chess champion's life, but their cover was belied by muscles bulging out of short-sleeved shirts, and hands too big and awkward for the elegant wooden chess pieces they had borrowed from the champ. They could have been tag team wrestlers.

In the early months of 1991, Garry still did not regard Moscow as home, and perhaps in part this explained the appeal of Klara's roomy flat, which was decorated with photographs and memorabilia of Baku. Klara's apartment was the heart of Garry's Moscow life. He arranged key political meetings here. He often met with Western journalists at his mother's, and once a week he tried to get in a two-hour session of chess at the dining room table with grandmaster Sergey Makarichev, his new trainer. In some ineffable way, ideas seemed to come together in the nurturing environment of her home. He watched CNN, pondered which variation in the King's Indian to play against Karpov in Linares, or gathered his thoughts for an upcoming meeting with Boris Yeltsin, while he ate his mother's aromatic chicken and his aunt Nellia's cakes. Many afternoons he took a short nap here.

He often wrote his political columns for the *Wall Street Journal* at his mother's desk, or at the dining room table. One afternoon while we waited for Klara's meal, he asked me to read his most recent article before he faxed it off. I had not read anything of his for some months. One year before, when he had started writing articles for English-language publications, his bold ideas had been awkwardly stated and amateurishly strung together. There had been little or no focus or momentum. While I read, Garry was impatient, glimpsing my way for a reaction. I was impressed. The piece was convincing and well-wrought. "I wrote it in five hours," he said, proud as a schoolboy. In a year, the improvement in his writing had been remarkable. Sometimes Garry composed in English, but more typically he wrote in Russian, had someone translate for him, and then closely edited the English copy. He had been studying articles in various Western publications for style and language. He particularly valued Abe Rosenthal's column in *The New York Times*, which he described as both informed and passionate. Garry worked at becoming more playful with his English. He would ask my opinion about a metaphor he had used in a speech or article, and if I didn't think it worked, he pushed me for a close explanation. Once, I found Garry analyzing a magazine article of mine. He read the beginning over a few times, with his lips moving. I was pleased and also nonplussed; he was scanning the paragraph for style. "Just take these two phrases out," he said. "Read it to yourself that way." He was right; the paragraph was leaner, tougher, with his deletions.

Klara spent much of her day administering the relief program for Armenian refugees which had been funded with the money Garry had received for the Korloff trophy. Every day Armenian refugees visited the apartment with stories of lost loved ones and of the impossibility of finding a meaningful life in Moscow. "We are nothing here. Nobody takes us seriously," said a young woman. Sons and daughters would report the death of a father or mother only weeks or months after the parents arrived in Moscow. "Died of a broken heart," was usually the given cause of a parent's death. But some refugees, such as Garry's aunt and grandmother, would not say a word about Baku. It was painful to recall, to be sure, but they seemed frightened to recount the tragedy, as though the telling would summon the monster to raise itself again.

Garry's driver, Kolia, was tormented with survivor's guilt. "My best friend at home was a dentist," he said. "I lived with him in his house. Last year, when I came to work for Garry, I left him alone, and my friend was murdered by the Azerbaijani hooligans. If only I had stayed with him." Like Nellia and Suzanna, Kolia believed that it was dangerous for Armenian refugees to think about home. "The pain is too great. You have to go through it to understand. My father died after Baku. He could not bear the loss."

Daily contact with refugees fanned Garry's hatred for Gorbachev. I also think that the abject misery of his countrymen had a paralyzing effect on the champion and in the first months after the Karpov match spurred his incessant travel from Moscow. In the office, Garry was always on a roll, but at his mother's his schedule was less tight, and sometimes this got him into trouble. It was at Klara's that Garry pined for Baku. He complained to his mother of feeling displaced, a stranger in a country where he was a national hero. One afternoon, when there were no appointments scheduled for the next several hours, Garry read the paper, counted the days until his next trip to Europe and the States, and then he paced. After a time, he talked with his mother in Russian, and his tone grew petulant. His restlessness built like bad weather. At this point in his life, Garry needed constant doses of action, travel, public attention, or else the walls caved in around him. The champion's face grew dark and he mumbled to himself. After a difficult stretch of silence, the phone rang. It was a journalist from *USA Today*, requesting an interview about the present political climate in Moscow and his views on Boris Yeltsin, whom Garry would actively support as Yeltsin made his bid to become Russia's first freely-elected president. Garry smiled broadly into the phone, and those of us in the apartment felt as if we had been reprieved from bad times. "My chess game is suffering," he told the journalist. "I cannot concentrate on chess. How can I? My country does not know the real meaning of democracy after seventy-eight years of dictatorship. But they know what they don't want. They don't want communism."

After the fifth Karpov match, Kasparov's life became a fast-paced global migration. Even when he settled in Moscow for a "lengthy" two- or three-week stay, he leaned to the West, making phone calls abroad to prepare for the next trip. For friends in any of the many cities he frequented, Garry was always arriving from some distant place or about to leave for another. He was on the road for three, four or five weeks, visiting scores of cities, shouldering a busy schedule of appointments the same day he stepped off an intercontinental flight. In his hotel room, he hefted his huge suitcase onto the bed with a prideful expression perhaps born of his recent international self-reliance—more and more often, he took these long trips alone. He sniffed the air in his room, deciding if he would stay here the next time he visited this city, and before racing off for a power breakfast, he sent his jackets and shirts to the cleaner and studied the detailed itinerary which was waiting on the desk, freshly faxed from Page's assistant, Antonia Bryson. If time permitted, he would call Andrew in the London office, or if Andrew was not in, check with Antonia, an empathetic woman and virtuoso juggler of intercontinental scheduling, to inquire why there was, God forbid, a two-hour break in his day without appointments or if there was a more direct route to Barcelona the following Wednesday.

His schedule was grueling, relentless and, to a large degree, self-imposed. "It is my duty," he said in the spring of 1991, referring to the endless string of chess exhibitions, goodwill speeches, meetings with politicians about promoting the game in their countries (and more and more press conferences and speeches about the politics of the Soviet Union), as if there were a book of rules about being a responsible world champion and someone above were rating his performance. In fact, it was Kasparov himself who was, in effect, writing the first primer for the modern world chess champion. In the past, with the exception of a short period in Bobby Fischer's life, world chess champions had not been highly visible in the West. When known at all here by the general public, they were usually regarded as brilliant eccentrics existing in their own world of dry calculations. Kasparov wanted to smash this caricature. He had said, time and again, that it was his duty as world champion to transform chess at the highest level into a full-blown professional sport, and to accomplish that he needed to make the game come alive for a large Western public. He was frequently on European television, and in the States he appeared on such shows as *Larry King Live, Tonight* with Jay Leno and *Late Night with David Letterman*, to spread the word of chess and anticommunism.

During a more recent trip to New York, Kasparov explained his nonstop schedule less piously. "I have to make a living," he insisted, like a traveling salesman. His main products were chess, political enlightenment in the Soviet Union, and, of course, Kasparov himself. If he didn't show up with his wares, no one would buy. Growing more urbane and understated since becoming a regular commuter to the States, and also as he approached the venerable age of thirty, Kasparov was apt to complain about the incessant traveling, the cramped seats, the crumpled clothes, the layers of jet lag. I didn't believe this new, sophisticated traveler talk. He loved the life. For his days to have meaning, Kasparov must make bold, even potentially historic moves.

The goings and comings were emotionally alive for Garry. The first meetings in town with old friends were little celebrations. There was a warm hug, an eager trading of news. Garry had been renewed by his travels and the initial flood of great expectations for his newest ventures. It was great to see him. These appealing moments of camaraderie were perhaps the best part of a trip for Garry.

When he flew into New York, I sometimes picked him up at the airport. Before he spotted me, I could see him through the heavy glass window, struggling through customs with his immense suitcase in one hand, briefcase in the other. Kasparov was aglow with the excitement of the hunt. He greeted me smiling, eager to speak of this or that, and soon we were practically running to my car while he toted the seventy-pound valise. During the ride to New York, he listed the rich and famous people he would see in the next three days. Bill Buckley, Bill Bradley, Donald Trump, Henry Kissinger, Ted Field, Warren Buffett. Had I heard that assemblyman Richard Brodsky was pushing a bill through the New York state legislature to make chess part of the curriculum in the public schools? Chess would surely sweep across the land. Communism would fall. Always these trips began on a note of tremendous optimism.

Of course, it was not simply duty and money that kept Garry running. There was escaping the malaise of Moscow, the thrill of the race to distant places, and the almost sexual promise of meeting strangers with stimulating ideas, lecturing to newspaper editors, bantering with television talk show hosts, making business deals, moving on to distant chess exhibitions, where at the press conference he would invariably shock the mayor and the organizer with his strong political views. The *enfant terrible* with the graying hair, leaving a trail of editorials behind him, stirring pots in continent after continent.

Garry rarely deviated from his long-range schedule. If he told me that we would meet for breakfast on a given day three months later at the Regency Hotel, he would be there. Just as predictably, however, he would arrive at our table a half-hour late, harried, looking at his watch, in mid-sentence about what we had talked about twelve weeks before, promising me that there was plenty of time for my journalistic questions, urging me to relax while we ate smoked salmon and speed-talked politics, because he was not yet in the mood for chess talk. "Please relax, Fred," he pleaded while he threw down his food. He was already late for a meeting with a multimillionaire who he hoped would support one of the humanitarian causes Kasparov sponsored in Russia. During his trips, Garry was frequently in a condition of ecstatic chaos.

One afternoon, a couple of months after the match, we were seated in his living room at the Regency Hotel, several hours before he and Masha were scheduled to fly back to Moscow. We were working on an article for *The European*, while Lev Alburt leafed through a magazine and drummed his fingers, waiting for a chance to discuss political ideas with Kasparov for an article he had in mind. Garry was expected at *The Wall Street Journal* in forty-five minutes, and from there the limousine would drive him and Masha to JFK. He would have to be very sharp to get it all done, but he was inspired by the challenge. Garry loved to propel himself out of New York with a brilliant last-minute flurry.

The phone rang. "Oh my God," said Kasparov. There was a Spanish television crew downstairs in the lobby. He had completely forgotten the appointment. Kasparov was in the midst of playing a game against a television audience in Spain. A film crew found him, wherever he was in the world, to televise each move and his comments about the progress of the game. "Masha, find my pocket set!" he called to his wife, who was in the bedroom, packing. During the previous hectic week of travel and appointments, he hadn't taken a minute to consider his move. And to make matters worse, Kasparov had a bad position with the black pieces. He hadn't taken this exhibition seriously. He had been led to understand that an audience of amateurs would decide each move, to play against him by consensus. Kasparov could win such a game in his sleep. But this audience was playing very professional moves, and Kasparov suspected that there was a committee of grandmasters working in the wings. "Masha, bring my set." She couldn't find the set. "Oh shit, oh shit." He looked up at the ceiling recalling the last move played against him. What to do? He moved the pieces in his head. His position was dire. Masha ran into the room with the pieces. Garry quickly set up the position. Then he noticed my alarmed expression. "Garry, we need to fax our article to London in four hours or we won't make the deadline."

This week's move by the studio audience was a deep positional sacrifice of a pawn, a move worthy of Karpov. "What amateur would play such a move?" he said to Alburt, who coughed and nodded, as if this moment held historical significance. Which it did. The world champion was on the verge of losing to a television audience of amateurs. "Ridiculous," said Masha. But actually, the idea of losing to beginners made Garry and Masha giddy. It *was* so ridiculous.

What to play? Garry stared at the set. "I can sacrifice the piece for the attack, and maybe die quickly, or just continue with this complicated position, where I am worse, and torture myself for a few more weeks. Unbelievable." Alburt coughed. "Don't worry, Fred. We will finish in the limousine." The phone rang again. Kasparov answered impatiently, raised an incredulous eyebrow. A knock on the door. The film crew carried the camera and gear into the room. "It is a great idea, but I won't participate," said Garry into the receiver. On the phone from Madrid, a journalist wanted Kasparov to take part in a political demonstration against apartheid rule in South Africa. "It's a great idea, Ricardo, a great demonstration, but I won't participate. No, I understand what's happening in South Africa, but what's happening in my country is also important, and I have to play a little chess, too. . . . You don't understand . . . I don't like Nelson Mandela . . . Ricardo, please. Chess yes. Politics no. For now I will only do politics in my own country. I'm interested in chess projects. That's it. I'm a human being, too, and there's only twenty-four hours in a day."

By now the crew was set up in the living room and Kasparov was seated in the lights, neatening his tie, composing his face. "Unbelievable," he muttered. "Maybe if I had some time, I could save it."

"Which move will you make?" I asked, seconds before they turned on the flood lights.

"I don't know yet."

Some weeks in advance of the 1992 National High School Scholastic Championship in Kentucky, Garry called my house from Europe to say that he would meet Josh, Bonnie and me in Lexington. There would be a thousand teenagers competing in the event, which Kasparov saw as a splendid opportunity to promote chess in the United States. He would give interviews and pose for photographs with the players. Besides being treasured souvenirs, many of the photographs would find their way into local newspapers across the country. In addition, Garry would bring a suitcase filled with his colorful hand-made chess sets for very young children. If he discovered a market during this trip, Garry planned to set up a factory mostly employing Armenian refugees.

The trip was a divided experience for him. When he first entered the playing hall, the atmosphere was electric. For the teenagers, the world champion's beaming athletic presence suddenly invested their pieces with great importance. As one might have guessed, all the young chess players wanted their photographs taken with Kasparov. The line for snapshots with him curled through the maze of halls, past the restrooms and around several large conference rooms. The champion began with great energy, shaking hands with each student, the electronic flash catching his broad ambitious smile. Then Garry invited a little discussion about the student's chess life. If he presented one of Kasparov's books or the tournament program, Garry wrote a short personal message and autographed it.

Hours passed, and he repeated this routine, again and again. He hadn't considered how long it would take personally to greet five or six hundred students and to pose affably for photographs. After several hundred smiles and greetings, he wanted to stop. But it was impossible. There were hundreds more lined up for photographs. Kasparov had become Santa Claus at Macy's. By now, a secondary line had formed to the side, where kids waited until Garry was free for a few seconds and could scribble his autograph. He began to recognize repeaters on this line. He realized that half of the scraps of paper with his name would end up in the trash. He tried to check his querulousness. By the evening, he looked tortured. His smile was a grimace and he could no longer bear to speak with the kids. "No more photographs," he whispered hoarsely to an assistant to the organizer, and when the man looked stricken (the winners of trophies had been promised a photo with the champion after the awards ceremony), Kasparov relented. He reminded himself that during the following week, his picture with smiling kids and chess trophies would be in newspapers all over America. But Garry felt appalled at being handled, posed, flashed, forced to stand in place for ten hours.

In his hotel room after dinner, Garry pushed himself to be decorous, as he pulled a chess stacking toy for toddlers, colorful children's chess pieces, and a hand-crafted pocket set out of his suitcase and showed them off to several of the coaches. Everyone admired them, although the men, all chess lovers, were dumbstruck at finding themselves being solicited by the world champion, and had difficulty focusing on the sets themselves. What exactly was he proposing? Should they order a few sets, or were these chess wares already destined for Bloomingdales? As Andrew Page had pointed out, Kasparov was too proud to make his sales pitch clear. It was a tough weekend for the chess salesman. Kasparov left Lexington, Kentucky, with praise for the craftsmanship of his samples, but no concrete sales. Nothing specific with which to go back to Moscow to open a factory.

On the short plane ride from Lexington to Cincinnati, he and I chatted about Bill Clinton and the smart, tough economic strategies of Ross Perot. Though it was six months before the election and Clinton was behind Bush in the polls, Kasparov predicted that the Arkansas governor would be the next U.S. president, although his own choice would have been Bill Bradley. While we talked, he would lean over me every two or three minutes to look out the window, and I assumed that he was curious about the flat, Midwest farm country. Kasparov was much more chipper than one might have expected after the fiasco of the day before. He believed that his appearance in Lexington would be a publicity boon to U.S. chess, and he was already looking forward to key meetings the following day somewhere in Europe.

After climbing out of the small plane, we waited for my son. "Hey, Josh, what state are we in?" Garry asked. "Ohio. We're in Cincinnati, Ohio," Josh answered in a what-kind-of-question-is-that tone of voice. He knew that Garry was a whiz at geography, but "Cincinnati" was plastered over airport signs in every direction. "You know, Josh," Garry replied, "we never flew north of the Ohio River. If that's true, we must still be in Kentucky." In the terminal, we asked, and, indeed, the Cincinnati airport was located in Kentucky.

While we waited for our connecting flights, Garry watched Josh and several younger children from The Dalton School's team play a variety of chess called "bughouse," in which four players split into teams and play adjacent games, with team members passing captured pieces to one another to augment their attacks. The games are hilarious and completely chaotic, with players slapping down extra queens and rooks. Kasparov had never seen bughouse before, and he was delighted by the intensity and joy with which the kids played. Some people stopped to take Kasparov's picture and he didn't mind at all. His expression was mellow and satisfied.

After twenty minutes or so, his flight to New York was announced. Waving goodbye to the kids, and giving Bonnie a hug and a box of chocolate-covered cherries the organizer had left in his room, he hefted the large valise, heavier even than usual for all the handmade wooden chess sets, and then turned around with a smile to say, you see, I'm off again. A half-dozen of us watched him struggling with his luggage down the long corridor to continue his selling trip in New York and several European countries.

10

LINARES

When Karpov and Kasparov squared off for their eighth-round game in the Linares International in the south of Spain, Kasparov was a full point behind the leader, Soviet grandmaster Alexander Beliavsky, and Karpov had already lost three games and was completely out of contention. Apparently, the marathon world championship had taken something from both of them. Karpov did not look like the same man. His face was washed out. His hair was stringy, unkempt. He had the look of someone who had been under great stress for a long time. Staring up at the leaders, Garry had become tense and distracted. "I can't get the Speelman game out of my mind," he said, an hour before playing Karpov. "If I had won that game . . ."

In the fifth round, he had mishandled a completely winning position against the British grandmaster, and had had to settle for a draw. He had played very uneven chess through the first seven rounds. In the first round on February 22 against twenty-one-year-old Vassily Ivanchuk, Garry had been overwhelmed. "It was the worst game of my career," he said. Ivanchuk had dominated Kasparov from start to finish. For hours afterwards, on television monitors in the playing hall of the Hotel Anibal and in the pressroom, a computerized animation replayed the deadly flowing progress of Ivanchuk's pieces picking apart the world champion's position, again and again this utter annihilation. Four rounds later, Ivanchuk had eked out a win against Karpov. It was the first time that one man had ever beaten both Ks in one tournament, and though Ivanchuk went into the eighth round trailing Beliavsky by half a point, journalists in Linares were fawning over the introverted Ukrainian. Along with original ideas in the openings, he was demonstrating a Kasparov-like feel for imbalanced positions, and, when it was called for, he defended ferociously. As the tournament continued, chess writers began to speculate that the next world champion was likely to be Ivanchuk, and that it could happen as early as 1993.

In round seven, Kasparov had taken out his frustration on sixteen-year-old Gata Kamsky, who was having a terrible tournament. Garry crushed the teenager in twenty-two moves, spurring players to wonder if Rustam would continue to claim that the world champion was terrified of his son. But the lost opportunity against Speelman kept working at Kasparov. "An amateur could have won that game," he said, showing the position to Josh, who had traveled with me to Spain. With an incredulous expression on his face, Garry demonstrated a half-dozen winning plans that for some reason he had failed to employ. It is Kasparov's manner to look back at his mistakes in utter disbelief, as though they were the work of another man. "Unbelievable," he muttered.

When I asked him if he had trained for this fantastic tournament, Kasparov answered dryly, "Yeah, I trained. I trained giving political speeches." But, I thought, this was just the situation that he relished: Things were going badly. The other players were beginning to count him out. The press was focused on Ivanchuk. And then summoning his rage and determination, the world champion would elbow through the pack like Achilles to win. "I'm in a bad mood," Garry repeated a few times before the Karpov game, which made me think that he was primed for his charge.

Driving south from Madrid, Josh and I had watched Linares arise unexpectedly from a sleepy green countryside of rocky foothills, grazing sheep and olive trees. Had we traveled here from the south, we would have passed fighting bull–breeding ranches. "The strongest tournament in the history of chess played in the middle of nowhere," said Garry, as though this explained his poor performance. But Linares was a town rich in traditions. On the twenty-eighth of August, 1947, the incomparable Manolete had died from a horn in the heart in the Linares bullring, which was only a few blocks from the small but commodious Hotel Anibal. There, each year D. Louis Rentero Suarez, a local businessman who had amassed a fortune building a chain of grocery stores, held what he endeavored to make the strongest and bloodiest chess tournament in the world.

Rentero, a lifelong aficionado of the *corrida de toros,* had been an ardent chess impresario since 1978, and it would seem that he had borrowed from his first love to enhance the second. In Spanish bullfighting, if the bull does not fight bravely, he is hissed and booed by fans, and killed quickly by the matador. Grandmasters who accepted Rentero's hefty appearance fees to come to Linares, even ones who had a reputation for drawing many of their games, understood that they had been invited here to fight. If a grandmaster did not have the stomach for battle, and accepted a quick, peaceful draw, he risked a severe tongue-lashing from Rentero, and the likelihood of never being invited back. Rentero was known to reward players with envelopes containing big bills, following victories with hair-raising sacrifices. In large part because of Rentero's strong hand, this annual event produced a higher percentage of decisive games than most grandmaster tournaments. His identification of a common beauty and brutality in chess and in the *corrida* had taken root in the town, where local folk had become crazy for the royal game. Along the streets of Linares, there were colorful bullfight posters advertising upcoming events here and in neighboring Baeza, and beside them the elegant poster of jousting knights proclaiming this year's Linares International to be the strongest tournament in the history of chess. The young children of Linares grew up daydreaming of becoming either bullfighters or matadors of the mind.

Local kids were delighted to meet my son, who at the time was a fourteen-year-old chess master. Each evening, after the games, Linares teenagers lined up in the lobby of the hotel to play blitz against Josh, who found it eye-opening that chess was so valued here. At an age that Garry described as half-child, half-man, Josh lived a relatively normal teenage life. He was a good student. He looked forward to school dances and was a starting guard on the Dalton eighth-grade basketball team. Up until now, with only a modest amount of his time devoted to study, his chess life had flourished, along with his jump shot. Since the age of nine, he had more often than not been the highest-rated player for his age in the United States. He had won four scholastic national championships and, soon after returning to the States from Linares, he would win two more, the high school national championship and the U.S. cadet, or under-16, championship.

But Josh knew that, relative to the grandmasters in this tournament of tournaments, he was a raw beginner. Much more than an amateur, a chess master could appreciate how very hard it was to become as good as the worst player in Linares. It was not unlike a star high school basketball player gauging the distance between his game and that of an NBA all-star. The young ball player who could hit the jump shot from fifteen feet had yet to prove that he could learn to do it from twenty feet, with bigger and stronger players draped all over him. A world-class grandmaster-in-progress must come equipped with the imagination to create unexpected and resonant ideas, along with a powerful calculating brain. But there were hundreds of talented young chess players around the world, much as there were eager kids in every city seemingly born with beautiful moves to the hoop and a tremendous vertical leap.

At fourteen, Josh was aware that the next big jump in chess would come not so much as the result of talent as from greater commitment and training. During the past year or two, Josh had noticed that his appetite for study had steadily increased as he had gained a deeper understanding of the game. But my son was still far from sure that he wanted to spend a full working week studying chess. And perhaps forty or fifty hours a week would not be enough. Gata Kamsky studied twelve hours a day. When Valery Salov, another grandmaster competing in Linares, was in deep training, he worked twelve to fourteen hours a day. There was no cultural precedent for an American youth to lean upon to make this kind of commitment. If an

American boy were to study chess twelve hours a day, he would be considered misguided or crazy. I suspected that this trip to Linares might make Joshua's life more complicated. Before coming here, the chess tournaments he knew were inelegant events in the States. In Linares, and a handful of other elite tournaments around the world, players were catered to like royalty, and the worst player would earn several thousand dollars a week. While Josh watched this altogether different chess experience, I knew that he would be measuring his potential and deciding if he wanted this life for himself.

In the Hotel Anibal, the fourteen grandmasters played on a modestly-raised stage at the end of a large room. About a hundred paying fans followed the action on computerized displays that were located behind each of the games and showed the current position, along with the remaining time on each player's clock. At the beginning of games, there was a jaunty, almost relaxed atmosphere on the stage, with players smiling at friends in the audience, while a waiter served them coffee, tea or soda. After thinking and making a move, a player might stand up from his board and begin to pace in an alley between the tables and the computerized display boards. There were often four or five players pacing at once, and for the most part they seemed oblivious to one another, but occasionally a few of them would stop to chat or joke around. As the games became tense and complicated, the pacing grew more intense, with grandmasters furrowing into their positions as they walked. One or two of the grandmasters were in the habit of picking up the pace after coming upon a promising idea. This was infectious, and quickly, four or five of the men, calculating deeply with eyes staring faraway or even rolled toward the ceiling, raced the length of the stage, then wheeled sharply and dashed back the other way. Kasparov was the best pacer. He was the fastest, but more, his gait had a relentless, biting quality, and he wagged his head, sneering at games as he passed them. It was a fast and angry walk, and more than once I noticed a player skip out of Kasparov's way.

At the start of the eighth round, Gata Kamsky's father, Rustam, approached the elderly lady assistant to Mr. Rentero, complaining of chest pains. They soon left for the hospital, leaving onlookers in the lobby concerned, although some of the players were skeptical. Gata was playing very poorly in this tournament, losing game after game, and for each defeat, the father and son precipitated a controversy. Early on, Rustam had ordered Gata not to drink from the large opened bottles of mineral water, because, according to one of the players, Rustam believed that Kasparov's assistant, Alexander Shaka-rov, was looking for an opportunity to poison Gata. Each round, there was a big argument about Gata's score sheet. In the Linares tournament, it was a rule that at the conclusion of the game, each player must turn in his signed score sheet, but the Kamskys had decided that the rule was unprincipled and they refused. Some play-ers said that Gata and his father were getting fifty dollars from a collector in New York for each score sheet. But others believed that Rustam was just making trouble. Gata wrote formal letters to Ren-tero, claiming that he was being harassed during games about this rule, and Rentero was furious. "If they don't produce them, they won't get their money," he said before the eighth round, but he had decided not to tell the Kamskys this until the end of the tournament, for fear that they would drop out before the end. "I'm not going to allow this sixteen-year-old kid and his father to ruin my tournament."

Apparently, creating controversy was Rustam's double-edged tac-tic to wake up Gata, who was quiet and placid by nature, and to distract Gata's opponents. But in Linares, despite Rustam's imagina-tive diversions and his evil-eye stare at his son's hated opponents, Gata continued to lose and was mired in last place. At the hospital, the doctor had found nothing wrong with Rustam, and when he was asked to pay for his examination, he became enraged, claiming that he had been forced to come to the hospital against his will by Mr. Rentero's assistant. An hour after the start of the eighth round, Rustam was back in the hotel and once again complaining that the score sheet harassment had ruined Gata's chances in the tournament. He returned to the playing hall in time to watch Gata blunder his eighth-round game against Jonathan Speelman.

As for Kasparov and Karpov, they played one another as though their fighting hearts were somewhere else, perhaps still back in Lyon in their three-month struggle. Neither player was willing to take any chances and their game was a lackluster draw, the 113th played between these world champions. Within seconds of the handshake, they were both smiling, walking quickly off the stage to go to the analysis area. With grandmasters and journalists jammed around their table, Karpov and Kasparov moved the pieces and spoke softly to one another. Karpov giggled. Garry smiled handsomely, sitting erect at the board, as though a photographer were taking cover shots.

The postmortem is a venerable tradition. It is an opportunity for players who have been guarding the most exquisitely-crafted secrets to share them, to learn how closely the opposing mind had shadowed the decisive plan and the scores of other plans that had been rejected. It is a time to learn from mistakes, and for the loser of a game it is a form of catharsis. Working through interesting ideas begins to make the loser feel whole again.

But for Karpov and Kasparov, it was a larger occasion. Dialectically, each had shut the other out of his life. The number one and two in the world could never be friends, but the postmortem was a singular opportunity to explore one another, apart from the statements they had made in anger and for political effect, and apart from the hype of journalists. Garry was a virtuoso in this hour-long analysis session. He pointed his forefinger at a thousand squares, dismissed deep possibilities with a raised eyebrow. But occasionally Karpov demonstrated a powerful move and Garry nodded without argument. I said to one of the grandmasters that Garry seemed to see much more than Karpov, and the man answered, "Yes, but it is Garry's manner to tell everything that he sees. Karpov will only tell a little." Although twenty people surrounded them, the two world champions acted as though they were alone. During one stretch, grandmaster Ljubomir Ljubojevic, a loquacious man and a bold attacking player, kept interrupting with plans that he couldn't keep to himself. Finally, Karpov said. "Yes, we know," in his most imperial and dismissive voice.

After this session, Josh and I went with Garry to his room. He and Josh looked at chess for an hour before Garry's meeting with Bessel Kok. Bessel was in Linares for a GMA meeting to be held the following day, and was coming to Kasparov's room to give him a briefing. I was not sure what Garry expected from the GMA meeting, but the prospect of talking with Bessel had an uplifting effect. Although Bessel had become an adversary, it was clear that Garry retained some attachment for the older man. On another occasion, I had been visiting Kasparov in Moscow before he left for Spain to participate in a symposium with Kok and several others. One morning while we were in the office, Garry had received a fax saying that Bessel was canceling his appearance. Garry had made no attempt to hide his disappointment. While Garry sorely wanted to defeat Bessel in their political fights, he nonetheless enjoyed having Bessel in the game. Bessel's was one of a half-dozen friendships with successful, middle-aged businessmen Garry had cultivated in the West. Perhaps because Garry, in his own words, "doesn't have the right character for business," he was drawn to men who did.

Bessel came with a briefcase of disturbing news. In the meeting tomorrow, the GMA would consider a proposal by Gata Kamsky to require the world champion to play in the candidates cycle—to compete in the elimination event to determine the final contenders to play for the world championship—instead of simply defending his title against the winner of the candidates, as was the current practice. In addition, they would probably vote to do away with adjournments in the 1993 championship, a rule change Kasparov opposed. And finally, they would almost surely vote against offering the world champion any appearance money to play in future GMA tournaments.

During dinner, Garry brooded over this news. To force the world champion to play in the candidates cycle was sheer lunacy. It would mortally compromise the mystique and prestige of the institution of world champion. The world title event, as presently constituted, was the only bankable commodity in the chess world. If an organizer could no longer count upon a reigning king, the best chess mind in all the world, to defend in three years, how would he ever entice sponsors to put up millions? Needless to say, Kasparov would never acquiesce to such an arrangement, and most likely the GMA would vote the plan down, but the fact that it was being seriously considered was a slap in the face to Garry, and an indication of the widening gulf between him and much of the world's chess elite. Also, by telling Garry that they were not going to pay him an appearance fee to attend GMA tournaments, the organization that he had created was saying, in effect, we don't want you and we don't need you.

In the meeting the following afternoon, that attitude was made manifestly clear. The GMs voted down the Kamsky proposal, but the English grandmaster Nigel Short, a hero in his country since showing great chess promise as a young boy, was pudding-pleased to announce that the GMA would not be offering appearance money to Kasparov, because it would not be democratic. Nigel flashed a cherubic smile, while describing the wrongfulness of treating Kasparov differently from any other grandmaster. Bessel appeared pained. He knew that he was dead in the water in the chess management business without Kasparov. Without Garry's charisma and ability to attract commercial sponsorship, GMA tournaments were destined to fail. Bessel came to Garry some hours after this meeting with an offer to pay him money under the table to play in GMA tournaments. Garry refused. Several months later, when Bessel resigned as chairman of the GMA, it was interpreted in the chess world as the effective end of the organization, but in fact, the GMA had committed suicide in Linares.

Fred Friedel, the brains behind ChessBase, was close to Kasparov, as well as to many of the top grandmasters who disliked the champion. Friedel pointed out that the erosion of Garry's popularity among the chess-playing elite predated his disputes within the GMA. "When Garry first won the title, he was a hero," said Friedel. "Everyone loved him, and Karpov was universally hated. But after several years, the complaints began: Garry is trying to take control of everything. He will not allow dissidence. His behavior at tournaments is bad. He is completely egotistical. Top players have been remarkably blind to the money and prestige Garry has brought into chess. They don't like him. They say he is a tyrant. Well, of course Garry does have a tyrannical side. He likes to have his way and he is an outrageously impatient man. His mind wanders if people beat around the bush. But he is also resented because of his worldliness. Chess is only a part of his life, and this is unusual for grandmasters, and they find it disturbing. One must have a sense for Garry's day and the scope of his life. When he is visiting Germany, he often meets with fifty or more people in a day. For the first twenty, he is quite polite, but after this he is in a haze and it drives him crazy listening to a long prologue. His critics say that you cannot argue with him. But this is simply not true. We have argued about many things. I tell him that he makes mistakes with the other players, allows himself to be misunderstood. At tournaments, he hangs out only with his friends. I tell him all the time to mingle with all the players, and he says this is like socializing with the enemy. They dislike him openly and he finds fraternizing hypocritical. Garry says, fine, you don't like me, do without me."

The groupings and body English of the grandmasters in the players' dining room at the Hotel Anibal were suggestive of Kasparov's increasing isolation in the chess world. After the Karpov game, Garry sat at a table with Alexander Shakarov, Josh and myself. He rarely ate with other players. Three or four tables away was the English grandmaster Jonathan Speelman, joined on this night by grandmaster Nigel Short, who had visited Linares for the GMA meeting. They nodded and forced a smile our way. "They hate me," commented Garry, while he chewed his swordfish. Spassky, also in Linares for the GMA meeting, did not say hello. At a nearby table, eating alone, grandmaster Salov nodded, and then for the next three courses avoided eye contact. At another table, Gata and Rustam Kamsky sat with Karpov, and eventually they were joined by Ivanchuk. The Kamsky-Karpov table radiated loathing, although Ivanchuk existed apart from it. During meals, Rustam, showing his gold front tooth, would glare for long malevolent minutes at Garry, while Gata stared at Josh. What to do at such moments? Smile urbanely? Try to ignore them? It felt awkward to eat Paella Valenciana while being murdered by a stare. One night, Josh tried to stare Gata down and failed miserably; after a half minute, his eyes fell back into his spaghetti and meatballs.

Karpov and the Kamskys had become good friends, chatting after rounds and usually dining together. "They deserve one another," said Garry glumly. Apparently, the friendship had begun a month earlier at the Reggio Emilia tournament in northern Italy. "It was like evil being drawn to evil," recalled Mikhail Gurevich, who had also played there. "They were together all the time. It was there, I am certain, that Karpov hatched the plan to have Kamsky formally propose that Kasparov must enter the world championship cycle at the candidates level. Karpov knew that the idea would infuriate Garry, and perhaps throw off his chess. A sophisticated and clever idea. Rustam has a primitive mind and could never have come up with it on his own."

"They all hate me," Kasparov said, assessing the dining room as though it were a chess position, the white king and a few pawns surrounded by powerful attacking pieces. When I suggested that he was going a little overboard, and mentioned his warm relations with grandmaster Artur Yusupov, whom he often joined for a chat after dinner, Garry answered, "We also have our ups and downs. There are jealousies that do not go away," alluding to a period when they had both been developing young players in the USSR, and Yusupov's considerable potential had been largely ignored because of Kasparov's show-stopping genius. Of course, Garry did have friends here. His relationships with Alexander Beliavsky, Mikhail Gurevich and Boris Gelfand were quite warm, but he was thrown off balance by the chill and glare from other tables.

On another evening when Garry came into the dining room, Josh and I were sitting with Anand and Gelfand. Garry looked upset, his little island was disappearing, and we excused ourselves to join him. A little later, Gelfand, a soft-spoken and soulful young man who spent his off-days reading the short stories of Isaac Bashevis Singer, came over and joined us. Soon he and Garry began talking about a proposed rule change for next year's Linares tournament, which called for drawn games to be decided afterwards by a speed game. Garry impatiently declared that this made a mockery of serious chess, and that he would not play in the tournament next year if the rule were passed. Gelfand, who was also against the rule change, was annoyed with Garry's heavy-handedness and quipped, "Okay, then I'll vote for it." Garry jerked back, as though slapped. He liked Gelfand, and this little joke had hit a bruise. Though he might try, Garry lacked the talent to be a regular guy.

"A lot of the players dislike Garry because he is such an absolutist," observed Gelfand, at the time the number-three-rated player in the world. "He doesn't have a knack for compromise and is always starting wars over everything."

Nonetheless, Kasparov was more bemused than aggrieved by the hostile atmosphere in Linares. He was a man with much too much on his plate. While struggling hard to win here, like Karpov he was still depleted from the world championship. He had ambitious plans for promoting chess worldwide and yet the chess world appeared to be slipping away from him. But in the larger scheme of things, none of this seemed important. In the past month, events in his country had started to move at shocking speed. How important was the Linares social atmosphere when Gorbachev and Yeltsin were primed for violent confrontation? On February 1, Gorbachev had declared a state of emergency, promising that he would use the army and navy, whatever force was necessary, to control demonstrations. "A state of military emergency was decreed for mass civil rallies," wrote the journalists Solovyov and Klepikova in their biography of Boris Yeltsin, "that is, for anti-Kremlin, pro-Yeltsin rallies and demonstrations. The Kremlin was moving from a passive defense to an aggressive one. It was really a putsch, but a slow, gradual, veiled one."

Before leaving for Linares, Kasparov had met twice with Yeltsin to discuss events of the day, and specifically to offer advice about how Russian diplomacy might influence the Bush administration to be more passive toward Gorbachev and more encouraging of the mounting democratic movement. "Yeltsin was not aware of the situation in the States," said Kasparov. "He did not know very much about the American system of government and the entrenched alliances of American politicians, but, unlike Gorbachev, he was a good listener."

For some time, Yelsin had been blocked from appearing on state-controlled television, but on February 19, three days before the start of play in Linares, he was on the evening newscast. "In 1987, I warned that it is inherent in Gorbachev's nature to strive for absolute personal power," said Yeltsin. "He has gone far in that direction; he has brought about a dictatorship under the pretty name of President's Rule. I dissociate myself from the president's position and his policies, and I call for his immediate resignation."

When Kasparov wasn't playing or preparing for his next game, he was listening to Radio Liberty on his little Grundig. There were plans for a demonstration in Moscow against Gorbachev's repressive policies, with an expected turnout of over one million people. Would Gorbachev allow it? Could he stop it?

"Gorbachev underestimated the anticommunist resistance among the population," said Garry. "People were so fed up with the communism. For years, they expressed it in kitchens, in private discussions, in jokes about Brezhnev, anecdotes about communism. But suddenly it went to the streets. Now it is an explosion. Gorbachev does what he can to stop it. On February 2, I gave a speech in front of two hundred editors of local newspapers and they all complained of the new censorship. In the state-controlled press there was practically nothing [about the match with Karpov]. If Karpov had won, it would have been on the front page—it would have been interpreted as a great victory for communism. The television in my country today is like it was twenty years ago. It is practically impossible for Yeltsin to get on. They have closed the independent TV in Siberia. . . . The day before I left for Linares, I gave a very tough interview with journalists from two major liberal newspapers. It hasn't appeared yet. I don't think it will. . . . Bush, of course, has no idea what is going on in my country. Here's a joke today in Moscow: Because of the anticommunist coup, America has stopped the food supply."

Before the start of the Linares tournament, some Western grandmasters had complained of the unfairness of inviting nine Soviet players to a tournament of only fourteen. But it was the only way that Rentero could put together a category 17 event. The Soviets, with an average rating of 2679, were needed to compensate for their weaker brothers from the West, in order to bring the average of all fourteen to the needed 2658. Western grandmasters had long been chagrined and jealous of Soviet dominance in the chess world, and rightly worried that the Soviets would win all the tournament prize money. In exquisitely elite renderings of affirmative action, Western grandmasters had lobbied to restrict Soviet participation at Western events. But in the early spring of 1991, world politics would soon eliminate this issue of chess politics. Although no one beside Kasparov would have predicted it, there would never again be a Linares tournament fielding even one "Soviet" grandmaster.

A compelling subtext in Linares was the confusion and unhappiness of the Soviet players, a close fraternity of great sportsmen that was breaking apart almost by the hour. In the evenings, players from the USSR talked about the meaning of the massive demonstrations at home, and the impossibility of getting food in Moscow, but mostly they tried to decide whether or not they should leave the country. Mikhail Gurevich had already moved to Brussels with his wife and baby daughter. He explained that, for a chess professional, Western Europe had become the most interesting place to live, but that more importantly, he feared for the safety of his family in the USSR. Valery Salov was planning to move to Barcelona. Boris Gelfand wondered whether the United States or Belgium offered the best opportunities for a chess player. Those Soviet players who had not emigrated were a fearful and confused group.

Perhaps the sting of the dining room contributed to Kasparov's chilly view of the plight of Soviet grandmasters. "The top players are leaving my country because they have lost all confidence in the regime," he said. "During the stagnation period, they were a well-off group. Comparatively speaking, they lived a good life. There were privileges for a top player who aligned himself with the system. You could travel to the West and, returning with Western currency, there were things to buy. But now it doesn't work anymore. The country is in chaos, the inner connections have broken down. You have to understand that, by and large, players didn't care about politics. They want to study chess. They don't want to worry about finding food or if the flat will have heat or being murdered in the street. They had connections with the Sports Committee, and when they needed to go to a training camp it was arranged. But now the system has collapsed and there is much less state support. Soon it will disappear altogether. Many feel the need to leave. The players must make a new life for themselves. You must also understand that this is happening throughout the Soviet sports system. This system was carefully built as a tool for communist propaganda. The most talented young girls and boys were trained like dogs to prove that the best sportsmen were communists."

Kasparov's ninth-round opponent, Alexander Beliavsky, four-time Soviet champion, was in first place, leading Kasparov by a point and a half. Along with Ivanchuk, "Big Al," as he was affectionately called by some grandmasters, was playing the best chess in Linares. He was pushing for the win in game after game, sacrificing material, unveiling opening novelties he had painstakingly prepared for months at home in Lvov in the Ukraine. So far, Beliavsky was playing the tournament of his career, and if he could win ahead of Kasparov, Karpov and Ivanchuk, it would be the crowning success of his chess life.

On the white side, Kasparov had to take this game if he was going to claw back into contention and possibly preserve his phenomenal tournament record. This was a very big game in Kasparov's career. "Of course, Garry is a genius," commented Leontxo Garcia, Spain's foremost chess journalist, before the start of play. "In the past, he has always been able to win the big game. This quality is what has separated him from Karpov."

There are occasional games during which Kasparov appears sublimely calm. He considers variations as though captivated by an internal music. Even as he attacks, his expression remains peaceful, sometimes beatific, and there is an easy sway to his body when he walks off stage between moves. This was such a game. Beliavsky played with hardly a glance at the champion, as though watching him would be a jinx. In the opening, Kasparov sacrificed a pawn for control of the center, and the advantage of playing with two bishops against Beliavsky's knight and bishop. He slowly limited Beliavsky's piece activity with perfect placement of his pawns. Then Kasparov stunned many of us by trading queens. It was a move which superseded time-honored principles. All good players know that when you are ahead in material, it is wise to "trade off," since the advantage tends to become decisive with fewer pieces and pawns on the board. When you have a positional advantage, however, you try to avoid trades, while slowly improving your position. This squeezes an opponent's army into less and less space, forcing his big guns onto squares where they have little or no range and harmony relative to one another. In trading queens, however, Kasparov had exercised the highest positional judgement. Looking far ahead, he'd seen that by giving up his queen, he would even further cramp the effectiveness of Beliavsky's army. Nine moves after the trade, Beliavsky's misplaced pieces could no longer defend his pawns.

That evening, Kasparov was ecstatic. He had done it again, found the magic for the big game. When he walked into the dining room, conversation hushed. In the face of genius, jealousies and angers receded, for the moment at least. With four rounds to go, Kasparov had pulled within a half-point of Ivanchuk and Beliavsky, and seemed once more destined to win. All the great players here could feel the inevitability of Kasparov's charge. Yusopov and Salov offered courtly congratulations. Kamsky and Karpov ate sullenly, but all the others listed Garry's way. I again recalled Lev Alburt's description of Garry's approach to life and chess: "Garry has an internal urge to create wonders, to put himself in lost situations and then to make a Houdini-like escape. He does this because he has learned that he can make a miracle at the last moment, and this is dangerous, because miracles don't always happen." But in this greatest of all tournaments, without training properly, Kasparov was once again making a miracle. "Garry is a unique character," offered Michael Gurevich, who was playing badly and marvelled at Garry's energy as well as his art. "After being with Garry for all those months helping him prepare, I'm still not the same. I'm worn out, still recovering."

After dinner, players came over to our table and chatted about their games. Toward his colleagues Kasparov was kind. To Josh he carefully explained his reasoning behind the exchange of queens. The Yugoslavian journalist Dimitri Bjelica came from Karpov's table to give his lengthy congratulations, and then ceremoniously announced that this great and seemingly portentous win had come on March 9, Bobby Fischer's birthday. Bjelica had made a movie about Bobby nearly twenty years before and the hotel management was planning to show it later that night on one of the television channels. Josh, Garry and I decided to watch.

At eleven, Garry was in his bedroom, late as usual, and Josh and I were in the sitting room in front of the television. The film came on, grainy and amateurish; there was Bobby Fischer, smiling shyly like a neighborhood friend you hadn't seen in a quarter of a century, and suddenly it felt so good to recall the drawl of his words, the relaxed slope of his shoulders. When this film had been made, Bobby had been about Garry's age, but Fischer seemed much younger and less worldly, a big puppy, eager to please. He still had his whole life ahead of him. This was before the legend of Bobby Fischer had consumed and disfigured Bobby.

His answers to Bjelica about the merits of past world chess champions were hesitant and understated. It struck me as prescient that Fischer spoke so tenderly and uncritically of the nineteenth-century American player Paul Morphy, whom he considered the greatest natural talent of all chess players. These two shared more than chess greatness. In 1859, following a year of chess-playing in Europe, during which Morphy had trounced the best players in the world, the twenty-one-year-old had returned to his country as a great hero, celebrated in newspapers and poems and feted by politicians and college presidents, much as Bobby had been after defeating Spassky in 1972. But soon after this triumphant return, chess had become abhorrent to young Morphy. The remainder of his life had been tragic. He'd become a recluse, paranoiac, tormented by inner demons. Likewise, after beating Spassky, Bobby Fischer had disappeared from his adoring public, hiding out in grimy rooming houses, wearing disguises, clearly a person dominated by delusions. Bobby had the fillings in his teeth removed so that he could not be insidiously influenced by radio signals. For twenty years, he ranted to his friends that the Jews had persecuted him throughout his career, making it impossible for him to defend the world title. Several of the great world chess champions featured in Bjelica's film—Morphy, Steinitz, and Fischer—had been afflicted with mental illness.

After the movie had been playing for five minutes or so, Kasparov came into the room and sat at his chess board. He set up the pieces with the black side closest to himself, his back toward the television. He was cleanly shaven, and wore a black turtleneck sweater, dark slacks and loafers. He had dressed for Bobby. Two hours earlier, in the dining room, Garry had been gregarious, accommodating, but no more. His visage had turned severe and intimidating. He was possessed by some inner resolve, eyes set deep and merciless, as before a critical game. He moved the pieces to an opening position and studied it. He made a few more moves. He took a sip from a cup of tea and stared at the position. The movie had played for ten or twelve minutes before Garry turned and looked at Fischer.

Bjelica asked Bobby how he would do against Morphy. Bobby's answer was noncommittal and self-effacing; he moved the pieces on a board to a position from a game of Morphy's. Kasparov looked back at his opening setup and moved a piece. He was preparing for tomorrow's game against Jaan Ehlvest. He sipped from his tea. Garry looked back at the screen for a minute or so, and then raised a pinky, enough of this. The happiness over today's win against Beliavsky was a dangerous indulgence. If he lost tomorrow, the Beliavsky game would be meaningless. He began turning through the *Informant* for the most recent games of Ehlvest.

"Bobby, do you think that Paul Morphy played better than you?" Bjelica pressed.

Fischer giggled. "I don't know. We both won." Despite Bobby's charming, shy manner, he had an inner strength. Fischer had beaten Spassky without the help of coaches, while Spassky had had the benefit of a factory of Soviet grandmasters for opening preparation and adjournment analysis.

Soon Fischer began speaking of the first official world championship match, which had been between Wilhelm Steinitz and Johannes Zukertort. Fischer was kind in his assessments of their play.

"Zukertort-Steinitz? Compared to modern players? Incredible," answered Kasparov derisively. To Josh, he added, "First category," meaning that those early games were amateurish by modern standards. Fischer was proving to be too strong a presence to ignore. Kasparov turned in his chair and watched the screen. He cocked his head to the side, and there was a flush of color on his nose and cheeks. He seemed to be thinking beyond the discussion of Steinitz. How could he not wonder who would have proven the greater player if he and Fischer had been contemporaries? After all, they were the two greatest of all world chess champions. Each had raised the game to a higher level. Each had played matches replete with political symbolism. In the United States, Bobby's 1972 defeat of Spassky had been interpreted as a victory against communism, much as Kasparov's recent defeat of Karpov had been hailed by democrats in the

Soviet Union as a political victory. After beating Spassky, Bobby Fischer had been an all-American hero, a role model, much as Garry was in his country.

"This is not a serious discussion," Kasparov said, back in the moment. "These older world champions are playing poor chess. They cannot be held to a modern standard."

"Capablanca was one of the best of all time," said Bobby.

"Nonsense," answered Kasparov. "Bobby says that he is not sure he could have beaten Capablanca. Ridiculous. He would have won easily. To compare players from different eras makes no sense. My games against Karpov would not be understood by the great players of the nineteenth century. If you took someone like Ljubojevic, who will finish near the bottom in Linares, and put him back into the twenties, Capablanca's time, he would have been world champion without a question. The only way to judge the old players is relative to the other players of their period. Fischer was far ahead of the other players of his day. By this measure, I consider him the greatest world champion."

Having said this, Garry turned back to the chessboard and, after a few minutes, Josh joined him. They were soon immersed in a variation that Garry was preparing for tomorrow. While Garry and Bobby had been squabbling across time, Josh had been listening closely. Now he looked very serene analyzing with Kasparov. The position was more engaging to both of them than the talk on the television. Bobby spoke on and on, and neither of them listened. But maybe Garry listened. Around midnight, Bjelica was interviewing Miguel Najdorf, the world's oldest grandmaster. Garry was staring at the ceiling, trying to evaluate a position many moves ahead. "Garry Kasparov," said Najdorf. "He's another Bobby Fischer." Kasparov shook his head, no, no, no.

Against Ehlvest, Garry played with the same dark resolve he had brought to the Fischer documentary. Ehlvest played tentatively and Kasparov overwhelmed him with the black pieces. Kasparov's intimidating physical presence at the board set him apart from the other grandmasters here. Confronted by his glowering look, an opponent lost confidence in his own ideas and was more apt to play wimpy moves. In contrast, Speelman and Anand, who were creating unexpected magic in Linares, looked like butterflies at the board, lithe and uneasy. Yusopov was big and soft, oozing gentleness, between moves smiling sweetly at his young pretty wife, Nadia, who sat in the audience. Ivanchuk, a genius to be sure, was a nervous wreck. Gelfand exuded kindness and goodwill. Salov was burdened with sadness and self-doubt. In the tenth round, Beliavsky, a decorous man, had forgotten to shave and brush his hair. He sensed that he was being left behind. Karpov was only half himself. He spoke in whispers and avoided eye contact. Maybe he would never fully recover from Lyon. It was hard to imagine any of the other players here overcoming the sheer strength and resolve of Kasparov. After the tenth round, Kasparov, Beliavsky and Ivanchuk were tied for first, and most people expected Garry to win.

Garry was in terrific spirits. After the game, he had called Moscow and learned that a million people had lined the streets around Red Square, calling for the ouster of Gorbachev. "Communism will die softly, without bloodshed," he said at dinner.

We walked from the hotel to the pool hall. In the evening, Garry usually shot for a half-hour before going on his walk. After he beat several of the players at eight ball, I challenged him to a game. I won easily and then Garry didn't want to play another. I think he sensed that I had his number at this game and he wanted to retain his good spirits. That night, our walk along the main avenue through Linares was fast and furious, with Garry singing Russian folk songs in full voice.

Each morning after breakfast, and each night before settling into his room, Kasparov walked this same route, which took about twenty-five minutes. There were more interesting choices, through narrow streets winding past the bullring and little restaurants and food shops, but Kasparov always walked this same broad, central avenue. Going another way was unimaginable. A car ride in the morning to Baeza was out of the question. Part of this was a kind of puritanism; there was little time for fooling around between rounds. But more, Garry pushed against the habits of his day, he revved himself, built his energy and emotion for the games by bouncing against small, familiar constraints. Garry sat at the same table for breakfast, and across the room, the same one each night for dinner. He always walked into the playing hall through the same door. He wore the same green jacket. During the games, he first drank his coffee, then his fruit juice, always the same routine.

Actually, most players, except Kamsky, took their walks along the same central avenue that led through a shopping area and then into the countryside. The morning walk was a ritual of the tournament, players deep in thought waving like sailors as they approached one another going and coming. But Gata and his father went their own way. Gata was the only one here who did not analyze with his opponents after games. Rustam did not want him to reveal the key to his genius. "It is a shame about that father," said Gurevich. "If the father weren't spreading so much hate, one of us would talk to the boy, tell him things so he wouldn't lose so much." But it was Rustam's larger strategy to cultivate in his son the belief that it was the two of them against the rest of the world. Apparently, Rustam also demanded a daunting stoicism from Gata. Winning or losing, Gata sat at the board like a robot. After games, there was never joy or grief. On his face one saw mostly sallow detachment, and occasionally a fissure of discomfort or impatience. Emotional displays by the player were not allowed. But on some nights, those who lived near their room would hear Rustam shouting and the boy crying.

The morning before the eleventh round, I walked the narrow streets of Linares in the warm sun, past the cafés, bodegas and little homes sunny today with their shutters thrown open. In a few hours, Kasparov would play the brilliant twenty-one-year-old Viswanathan Anand, perhaps the biggest talent to emerge in the chess world since Kasparov, and the morning was bright and thrilling with the promise of their battle. Maybe today Kasparov would take the lead. Garry had said in interviews that despite Anand's soaring rating and fast vision of the board, the Indian player had deep holes in his game and would never make a serious challenge for the world championship. Such outspokenness, provocative and typical for Kasparov, raised the stakes of his games. But there were many little blood wars in Linares.

In the round after this one, Ivanchuk and Gelfand, the best young players in the Soviet Union, would square off, with the winner of this game sure to be touted as a world championship contender, and the loser returning to the Soviet Union feeling miserable and questioning his talent.

On Calle Parez Galdo Ventanas, I came across the bar called Lagartijo, a cathedral of bullfighting. The men of Linares came here to drink *cerveza*, snack on *tapas* and dream about the great *corridas* of the past and those coming up this spring and summer. On the walls were fighting photographs of lean, sad men, their bodies bent gracefully as bleeding bulls rushed past. These men had suffered terrible life-threatening wounds and had won victories that would be praised for decades. Linares was a town steeped in two blood sports, and I found myself recalling great chess tournaments of the past, even while I looked at photographs of famous *corridas* on the walls of the Lagartijo: San Sebastian 1911 with Capablanca and Rubinstein, Seville 1921 with Juan Belmonte, Linares 1947 with Manolete, Marbella 1965 with El Cordobes and Paco Camino, Palma de Majorca 1970 with Fischer, Seville 1987 with Karpov and Kasparov, Linares 1991 with Kasparov and Ivanchuk.

When I returned to the hotel, Josh was playing speed chess against all challengers in the pressroom and winning game after game. Mr. Rentero came by and said something like, young man, you'll be playing in Linares in a few years. We both felt unbearably terrific. We were finishing our late lunch in the dining room with Mikhail Gurevich when Kasparov walked through on his way to the playing hall. He stopped at our table for a moment, flashing his best smile, and the room brightened two shades. When he was gone, Gurevich commented, "Garry will come into the playing room like a big fighting bull. With a look around the room, he'll take all the space. Players will feel like jumping out of his way. I feel badly for Anand."

Even among the great players in Linares, Viswanathan Anand was considered one of a kind. Anand was a chess player who did not need time to think. Against Anand, grandmasters used their entire two and a half hours, while he required only ten or fifteen minutes to engineer his deadly assaults. While his opponents thought and thought, Vishy's biggest problem seemed to be boredom. He fidgeted, looked around, forced a show of interest. In blitz chess, against grandmasters, Vishy usually won using less than a minute on his clock. Indeed, Anand's talent for the game was so huge that some in the chess world felt that it might ultimately prove to be his undoing. With his gift for playing very good moves by instinct, it was argued that Anand was less inclined to struggle to find great moves.

Anand-Kasparov in the eleventh round looked to be a physical mismatch. Although twenty-one, Anand was much more boy than man. He was willowy, with soft brown eyes and a lighthearted manner. There was no anger, angst or threat in Vishy. Most days in Linares, he hung out with Josh, taking walks, playing table soccer and Ping-Pong in the arcade room, talking about school, sports, chess, joking around, being kids together.

For the first twenty minutes of their game, both Kasparov and Anand moved very rapidly through a long and much-studied opening line. To go with his astonishingly fast vision of the board, Vishy was also a theory hound. He had a great memory and knew everything there was to know about the opening lines that he favored. The first twenty-two moves of the game were all theory. But on the twenty-third move, Kasparov ran out of book knowledge and made a small mistake, giving Anand good chances to draw the game. Anand began to construct a fortress for his king. Garry hunkered down at the board, held his head between his two hands. He was wrenching deep into himself for a winning idea. For most grandmasters, winning or playing brilliantly involves an element of suffering. After fifteen minutes, Garry moved. Immediately, Anand's hand shot out, but he brought it back, looking embarrassed. The other players were always saying to him, Vishy, you must learn to think a little before you move.

But while he paused, he didn't think. He looked around at the other players and then out at the audience. He gave Josh a silly grin. While Kasparov tried futilely to create complications in an arid position, Anand paced the stage, and each time he sat following Kasparov's move, it was almost unbearable for him not to volley back his reply instantly. He would stall for a minute or two, glancing at the players sitting nearby. Beliavsky was making faces of mental anguish. He was being mated by Salov. Gurevich was being slowly squeezed to death by Ivanchuk. When the waiter came by with Garry's coffee, the champion waved the cup away. He was thinking like a turbine, but could not come up with a winning plan. Vishy held his head, imitating Garry, trying to think longer and harder, but his eyes flipped around the stage. He looked up at Kasparov, trying to figure him out. He liked Garry, but found his seriousness and petulance annoying. This game was so easy for Vishy. He seemed like a man straining for something to do with himself while he waited for Kasparov to make up his mind. When they agreed to a draw after twenty-seven moves, Kasparov had used a full hour more on his clock than Vishy. Afterwards, the champion was disgusted and muttered that Anand had been lucky. "Why do you say that?" asked Anand, with a smile and twinkling eyes.

"What would you have done here?" Garry said, showing the correct continuation on the twenty-third move.

"I would have thought for a minute and come up with something," Anand answered playfully.

After the eleventh round, it was Ivanchuk who had forged into the lead. Anand, with an eye and ear for the absurd, referred to the Ukrainian as "Chucky," and noted that he was not your average neighborhood fella. At the board, Ivanchuk rarely looked at the pieces, staring instead at the ceiling, envisioning the game in his head. At least in Linares, the gifted grandmaster was all chess. Pale and mumbling, with eyes upturned, Ivanchuk calculated variations while walking in the halls, or distractedly bouncing on one leg in the lobby or while eating with Karpov and Kamsky.

In the dining room, players' moods changed dramatically from one evening meal to the next. Following the Anand game, Kasparov picked at his food and wouldn't answer when I spoke to him. He felt the tournament slipping away from him. And also Anand's lightness of being had been infuriating. "You're twenty-seven years old and world champion. It's not so bad," I tried at one point, but he didn't respond. Garry pushed away his plate, and with a toothpick in his mouth, he turned sideways to the table, so that he would not have to look at us. It was blistering to sit across from him like this. Josh felt trapped and angry, trying to eat his meal.

At a nearby table, Beliavsky sat, holding his head between his hands. He had started this event winning game after game, but now he had lost two of the last three, mated like a patzer by Salov this afternoon. Beliavsky had been jilted by the chess muse and all the earlier winning meant nothing to him. He was smashed, finished. Salov, a sad man by disposition, was brightened greatly by his bishop sacrifice and clever win against Beliavsky. "*Mas queso,*" more cheese for my spaghetti, he said jauntily to the waiter. Salov was looking forward to an evening of billiards with Vishy, who was also pleased after having held off Gazza, which was what he called the world champion. Nearby, after a hard-fought draw against Yusupov, Gelfand was pleasantly engrossed in his book of Isaac Singer short stories. In the following round, he would play one of the biggest games of his career against his arch-rival, Ivanchuk.

In a far corner of the room, Mikhail Gurevich sat by himself, smoking a cigarette. He had sealed in a losing position against Ivanchuk. He had been so hopeful this afternoon, going into the round. A win against Ivanchuk would have redeemed a poor performance in Linares. Following dessert, which Kasparov didn't touch, Garry walked to Gurevich's table and lectured to his friend about how he could have drawn the game—which would have improved Kasparov's chances to win the tournament. Kasparov's bitter critique was yet another blow. When I had first met Gurevich in New York at the beginning of the Karpov match, he had been a bold, confident man. The timbre of his voice was deep and compelling. He believed that he was as good as any player on the earth, besides Kasparov, and in New York he had held his own in analysis sessions and practice games with the world champion. Now, with a poor performance in Linares following his mediocre play in Reggio Emilia, he was utterly depleted, sadness manifest in each glance and in his drooping posture.

The dinner following the twelfth round was memorable because of Gelfand. Boris Gelfand was an optimistic twenty-two-year-old with a wonderful, wry sense of humor. He was wise beyond his years, and though he was the number three in the world, for the most part he maintained a sensible perspective about his chosen career. "It is a day for life, not chess," he would say, when the sunny blue sky was an entreaty for tennis or hiking in the country. But the game this afternoon had crippled him. Ivanchuk had played a novelty in the opening and Gelfand had answered with terrible mistakes. When Kasparov had gotten up from his own board to take a first look, he had scowled and shook his head, no, no, no, no, no. His censure was something that a young player was likely to remember. All of Gelfand's pieces were on the wrong squares and his queen appeared to be trapped. Meanwhile, Ivanchuk was rocking back and forth in his seat and mumbling as though he were reciting a prayer. Kasparov had paced two lengths of the stage, hoping that first appearances were deceiving, then stopped again in front of Gelfand and pulled his fingers through his hair. He then made this bitter, incredulous expression, how could you do this to me, Gelfand? All of Garry's friends were losing to Ivanchuk, giving the tournament to Ivanchuk. This game had been billed as a contest between two possible world champions, and Gelfand had resigned after only eighteen moves. It was a nightmare. In chess circles throughout the Soviet Union, people would conjecture that this game could be a turning point in two careers.

Gelfand was a gangly fellow, and in the dining room following this humiliation, his angles were all wrong. He hid behind a local newspaper, with one shoulder slung six inches below the other, his neck bent uncomfortably. Gelfand's kind face had broken out with pimples. When he tried to thank the waiter for his tea, he slurred his words. And then his hands wouldn't work properly and he poured the scalding tea all over himself. "It was terrible," he said quietly, when we met later. Watching him in this condition made me afraid for my son. What if he decided to do this with his life? Gelfand was ranked third in the world. One day he was a hero, a god. The next he was a fool, humiliated, distraught, vanquished for the loss of a tempo or a piece on a wrong square.

Winning was the only medicine. Each night the victors came to the dining room with appetites braced by the sweet illusion of endless winning. The walk the following morning was propelled by winning, and the preparation for the next round seemed majestic and irrefutable. Even for Kasparov, it was like this. It was the life of a salesman. There was no tenure. As a chess professional, you were only as good as your last good sale, your last victory. But when you were winning, you could not recall the feeling of losing. Such highs and lows. Josh says that, after a tournament, trying to pull himself back into the prosaic school life is a torture. "Living this life is a drug," Kasparov says.

As a chess father it has been this way for me, as well. I feel like a child again, giggling, soaring high above the worrisome world while Josh is moving in for the kill with his pieces. When our boys are winning, it is redemptive for me and Klara. When Josh was nine or ten, I said to myself maybe we'll back off on chess a little when he is fifteen or sixteen. Now that he is a teenager, I say, what is the harm in giving it five or six more years? The beauty and rush of his chess success not only masks the dark ironies of the life, but it impedes time, helps me forget that he is no longer a child. I forget that as a teenager Josh watches the deep maneuvers of the world's best with the game already beneath his skin, that he will do the choosing, not me.

Kasparov's response to winning against Ljubojevic in the twelfth round was manic, and jangled like the game itself. "I don't know how I feel," said Garry while he ate. "The winning, losing, and winning happened so fast. You need time to understand it, to know how you feel." For most of the game, Garry had played beautifully, but then on the verge of putting it away, he had overlooked a little combination and blundered his rook. Ljubojevic, a powerful and creative player, was stunned to find himself suddenly defeating the world champion, and in time pressure, Ljubojevic fumbled and lost like a beginner. Garry had won this game with big help from good luck. In game after game here, he was getting hit with big blows. Going into the last round, although he remained within a half point of Ivanchuk, Kasparov was vexed and uneasy.

There was also irritating news from abroad. Garry pointed to an article and photograph in a French newspaper, and shook his head in disbelief. "Do you see what I tell you, Fred?" The photograph showed demonstrators in Moscow: the article reported that 300,000 people had rallied against Gorbachev, a carefully-organized group of Yeltsin's supporters. Garry's mother and several friends had called from Moscow to say that over a million had turned out. Kasparov reflected bitterly that it was typical for the Western press to censor or soften examples of Gorbachev's waning popularity. "Yeltsin will replace him soon. Definitely," said Garry. "He has enormous popular support. Maybe higher than Mr. Bush has in America."

To win the Linares tournament, Garry had to beat Yusupov in the last round and Timman had to beat Ivanchuk. He would still tie for first, and hold on to his ten-year tournament record of first-place finishes, if he won while Timman and Ivanchuk drew. If Ivanchuk won, it was all over. Kasparov, who held strong reservations about Timman's play, went into the last round feeling pessimistic. While Garry played his game, he constantly monitored the other. Ivanchuk went for broke, attacked and didn't mind Timman taking a few of his pawns. They quickly achieved a wild unbalanced position which could have gone either way. And then, with Ivanchuk pressing hard, Timman wisely agreed to a draw.

At this point, Kasparov's position against Yusupov was at best equal. Garry looked at his docile army and made a classic wide-eyed face, Kasparov, how could you abandon me in this strongest tournament in the history of chess? Karpov came by and looked for a long, pleased minute. It was one of the only times in this tournament that Karpov had paused in front of Garry's board. For the most part, living in this small hotel, each of these perpetual antagonists had pretended that the other did not exist. Passing in the hall or on the stairs, they didn't say hello or nod. Then, on move thirty-three, Garry sacrificed a knight, straining to make gold out of straw, but Yusupov defended carefully, refusing to allow Garry a leg up. After nearly each move, Yusupov cast a sweet smile of assurance at his new bride, Nadia, who sat in the audience, nervously wringing her hands.

After forty moves, they agreed to a draw. And Garry let out a long breath. The burden of the winning record was off his shoulders. DiMaggio must have felt this way when he went 0 for 4 after hitting in fifty-six games straight. During the postmortem, all the tension was out of Garry. He seemed to yield to the softness of Yusupov's disposition. He smiled a little while they moved the pieces, and nodded yes when Yusupov explained his thinking. I suspected that

Garry was a little pleased for Yusupov, whom he respected greatly, but when we walked back to the room, Garry remarked, "It's a pity, the first time I've lost since 1981." Of course, he hadn't lost. He had finished second instead of first, but to Kasparov that was losing.

"I don't think it's so terrible," I said. "I mean, there's something human about it, and you seem okay. You don't seem as down as I thought you would be."

"Maybe it shows that my luck is turning the wrong way," he answered.

At the awards ceremony, Ivanchuk was absorbed in a deep calculation, and seemed confused when they asked him to come on stage. Having played so fantastically, at the outer reach of his imagination, ideas were still coursing through him, and impositions of the outside world were unsettling. On stage, he quieted himself, rocking from leg to leg, and then he looked to the sky and began moving his lips.

For some reason, Kasparov's regular table was occupied and we found ourselves eating our last dinner in Linares closer to Karpov, Ivanchuk and the Kamskys. Gata had finished in last place with only two and a half points, but father and son looked happy. The hated King Kasparov had lost. Also, they had analyzed the cause of Gata's poor performance, and in interviews with various chess magazines, the Kamskys would explain that Gata had played badly in Linares because Garry Kasparov had poisoned his food. Before the first course was served, while Garry was out of the room to answer a phone call, Rustam Kamsky rose from his table and offered a toast. "Ivanchuk is the world champion. This tournament is the real world championship. Kasparov is finished. Kasparov is finished." Shakarov raised a finger to his lips and whispered to me, "Don't tell this to Garry."

Garry looked content. The tournament was over and he had made a discovery. He could lose and still feel alive. He seemed to revel in this unspoken, unexpected idea. He felt terrific. He looked around the room, drinking in the scene. It was great not to have to battle against Ivanchuk or Karpov tomorrow. He slouched at the table and nodded his head, not so bad, life's not so bad. After a time, Dimitri Bjelica came over and asked Garry a couple of questions. But Dimitri didn't seem very interested in Garry's answers, and soon he interrupted to describe an interview with Fischer in 1971. After he left our table, Garry reflected, "That was the most important time in his life, and now he lives to re-create it. He is always sitting at Karpov's elbow or mine, asking questions, but he doesn't really care what we say. He is in the past with Bobby. He reminds me of a man I met in Reykjavik, Iceland, a few years ago. He was Bobby Fischer's driver during the championship in 1972 and they became close. Every time I would say something to this man, he would bring up Bobby. He couldn't listen. He wasn't living in the moment. It occurred to me that this man was completely safe. The Fischer relationship was the single important moment in his life, and now he and Bobby were protected by time."

An hour later, Garry and I were standing outside with his bags. It was raining lightly. "It's a colorful group, don't you think?" he said, gesturing toward the hotel. "Even Kamsky. The father is a character. The chess world is better for him being there." It was ten-thirty at night when a small sedan pulled up in front of the hotel. Garry shook hands warmly and climbed into the back seat. We would meet in New York in four weeks, he reminded me, dinner at Shun Lee Palace. He yawned. Garry would sleep like a baby in the back seat. In four hours, they would arrive in Madrid. Tomorrow morning, Kasparov had a press conference and a television show. He waved through the window, happy to be on the road again.

EPILOGUE

On June 9, 1991, three days before Boris Yeltsin would become Russia's first democratically elected president, Garry Kasparov, dressed in blue jeans and a sports shirt, stood on a platform about to address a cheering crowd assembled in Moscow's Manezhnaya Square. "Citizens of Moscow," he began, and then for the first time appreciated the immensity of his audience. There were at least 250,-000 people spread out in front of him, acres of people, swaying with the anticipation of democracy, wealth and good times—no more Gorbachev, no more food lines. Kasparov's face went white. For three or four seconds, he could not recall his words, and then he burst into a flabbergasted smile. Look where I am. This boy from Baku. A wood pusher. The champion began to speak, at first hesitantly, but soon the words were pouring out of him: "This is the final stand against communism. It is a moment when we all must be united. Our opponents will do anything to win."

The crowd loved him. "On June twelfth, we will close a shameful page in our history and we will go onto the same road with all civilized people." There was thunderous applause and cheering, political banners waving. The Kremlin rocked with the chant, "Yeltsin, Yeltsin, Yeltsin." Garry was charismatic, a political rising star.

Three days later, Masha, Garry and I walked from their little apartment to the neighborhood polling place, a technical school which was dank and in need of repair, like all of Moscow. People standing on line ahead of us were in festive spirits. Nearly everyone was voting for Yeltsin. In New York I had seen Garry use his celebrity to go to the front of the line, for example, when he needed to pick up a visa at the Spanish embassy. But not here, not today. Waiting his turn on election day had symbolic importance to him. When it was his turn to vote, he showed his passport to prove his citizenship like all the others on line, though the lady in charge tittered over Kasparov, whom she recognized immediately. Garry was very proud this day, but also cautious, as though recalling winning positions that he had failed to win because of overconfidence. "June twelfth is an historic date because communism has lost, but democracy hasn't yet won."

We walked back to their apartment past a little lake that must once have been lovely but now was littered and slimed with motor oil. Garry was pensive. He kicked at the water's edge. "It's nice here," he said, not noticing the bottles and cans. He was somewhere else. He threw a rock into the lake. "I have a story for you," he said. "It's about my father." The word caught in his throat. Garry almost never referred to his father, and whenever I asked him what he remembered of his father, he would brush me off: "It was too long ago," or "too painful."

"It's a classic tale," he said looking for a way to begin. "It's about three friends, all Jews, all the same age. They lived next to one another in Baku. They were really great friends. David Zaferman, Bob Korsh and my father Kim Weinstein. While growing up, they were always together. All three attended the engineering institute in Baku. When one of them did his apprenticeship in Western Siberia, the other two came along. They loved the company of one another. Eventually they all married and still they remained friends, visiting one another, talking politics. They hated the Soviet system, but probably my father was the most forthright. He would criticize the system in public and was forced to change jobs several times because of his politics. He really hated the communism. He was always arguing with my grandfather about it. One time his strong views almost cost the marriage. My mother had an opportunity for advancement in her work but to be promoted she had to join the party. My father told her, 'If you join the Communist Party, we are divorced.' In 1965, my father wrote in his diary that in twenty-five years, there would be no more communism in the Soviet Union. His two friends said that he was crazy," Garry nodded his head deliberately. "He was wrong by one year.

"My father died in January, 1971, when I was seven. That year his two friends brought flowers to my father's grave on his birthday, then again on the second of May, a day when people do this in my country, and once again the following January on the date of my father's death. Then in 1972, David Zaferman decided to emigrate with his family to Israel. Before he left he asked Bob to bring flowers to the cemetery for him. Bob took this as a sacred responsibility. Always, on these days there were two pots of flowers on my father's grave, and sometimes I came to the cemetery in the early morning and saw Bob Korsh there.

"After the genocide in Baku, we lost track of our friends. People were scattered to the wind. Not only Armenians. There was also a Jewish exodus from Baku. Jews tried to get to Israel. Baku was a dangerous place to live. My mother and I often thought of the graves of my father and of my grandfather. Who would care for them? Probably they would be desecrated. In Baku, everything was fouled.

"A few days ago, I was at my mother's and one of the bodyguards said, 'There is an old guy looking for you.' My mother had an intuition that it was Bob Korsh. A few minutes later, they found him wandering on another floor in the building and brought him to us. Bob said to my mother, 'I wanted always to live in my native city. But I'm old now and the city is empty.' Bob was a lost person, like many refugees from Baku who are now in Moscow. 'Klara, when they started the riots and murder, I began to cross out the names of my friends and relatives from my address book,' he said. 'One day this past April, I opened the book and I didn't find any more names. They were all crossed out. Then I understood I would leave Baku, Klara.'

"A very short story," said Garry. "One day he opened the book and there were no more names. 'Please, if you go back there put two pots of flowers on Kim's grave,' Bob said to us, but we won't go back there. This will be the first year there will be no flowers. The first year of no communism."

As we walked from the lake, Garry was crying. He opened his wallet and stole a look at a photograph of his father, whom he barely remembered.

No names in the book. What a time this past year and a little more had been for him. He had lost his home and managed to hang onto the world championship. He had predicted the fall of communism and then had become a player in that very drama. For Garry, June was an ending and a beginning. Masha was pregnant. Such a happy idea. Such lows and highs. Perhaps a son would drive away some of the sadness. "But a little girl would be fine," he insisted. "The most important thing is for it to be healthy." We came back to their apartment. We ate and then talked for hours. We were interrupted by a phone call from an official of the Kenyan Chess Federation. The man had been calling all week and had finally reached Garry. "Come to Kenya," he said. "You'll go on safari." The idea seemed outrageously funny to all of us.

Earlier that week, I had visited Arkady Murashov, at the time a People's Deputy, who would later become Moscow's Commissioner of Police. "Garry is one of the brightest political figures in the Soviet Union," Arkady had said to me. "He gains respect among intellectuals here by the day. His one drawback is time. If he were to give up his chess life, he could do anything he wanted in Soviet politics." In June of 1991, it appeared to many that Kasparov was poised to do just that. In the weeks after Linares, Kasparov did little studying. He was inflamed with Yeltsin's election. At the beginning of June, he had met with Yeltsin once again to discuss George Bush's reticence to accept the democratic movement, and Garry had described the lobbying effort of Gorbachev's people in Washington. Perhaps Kasparov would be part of Yeltsin's new government.

I suggested this possibility several days after the election, when Murashov joined us for lunch. "Now we have to build a new opposition to Yeltsin," Garry said, much to my surprise. "Yeltsin is the state. And the state is always the state. Oh, yes, Yeltsin was an important step towards democracy. But, when you listen closely to his speeches, he still uses some of the old communist rhetoric, and he has made compromises with the communists. Of course, we need an opposition to him. Here we don't have democratic traditions. We need this to keep Yeltsin honest, and to force him to move quickly toward democratic changes."

Garry had decided to oppose Yeltsin even before the votes were counted. With Gorbachev down but not yet out, Garry already craved a new battle. In fairness, other leading Moscow democrats argued that an opposition to Yeltsin was essential for nurturing this fledgling democracy; nevertheless it was in Garry's nature to seek the boldest alternative, to be at the forefront of the movement. Garry had little patience for negotiation and compromise. Several months earlier, when Democratic Russia, the political movement that he had helped to create, adopted a cautious middle-of-the-road platform, Kasparov promptly resigned. The plodding labor of tearing down the *apparat* and building a new government was inimical to his personality. Being a People's Deputy or Yeltsin's Secretary of something would be a slow death. But whether Garry would actually start an opposition to Yeltsin was another question entirely. I had learned long ago that for Kasparov the idea was more intriguing than the execution. He gained energy and momentum from new ideas. When propositions felt stale or fell back into the mainstream, he lost interest without remorse. Kasparov leaped from slow-moving trains. His enemies considered his wanderlust irresponsible and even immoral. Those who loved Kasparov knew him to be a Prospero, who needed to play new and original moves in order to play at all.

"What do you think Gorbachev will do?" I asked.

"I would prefer to have him out of the country. I think the perfect choice for him would be to join the faculty at Harvard," he said, trying to keep a straight face. "He could write a book, 'How I Killed Communism in the Soviet Union.' Some publisher will give him a six- or eight-million-dollar advance. I'm sure it would rise to the top of the best-seller list in *The New York Times Book Review*."

*   *   *

On August 19, when the coup took place, Garry was resting and studying chess in Malibu in a lavish rented house that had once been owned by Madonna. "It felt confusing and very uncomfortable hearing about this so-called coup from southern California," he reflected sometime later. "If I had been at home, I would have been with all of my friends in the Russian White House. But actually I could be more useful in California." During those momentous days, Garry spoke constantly with journalists and appeared on U.S. television. "I've never trusted the American press," he said. "*The New York Times*, the networks—ideology and preconceptions dominate their coverage. The American assessment of the coup was simply astounding. Everyone was convinced that *perestroika* was finished and we were back in the cold war."

On the second day of the coup, Garry was a guest on *Larry King Live*, along with Jeane Kirkpatrick and a Russian defector. "The defector, who had not been in Moscow for a long time, believed that the coup would fail but that it would be a lengthy process. Jeane Kirkpatrick said it would take forty-eight weeks. I said that the coup would be defeated in forty-eight hours." Jeane Kirkpatrick and Larry King both responded as though Kasparov did not have a realistic grasp of the situation. "I told them that Russian officers would not shoot democrats; even the KGB would not go against the people. I said the same thing on the *Tonight Show* to Jay Leno and on *Good Morning America*."

On August 23, Kasparov published an article in the *Wall Street Journal* suggesting that Gorbachev was himself behind the coup, a view that has gained acceptance among Moscow intellectuals. "I believe that Gorbachev was in favor of this military takeover. He definitely knew about it in advance," Garry said in September during a visit to New York, "but he wanted to be like Pontius Pilate in *Master and Margarita*, to keep his hands clean while it took place. So he took a little vacation in his dacha while men he had promoted to power did the dirty work. Obviously he was never in danger. His worldwide system of communication was never broken. He was never arrested. What kind of coup is that? If you follow the story, for the first two days Gorbachev was relaxed, swimming on the beach. He only became nervous on the third day when it became clear that the coup was failing. If the coup had succeeded, he would have come back and assumed absolute power.

"But it could not succeed. Not a chance. Although the reason was ignored by the CIA, by Western politicians and by the American media. The psychology of the Russian people had changed. A simple change. The entire communist system of power was based upon fear, but fear survives only if there is hope. For many years the population was afraid to lose jobs, afraid to be sent to labor camp; in the case of Soviet sportsmen, afraid to be barred from foreign competitions, to lose the opportunity to go abroad to earn hard currency. In the communist system there is terrible pressure not to lose something, even if it is a tiny privilege. If you have something in your life, you can lose it. The more you have, the more you are scared. During the years of *perestroika*, Gorbachev lost this critical control. With a little bit of freedom people could see. It was as if one morning people opened the windows and they saw the country was destroyed—its ecology was a disaster—Chernobyl. They can't earn enough to live decently; the economy is ruined; children are unhappy to see that their parents are lying every day to survive; it is a moral disaster. The country is falling apart, and the West is flourishing. We are expelled from civilization. This country of ours is a toilet seat. For seventy-something years, the people had been living a lie. With this realization, there was a sense of a disappearing future and a loss of hope. When there is no hope, there is also no fear. And that's the psychological reason that the coup failed. Hundreds of thousands were prepared to die. The military would have had to slaughter thousands, and they weren't prepared to do this. The coup failed in two days because there was a feeling of hopelessness and a lack of fear."

Following the failure of the coup, and the dissolution of the Soviet Union, Kasparov quietly changed his course, withdrew from the Russian political scene at a time when many thought he would become a leader. "Almost overnight there was no political life where I could find my place. I was not interested in fighting for positions,

for a corner of power. To stay in politics I would be obliged to fight
very miserable battles. And frankly, the Russian government under
Yeltsin didn't mean much to me. Too many compromises. I decided
to wait."

But perhaps more importantly, Kasparov was facing a crisis in his
chess life. He had become a beatable player. In May of '91, two
months after failing to win the Linares tournament, Garry embarrassed himself in the Euwe Memorial in Amsterdam, tying for third
with Karpov behind Valery Salov and Nigel Short. After this second
weak performance in a row, grandmasters were agreeing that Kasparov had lost the magic. "After Amsterdam, I realized that if I did
not change my life I would become an ordinary player," said Garry.
"I did not have enough energy to live both of these lives. But before
the election in Moscow, it was still impossible to focus on chess."
Following the coup attempt, there was a winning effort in Tilburg,
but then Garry failed once again in the Immopar Trophée, losing to
Timman in the final round. Next Garry played the Reggio Emilia
tournament in northern Italy and performed miserably. "Four tournaments in one year that I didn't win. At least I was making the other
players happy. When I lost to Anand in Tilburg, Timman and Short
were laughing. After Reggio Emilia, grandmasters were writing in
chess magazines, 'He's just another player. It's an old chess Kasparov
is playing. The game has passed him by.'"

But, despite the poor result in Reggio Emilia, Kasparov was once
again feeling the game come alive within him. For the first time in
two years, spurred by the glee of his peers, who had already committed him to history, Garry had begun studying systematically and
craved chess combat. Garry's next event was a simultaneous exhibition against the German national team of four respected grandmasters. The winner-take-all prize was a BMW. Chess aficionados gave
Kasparov almost no chance to win this extravagant event. "Before
the start of play, the Germans were figuring how they would sell the
BMW and share the money," remarked Garry. Charged by the
craziness of the challenge, Garry had studied the games of the
grandmasters for four days around the clock to unearth technical
deficiencies and psychological weaknesses which he might exploit.

The exhibition was played in front of 1500 spectators and was shown live on German television. The champion employed devilish tactics to make each of his opponents uneasy, ignoring one man as though he were contemptibly weak, while focusing like a laser on the other three. His moves probed the timidities and dark fears of each of them. Having decided that one player lacked courage, he cajoled him into accepting an early draw, which soured the mood of the German team. Switching from one game to the next, Kasparov created deep complexities, actually pressuring his august opponents on the clock, though each of them had four times as many minutes for thinking as he did. Garry outfoxed his opponents and then overwhelmed them with his power and speed. A stunning victory.

Throughout 1992, Garry studied chess, played in the world's toughest tournaments, and traveled almost monthly to the United States to help the organizer of the 1993 title defense, an American entrepreneur, Jim McKay, find sponsors for the event, which was to be held in Los Angeles. Garry believed that holding a world championship in California, with a year and a half to plan ancillary chess events and to arrange television coverage, would raise the sport to a new level, and he worked on the project with missionary zeal. When Apple showed strong interest in becoming the primary sponsor, he envisioned a great chess awakening in America.

In 1992 Kasparov played some of the greatest chess of his career. He won the Linares tournament with an overwhelming score, showed dazzling power and inventiveness in the chess Olympiad, where he played first board for the winning Russian team, played equally well in the European championship, won the Immopar Trophée, and finished the year with an international rating of 2805, the highest in the history of chess. Focusing more or less exclusively on the game, Kasparov left his major competitors in the dust.

Throughout the year, Karpov continued to struggle, most importantly eliminating himself from the '93 world championship by losing to Nigel Short in the semifinals of the candidates matches. For the first time in his career, Kasparov would be playing the world championship against someone other than Karpov. Following Ivanchuk's memorable victory over Kasparov in Linares, Vassily played up-and-down chess, his great talent hampered by bad nerves. Gelfand lost rating points, and although Anand and Kamsky continued to improve, by year's end even Kasparov's detractors were forced to acknowledge that the champion was in a class by himself.

But this lofty distinction brought its own problems. Apple eventually decided against sponsoring the world championship, and over the ensuing months, while Timman and Short prepared for the final candidates match, there was little interest among American corporations in sponsoring a big-money event in California between Kasparov and some foreign grandmaster who had little chance to make the match competitive. "No one cares about this championship match," said Garry, growing more frustrated with each trip to the States. "Nigel Short or Jan Timman, it's like no opponent. I find myself in the position of hustling around trying to raise this money, and people are thinking, what are you doing, raising this money for yourself?" Indeed, when Anand heard that Kasparov's challenger in '93 would be either Nigel Short or Jan Timman, each with a woeful record against the world champion, Anand commented dryly that such a match would be unfair and that Kasparov should play them simultaneously to keep the title. "This would be an interesting match," Garry said, his spirits lifted momentarily by the fantasy of an event that might generate some interest. "I think I could beat them both if the match were kept to ten games or less. After this they would wear me down." By the summer it was clinched that no major sponsor would finance a glitzy chess mismatch in California in 1993. As Bruce Pandolfini had predicted at the end of the last world championship, Karpov's fall from power had become a grave problem for Kasparov.

The next possibility unearthed by Jim McKay was to hold the match in Hamilton, Ontario, sponsored by the Canadian government. As Kasparov came to terms with this off-the-beaten-track venue, a diminished prize fund, and the likelihood that chess would not displace baseball as our national pastime in the fall of 1993, Bobby Fischer was suddenly back on the front pages of newspapers and on the nightly television news.

The Fischer-Spassky rematch, referred to as "The World Chess Championship," at Fischer's insistence, was held in the fall of '92 in the war-torn remains of Yugoslavia and was won by Fischer by a 10–5 score. Hundreds of journalists made their way to the island of Sveti Stefan, where the match began, and then camped in Belgrade for its conclusion. At Fischer's direction, the games were played behind a glass shield, and fans could barely see the moves. Photographers were, for the most part, not allowed to take pictures, and journalists who approached Fischer were sometimes harassed by armed thugs. This bizarre chess spectacle was organized by Jezdimir Vasiljevic, a banker and known war profiteer closely associated with Serbian president Slobodan Milosevic.

During Fischer's nine press conferences, he referred to himself as "the world champion," and called Kasparov a pathological liar, alleging that Kasparov had fixed all of his games with Karpov. He railed against Jews and spat upon State Department documents warning him of the penalties for violating sanctions by playing this match in Serbia. But for the majority of chess lovers around the world, the reemergence of Bobby Fischer eclipsed his off-color rhetoric and the disquieting juxtaposition of chess and genocide on nightly television newscasts. The Great One had wakened from a twenty-year sleep to reclaim his kingdom. This was Bobby's greatest chess trick since disappearing. Chess players were delirious to see the innovations he had conceived during his long respite, and they resisted the Hyde side of Bobby. One frail old Jewish lady with thinning hair, a long-time member of the Manhattan Chess Club, became enraged when I mentioned that Bobby was saying terrible things about Jews. "Why are you spreading these disgusting lies?" she asked me bitterly. "What do you have against him?"

Spassky proved to be a very weak opponent, and the quality of the games was so uneven that top chess minds are still uncertain of Fischer's playing strength, but in the excitement of the first weeks of the match Fischer fans tended to ignore Bobby's blunders and doted on his brilliancies. Players in Washington Square wanted to believe that Bobby was stronger than Garry, and they demonstrated Fischer's finest moments against Spassky as proof. In his commentaries, Seirawan extolled Bobby's play and pointed out that Fischer taunted Kasparov by playing improvements in lines favored by Garry.

But the real Fischer magic was his effect upon the general public. Overnight, people were interested in chess. All the television news shows carried stories about Bobby Fischer, and his games were analyzed on the news pages of the tabloids. One evening I took a taxi uptown, and the driver asked me what had happened in today's chess game. The guy who makes sandwiches at my neighborhood deli wanted to talk Fischer while he built my ham and cheese.

During the first weeks of the match, Garry tried to sound matter-of-fact about Bobby, but you could tell that Fischer was leaning on him heavily. "Bobby is playing okay, nothing more," he said to me, with a drawn face. "Maybe his strength is 2600 or 2650. It wouldn't be close between us. In fact, Bobby would lose a match against any of the top grandmasters today. If he were to try to play in a high-level tournament like Linares, one top player after the next gunning for him with the modern ideas, Bobby would die before the end of the event. It wouldn't be a question of winning or losing. Sometime before the end of the tournament, Bobby would *die*."

Of course, Kasparov felt jilted by the Fischer love-in, but more, he felt blindsided. While talking blasphemy, Fischer was, nonetheless, making millions of people curious about the game. Garry, on the other hand, was finding it impossible to interest a sponsor for the world championship. How could he not grind his teeth when he read that there were more million-dollar deals lined up for Bobby as soon as he finished off Spassky—millions to play against Judit Polgar, millions more to play against Anand? Journalists rarely asked Kasparov a question about his coming match against either Nigel Short or Jan Timman; they wanted his view on Bobby. He tried to be generous, but his public statements sounded stiff and ill-tempered. When asked about the quality of chess in the match, Kasparov said it was mediocre—in fact he considered it awful—two middle-aged has-beens playing bad chess for a five-million-dollar purse.

When asked if he would play Bobby in a match, Garry answered that he would, under the right conditions, yes, but he felt uncomfortable giving Fischer a podium from which to propagate his neo-Nazism. Many chess fans considered Kasparov's response querulous, and some took it to mean that he was afraid of Bobby. When Garry said that he had no doubt he would beat Bobby badly in a match, I believed him. But still, how could he not worry a little in the middle of the night? He would go into such a match burdened with the knowledge that pummeling fifty-year-old Bobby would not win him any more admirers than the Grinch who stole Christmas.

In fact, for Garry, Fischer's comeback was torture. At times he would speak of Bobby with a sneer on his face, "He's a weak player, he's a crazy man." I didn't want to hear these things from him. The jealousy of kings is very loud. Lest the game become trivial, Michael Jordan must not speak ill of Julius Erving.

"Garry, don't repeat the error of Spassky and Botvinnik," I said.

Garry smirked, and averted his face. "You know, I'm a pretty clever fellow. I know what to say," he answered.

"Forgive Bobby his craziness, and the weakening of his memory and tactics. You will be almost fifty soon enough. I know about being almost fifty."

"You are not old, Fred," he answered. "You are not old. *You* are not old. Do you hear me?"

"It's a shame," Garry said. "It's a shame he came out of retirement. It ruined his invincibility. His reputation is tarnished."

"No, I don't think so, Garry. Not badly." The little Jewish lady at the Manhattan Chess Club still loves him. Bruce Pandolfini still loves him. You should see Bruce's smile when he plays through Bobby's combinations. Bobby is in our blood. Josh and I would not be living the chess life today were it not for Bobby.

Garry knew this. He sighed. "What can I do, Fred?" He shook his head slowly, his mood softened.

"Maybe we could play," he said slowly. "I don't care what Bobby says about me. His political opinions are not very serious, because he is not responsible for what he says. It could be ignored."

Garry had changed a great deal in the three years since we became friends. He listened much more closely. He was not so impatient. He had been humbled a little by losing and considered that okay. He would admit that losing has broadened him.

* * *

After Fischer beat Spassky, the U.S. State Department announced
that Fischer would be prosecuted, and would face a fine and possible
imprisonment for violating sanctions. After receiving this news,
Bobby disappeared again, probably to somewhere in Serbia, from
where he could not be extradited, where he has always been loved
for his game and where his political views today seem no more
outrageous than those of his Serbian hosts.

Bobby Fischer brought Kasparov nothing but bad luck. By the end
of November, the Canadian government had decided that it did not
want to sponsor a world championship match. This decision made it
nearly definite that there would be no world championship in North
America in 1993. It was a stinging defeat for Garry. "A great failure
and disappointment," he said. "I spent a year and a half of my life
trying to accomplish this. I paid a huge price to be disappointed. In
December, I was quite depressed."

When I visited Garry in the beginning of January, 1993, at the St.
Regis Hotel, I expected to find a gloomy world champion, but I was
far from sure about this. Invariably, when I see him for the first time
in two or three months, he surprises me, shakes my confidence in my
most recent pages about him. He greeted me by picking me up off
the ground with a hard sweet hug. "Look at this, Fred," he said,
making a muscle. "I am down to a hundred and seventy pounds. I am
in training. Get Josh to come tomorrow morning. We'll see who can
do more push-ups." Garry was in such great spirits, full of new ideas.
He had just returned from Las Vegas and was negotiating with
MGM to put on a huge show in the desert in 1994 called "Man
versus Machine." Kasparov would play against the next generation
chess computer, a monster machine, much more advanced than the
current champion of computers, Deep Thought, which has defeated
many strong grandmasters. "This event will lead to other events. It
will interest huge companies." In one hour, Garry had a meeting in

the restaurant downstairs with four wealthy businessmen who were interested in chess promotions in the United States. "Before Man versus Machine, I will crush Nigel Short to keep my title," he remembered to add. Short had just defeated Timman to become Garry's official challenger in 1993. "Then I will challenge the American national team—four very strong grandmasters—Seirawan, Wolff, Christiansen, Benjamin. I wonder if Seirawan will swallow his pride and play on the team? . . . For money he will swallow his pride." This would be by far the most difficult simultaneous match ever attempted, and Garry was confident he could win. "A very strong group, but I like my chances."

"Why such optimism, Garry?" I needled. "Mostly things have gone badly for you of late. You know, sometimes I think our moods are more chemical than anything."

"Yes, chemical," he said, considering a moment. And then, imperturbably, "I feel very optimistic for 1993. I will play great chess. We will continue the work in the United States. Chess in the schools, yes.

"Then, in 1996 I will take the championship away from FIDE, make an independent promotion. . . . Campomanes will create a new world champion, but who will care about him?"* By now we had been speaking for about an hour and a half, and Kasparov was already twenty minutes late for his meeting downstairs in the restaurant. "Fred, you know there is still a small chance for the world championship in New York in '93," he said.

"What?"

"The four guys downstairs have interest. Probably it won't happen. We'll see. A small chance."

"Really?" I was thinking, why are you here now instead of down there? You're late! But I had long ago learned the answer to this question. Garry wasn't yet ready to leave. Garry would go down-

---

*About six weeks later, the 1993 challenger, Nigel Short, phoned Garry Kasparov and asked if he were prepared to break from FIDE and play their match under the auspices of a new professional chess management organization. Kasparov replied without hesitation, "I've been waiting for this chance for eight years, since 1985." They announced their intentions to the press and opened the bidding for the PCA World Chess Championship, to be held in September, 1993. This move would shake the existing structures of world chess management and may prove to be the death knell for FIDE.

stairs when the moment was propitious. From his manner I knew that
he wanted to talk more about his plans for the future. Then he would
probably glance at the newspaper and check his messages. At exactly
the right moment, Kasparov would stride into the restaurant with a
hard but detached expression, suggesting that he had been wrenched
from matters of great importance. It is both thrilling and intimidating
to meet the world champion for the first time. He is an historical
figure. You sweat, don't want to blow this opportunity. You can tell
that he won't tolerate small talk. His stare is calculating and cold. He
is making lasting judgements.

"Fred, look at this, will you," Garry said, and I half expected him
to pull a typed draft of a *Wall Street Journal* article from his jacket
pocket. I knew that I would have trouble concentrating on the article.
It is always nerve-wracking to be with Garry when he is late. I
wonder, should I be responsible and push him out the door or should
I revel with him in his naughty and blissful truancy? But it wasn't a
Wall Street Journal article that Garry wanted to show me. Garry
quickly peeled off his sports jacket, and, casting a quick grin my way,
he jogged a few bouncy strides across the room and suddenly
vaulted into a handstand. I had no idea that he could do this.

"I've reconstructed my optimism," he said from this unlikely position. "The engine is running again. Not so much energy as before,
but very steady. Watch this." Garry began doing slow push-ups from
the handstand position. "Bet Josh can't do this," he said. "I can play
better than I did in '92." Garry's face was red. He would be thirty
years old soon, no longer a prodigy. "Could never do this before,
Fred. Five. I can do five of them."

11/01 (14) 10/01
7/06 (28) 5/05
6/10 (33) 7/9
4/13 (35) 9/12
4/17 (41) 10/16